THE FIRST FAMILIES OF LOUISIANA

Volume I

Translated and Compiled

by

Glenn R. Conrad

Baton Rouge
CLAITOR'S PUBLISHING DIVISION
1970

Published and for sale by:
Claitor's Publishing Division
3165 S. Acadian at I-10, P. O. Box 239
Baton Rouge, La. 70821

TO

Sylvia, Martin, Alicia,
Margaret and Randolph
Conrad

INTRODUCTION

Between 1717, the year that Antoine Crozat abandoned his Louisiana concession, and 1731, the year the Company of the Indies returned operation of the colony to the French Crown, there occurred a most significant migration to Louisiana.

During those fourteen or fifteen years, thousands of Europeans, mainly Frenchmen and Germans but also Englishmen, Irishmen and Bohemians, quit their native land in search of a new life. Some of these immigrants voluntarily went to the colony, others did not. Some of the colonists were adventurers, a happy-go-lucky breed, but most were deluded farmers, soldiers and tradesmen. Still others were prisoners who were forced to go to Louisiana.

The fact remains, however, that regardless of why they sought the New World, these fearless people soon shared a common problem--survival. No matter their station in life, all of them--men, women, and children, freemen, engages, and prisoners--had to work hard to survive the perils of every-day colonial life.

Upon their arrival in America, after a hazardous journey across the Atlantic Ocean and the Gulf of Mexico, the colonists discovered that there was little more to greet them than a damp, forested land. Their task was obvious--begin the exhausting work of clearing the land. As the first and second years passed and their work of deforestation progressed, they experienced the simple joys of seeing their little homes become a reality and seeing their crops spring from the heavy delta soil. Tragedy, however, was always just beyond the horizon. Frequently they saw their ripened crops plundered by seemingly endless waves of blackbirds or they stood by helplessly as their grain, their homes, their meagre possessions were washed away by unpredictable floods and storms. Nevertheless, these hardy folk persevered between those years 1717 and 1732. They struggled for their new life and sometimes they failed. They died of overwork, malnutrition, fever, snakebite and the primitiveness of their enviornment. Some died of disappointment, pining for a France or a Germany they would never see again. Many colonists died fighting to protect their families and their homes from the first Americans.

Though death was a constant visitor, this intrepid group of minor noblemen, administrators, farmers, shopkeepers, soldiers, prisoners and vagabonds began the transformation of the wilderness they found into the heartland of America which they have bequeathed to their descendants.

What follows, then, are some of the lists which record the arrival, the pursuits, the joys and the sorrows of these first families of Louisiana.

These lists are copies of documents on deposit at the
Archives Nationales in Paris. The author is aware that
some of these lists have already appeared in several publica-
tions. It is the author's intention, however, to present
in a single work, and as completely as possible, a compila-
tion of the lists for the years 1717 to 1732. In order to
document sources of information, the Table of Contents pre-
sents the French archival citation of each document employed
in this work. All of the documents used can also be found
in the Louisiana Colonial Records Collection of the University of Southwestern Louisiana at Lafayette, Louisiana.

The author must mention the inevitable problems that
arose in the preparation of the work, particularly the problems of orthography and chirography. In order to solve
the problem of different spellings for apparently the same
personal name or place, the author adopted as his rule the
spelling that appears on the document. Thus the alert reader
will discover that the names "Kel," "Quel," "Quelle," and
"Kelle" are probably different spellings for one person's
name.

A greater problem was that of Chirography which rendered almost impossible, in some instances, a distinction
between certain letters of the alphabet, but particularly
between "u" and "n." For this reason a person's name may

appear as "Fion" in one place and as "Fiou" in another place. Whenever it was impossible for the author to judge the correct spelling, the alternate spelling with a question mark is placed in parentheses following the supposed spelling. Furthermore, the French phonetic spelling of the German names has, in some instances, rendered these names almost unrecognizable from the correct German spelling. An aid to discovering the correct orthography of these German names can be found in J. Hanno Deiler's monograph on the German settlers of Louisiana.[1]

Now, a word of advice, particularly to the inexperienced genealogist. It is always wise to corroborate information from as many sources as possible. Presented here are some major sources of geneaological information for the given years. The author could not include, unfortunately, the hundreds, perhaps thousands, of names that appear individually or in small groups in the great number of documents pertaining to other aspects of colonial life during the period under investigation. Further research, therefore, could reveal additional information.

Finally, the author has taken the liberty of presenting

---

[1] J. Hanno Deiler, The Settlement of the German Coast of Louisiana and Creoles of German Descent (Philadelphia:1909). This author will be privileged to prepare an introduction to a new edition of Mr. Deiler's monograph to be published by the Claiter Publishing Company during 1970.

as the concluding item "The General Roll of Louisiana Troops from 1720 to 1770." Inasmuch as this list indicates the ultimate disposition of many of the soldiers who arrived in the colony between 1717 and 1732, the author believes that it should be included in this work. Indeed, it is the author's hope that his overall efforts will shed further light on those gallant pioneers--the first families of Louisiana.

University of South-   Glenn R. Conrad
    western Louisiana
Lafayette, Louisiana
June, 1969

The <u>Archives Nationales</u> is the central repository for the archives and records of the French government. The archives from which the present material is taken is that of the <u>Archives Colonies</u> (abbreviated hereafter as AC).[1]

PASSENGER LISTS

[1]For a brief explanation of the arrangement of the French archives see chapter one, "The French Archives and American History," of J. Putney Beers, <u>The French in North America: A Bibliographical Guide to French Archives, Reproductions, and Research Missions</u> (Baton Rouge: Louisiana State University Press, 1957).

MILITARY OFFICERS

SOLDIERS[1]

[1]See also the lists of soldiers included with the passenger lists.

COMPANY OF THE INDIES

TABLE OF CONTENTS

Volume II

CENSUS REPORTS

BAPTISMAL AND DEATH REGISTERS

MISCELLANEOUS

OCTOBER 25, 1717

LIST OF PERSONS EMBARKED ON THE NEPTUNE,
DAUPHINE AND VIGILANTE BOUND FOR LOUISI-
ANA FOR SERVICE WITH THE COMPANY OF THE
INDIES OR FOR OTHER REASONS

(A) Employed by the Company of the Indies
(B) Concessionaries and their people
(C) Private Passengers
(D) Exiles
(E) Illegal Salt Dealers

Name	Occupation	Status
BONNAUD, Mr.	Clerk	A
A valet	Valet	A
A female Servant	Servant	A
GUENAUD, Mr.	Clerk	A
CHASSIN, Mr.	Clerk	A
MONTSUSIN, Mr.	Clerk	A
LEFEVRE, Zacharie	Laborer	A
LEFEVRE, Jacques	Laborer	A
SLACHENDRY, Jean de	Pitch maker	A
BELSAUGUY, Dominique	Pitch maker	A
DUQUERON, Joseph	Edge-tool maker	A
LURAT, Felix	Cooper	A
COSTIER, Jean	Cooper	A
BERARD, Mr.	Surgeon	A
A boy	---	A
TRILLARD d'AUVILLERS, Mr.		B
Two children		B
A clerk		B
A valet		B
LAUDRY, Mrs.		B
LA MOTTE, Mr.		C
BUG (?), Maximilien du		C
FOUST, Antoine		C
VALLET, Françoise		C
ST. JUST, Guillemain de		C
VILLEQUER, François		C
AMILLAU, Gabriel		C
BRELOU, Antoine		C
POITEVIN, André		C
PHILIPPE, François called DESPREZ		C
VALADON	Baker	C
BAU, Gabriel	Carpenter	C
PINAUD, Pierre	Carpenter	C

Name	Occupation	Status
CONIANT, Mr.		(D)
LE VRAY, Pierre		E
BROSSEAU, Jacques		E
ROULLIER, René		E
CHEOPILLOU, Jean		E
BUREAU, Jean		E
BEDOUINEAU, Jean		E
L'ECORCHE, Mathurin		E
RONDEAU, Pierre		E
BIGOT, Jean		E
TASBENRAU (SASBENRAU?), Charles		E
BARBIN, Jullien		E
RAYMOND, Thomas		E
ROGER, Mathurin		E
GIRARD, Jacques		E
LA MARIE, François		E
TRUCHET, François		E
GAZEAU, Guilleaume		E
CEBON, François		E
MAZIERES, Jean		E
DALIBOU, René		E
GAUTHIE, René		E
BONNET, François		E
LEPIN, Joseph		E
AVRIL, Charles		E
PISSOT, Jacques		E
GIRAULT, Silvain		E
METIVIER, Alexandre		E
MONTGAZON, Pierre		E
ROGER, René		E
BAHUET, Thomas		E
LAIME, René		E
GOUBAULT, Jacques		E
BOISSIMON, Jacques		E
RIDEAU, Charles		E
LE MOYNE, André		E
BOUET, Sebastien		E
LAURENT, François		E
GASCHET, François		E
LA MOUCHE, Jacques		E
FLANDRE, Pierre		E
DUBOIS, Jean		E
BONNET, Jean		E
PARMENTIER, Adrien		E
DIJON, Jean		E
LANGERONT, Louis		E
BRAZILIER, Louis called TOURANJEAN		E
BONNET, Gilbert		E
SIMONIN, Jean		E
BIOU, Guillaume, Chevalier du		E

Name	Occupation	Status
PIOT, Jean		E
SAUVANET, Pierre (called LE SACREUR)		E
LA NEUZILIERE, François		E
GRAPTON, Nicolas		E
PERROT, Toussaint		E
DAVID, Michel		E
BLANCHARD, Jean		E
MASSON, Pierre		E
PARINEAU, Jean		E
DUBOIS, Pierre (called CHERREAU)		E
LA PLAINE, Simon		E
BEAUJEAN, Christophe		E
LE FORT, Pierre		E
SIMON (called LA GRANDE JEANNE)		E
BARRE, Gilbert		E

MAY 18, 1718

LIST OF PERSONS BOUND FOR THE DE LA
HOUSSAYE CONCESSION IN LOUISIANA WHO
WERE FURNISHED FOOD AT LA ROCHELLE
FROM MARCH 29, 1718 TO MAY 16, 1718
WHILE AWAITING THE DEPARTURE OF THE
DUCHESSE DE NOAILLES.[1]

Name	Number of Days during which Food was Furnished
AT THE CAPTAIN'S TABLE	
DAMOIS, Marte (Wife of Sieur de la Houssaye)	36
HOUSSAYE, Charles Scourion de la	23
TIXERANT, Louis Gabriel	2
TIXERANT, C. Gabrielle	23
PARQUIER, Estienne	30
PERON, J. Baptiste	4
ROBERT, Antoine	6
L'AMIRAL, Henriette	42
MAILLEMAIN, Claude de	46
GRACES, Louis	41
BEAUPIN, Jean LES	43
ST. ROCQ, Jean Baptiste	30
AT THE OFFICER'S MESS	
LE MAYRE, Jacques	49
MARTEAU, Nicolas	49
GAUTIER, Bernard	49
VAUGY, Jean	49
BARNIERE, Nicolas	49
LA FERIERE, François	49
MARE, Mathias de la	49
LAMAURY, Pierre	49
LE BAUD, Pierre	12
BIDAIX, Simon	21
CROQUEAIN, François	49
SAUMER, François	12
CORDELAIN, Jean	12
HEMIN, Guillaume du	49
LAINE, Jean	49
DRAY, Martin	12
DUHAMEL, Charles	49
VINOIR, François	49
VIOLETTE, Jean	49

[1]The passenger list for the Duchesse de Noailles is dated May 25, 1718.

Name	Number of Days during which Food was Furnished
FALIS, Jean	49
LUNERAY, François	49
LUNERAY, Claude	12
LE COQ, Pierre	49
NAVARRE, Nicolas	49
DALEINIE, Louis	49
LENORY, George	2
SLACHO, Thomas	49
PATIN, Claude	44
L'AUGEVIN, Pierre	49
MARCHAND, Guillaume	49
JULIEN, Cristophe	49
LAINE, Jacques	21
LE FEVRE, Justinien	45
CHARLES, Jean	--
DEVILLON, Louis	49
CAPON, Michel	1
VILLARS, Ferdinand	49
DEAUDRY, Pierre	21
THIBAUD, Nicolas	12
GILBERT, Antoine	12
LA VALLEE, Nicolas	21
LE NOIR, Nicolas	49
PAYEN, Jean Baptiste	49
QUENETES, Jean	49
BRONZY, Marianne	43
PIET, Jeanne	41
PIET, Catherine	38
CHEVALIER, Marge	43
WABE, Romaine	7
NEVEU, Barthelemy	49
LA NOUE, Jacques	12
LE THUELLIER, Jacques	49
LIQUEUR, Jacques	49
LUZ, Aubin de	49
LE CONTE, Joseph	28

MAY 23, 1718

LIST OF PERSONS EMBARKED ON THE <u>MARIE</u>
BOUND FOR LOUISIANA FOR SERVICE WITH
THE COMPANY OF THE WEST OR FOR OTHER
REASONS.

Key to Status
(A)   Employed by the Company of the West
(B)   Concessionaries and their People
(C)   Private Passengers
(D)   Prisoners
(E)   Officers and Troops

Name	Native of	Occupation	Status
PREVOST, M.		Surgeon	A
RIFFAUT, M.		Stone-fitter	A
HORY, Abraham		Stone-fitter	A
LAIRE, MM. de (brothers)	Paris	Concessionaries	B
CHASTANG, M.	Nîme		B
ROBERT, M. Alexis	Paris		B
RUE, M. Antoine de la	Paris		B
ROBERT, M. Guillaume	Paris		B
ARGNON, Pierre	Vignolle		B
FRANCONY, Antoine	Geneva		B
CROZET DE MARETZ, Charles	Coligny		B
LE MORINIERE, Charles	Orléans		B
FASSIOT, Jean Baptiste	Reims		B
BRUNET, Jean	Lyon		B
BACHER, Jean	London		B
BERTHAULT, Pierre	Lyon		B
CARITON, Jean	Paris		B
VINAUD, Jean	Paris		B
MAYEUX, Laurent	St. Germain		B
CHAUMONT, Anselme	Paris		B
MILLIAT, François	Nogent		B
DUPART, Jacques	Condé		B
BERTIN, Jean Germain	Paris		B
BOCASSOT, Antoine	Paris		B
COURDON, Nicolas	Quercy		B
LEGER, Pierre	Chartres		B
CLAVIERE, Louis de la	Paris		B
COMMES, Louis de	Paris		B
LE FEVRE, Noël	Montmartre		B
CRISTIANNE, Louis	Paris		B
LE ROY, Mathieu	Cuilly		B
GARNIER, Jean	Sancerre		B

Name	Native of	Occupation	Status

CONCESSIONARIES (cont.)

Name	Native of		Status
LE GRAND, Gabriel	Paris		B
ROUSSEAU, Nicolas	Mantelan		B
DENIS, Jacques Charles	Paris		B
VALLET, François de	Versailles		B
GUIDER, Nicolas	Nogent		B
FLORAT, Antoine	Paris		B
AUBERT, Pierre	Lizigny		B
LA COMBE, Claude	St. Alban		B
ROUSSEAU, Louis	Villiers		B
SEJOURNE, Jacques Claude	Versailles		B
THOMAS, Louis	St. Leu de Paris		B
CHALIER, Pierre	Dunquerque		B
ADAM, Gilles	Paris		B
LE ROUX, Jean	Paris		B
CARON, Antoine Michel	Paris		B
LA CROIX, Jean Baptiste	Paris		B
LEVASSEUR, Claude	Paris		B
LE ROY, Louis Jacques	Paris		B
FOUTEL, Jacques	Paris		B
DUPONT, Jacques Claude	Paris		B
CORNU, Alexandre	Montfort		B
COLIGNOT, Jacques	Paris		B
BEAUCHESNE, André	Montfort		B
LAPLAUCHE, Louis	Dourlan		B
CARON, Jean	Peronne		B
LE CLERC, Robert	Chartres		B
OVENELLE, Antoine	St. Denis		B
BOUCHEREAU, Claude	Paris		B
BORNE, Antoine	Valencienne		B
JACOB (JARAN?), Robert	Prenay		B
BOURGEOIS, Jean Baptiste	Palisseau		B
VIETTE, Antoine	St. Germain		B
COUILLARD, Pierre	Argenteuil		B
FRETIN, François	St. Jean d'Angely		B
ROGER, Michel	Rion		B
ROCOURT, Jean du	Meulan		B
ROCOURT, Pierre du	Meulan		B
BARBARON, Martin	Rion		B
GRAVERET, Jean	Paris		B
ROBINET, Jacques	Paris		B
MEUNIER, Pierre	Paris		B
LE ROY, Noël	Paris		B
SEGRAIS, Brisse	Marcon		B
BRISSON, Germain	St. Jean Dumont		B
GAIGNEUR, Pierre	Paris		B

Name	Native of	Occupation	Status

WIVES & DAUGHTERS OF THE DE LAIRE GROUP

Name	Native of	Occupation	Status
ANDELYONNE, Marie	Marans	(She may have been the wife of Jean VINAUD)	B
GENTILLE, Marie	Teré		B
PARISIS, Catherine	Paris	(She may have been the wife of Jean BERTIN)	B
MILLIAT, Marie	Nogent		B
CAPRON, Marie Jeanne	Paris		B
PHELIPEAUX, Louise	Marans		B
GRAVELLE, Anne de	Isle de Ré	(Wife of Louis de la CLAVIERE)	B
AUBERT, Françoise	La Rochelle	(She may have been the wife of Louis de COMMES)	B

La demoiselle DU MARTRE

Name	Native of	Occupation	Status
BROSSARD, M.	Lyon	Concessionary	B
GRANDON, Denis	St. Quentin		B
CROMIERE, Michel de la	Paris		B
VELIEN, François	Diane in Lyonnois		B
QUNRELAN (QUINCLAU?) Thomas	Nantes		B
HILARET, Jean	Barbezieux		B
PRONDEAU, André	Selonzeau		B
DELAUNAY, Michel	Salle		B
CHAMEAU, Anne	St. Cloud		B
ISAMBERT, Toinette	La Rochelle		B
METIVET, Jeanne	St. George		B
LE GAIX (LEGOUX?), Sieur	Reims	Concessionary	B
CORFELIERE, Joseph	Loraine		B
ROBERT, Pierre	Poitou		B
JUYAN, Joseph	Nitré		B
CABILLAU, René	Liré in Anjou		B
DOUBLET, Pierre	St. Crespin in Champagne		B
TRIPLE, Silvain	Loches		B
VARIN, Remy	St. Thierry		B
BARRAT (BARRA), Jean	St. Jouy		B
LE PAGE, M.	Paris	Concessionary	B
DUVAL, François	Paris		B
LE JET (LEJEUNE?), Pierre An.	Paris		B
HERAULT, Jean	Oléron		B
LE MERCIER, Jean	Nantes		B
BOISLEAU, Condé	Fau in Poitou		B
TROUJON, Jean	St. Malo		B
HURLOT (URLOT), Laurent	Coulanges		B
AURARD, Jean	La Rochelle		B
REAL, Marie	Oléron	(She may have been the wife of Jean HERAULT)	B

Name	Native of	Occupation	Status

PRIVATE PASSENGERS

Name	Native of	Occupation	Status
LOCHON, M.	Paris		C
PERILLAU, André	Touraine		C
PREVOST, Antoine	Touraine		C
CHERRON (CHALON?), Jean	Blois		C
BAU, Anne du	Paris		C
MARECHAL, Jean Charles	Compiègne		C
LOUISEAU, Simon	Auxerre in Burgundy		C
MAGINET, Anne	Touraine		C
PREVOST, Anne Margarete	Touraine	(Wife of Antoine Prevost)	
ROGER, Mathieu	La Rochelle		C
SERVAN, Simonne	La Rochelle	(Wife of Roger)	C
ROGER, Margueritte	La Rochelle		C
BESSON, Michel	Angers		C
DEVALLEE, Jeanne	La Rochelle		C
BESSON, André	La Rochelle		C
GACHET (GARCHES?), André	La Rochelle		C
RIFFAUT, Sieur	Paris	Stone-fitter	C
GRANDIN, Sieur	Paris		C
VEILLERT (VALLERT?), M.	Paris		C
HORY, Abraham	Paris		C
DRILLANT (the elder)	La Rochelle		C
DRILLANT (younger brother)	La Rochelle		C

PRISONERS

Name	Native of	Occupation	Status
DESTOUCHES (called LA TOUCHE)			D
LA DOUCEUR (called CONFLANS)			D
LA FORTUNE (called ST. PIERRE)			D
ST. PIERRE (called PIERRE ROUGE			D
ST. SERVAIN (called LA FORME)			D
BEAUSOLEIL (called LA VALLEE)			D
CASTELNAUD (called JEAN DURAND)			D

OFFICERS AND TROOPS

Name	Native of	Occupation	Status
MARQUE, M. de la		Lieutenant. Commander of troops on board ship	E
PIGNOL, M.			E
BORDE, M. de la			E
DUMERBION, M.			E
DESBROSSES, M.			E
PALLICE, M. de la			E

Name	Native of	Occupation	Status

OFFICERS AND TROOPS (cont.)

<u>Sergeants</u>

BONCOEUR, de			E
MANDOLY			E
LE COMTE			E

<u>Soldiers</u>

DEGU			E
BATISTE, Jean			E
BALLEON, Cristophe			E
SILVESTE, François			E
GARDET, François			E
ARNAUD, Jean Baptiste			E
AUTERIVE, François			E
LORME, Joseph de			E
NIMAR			E
DESCHAMPS, François			E
COQUILLE, François			E
MICHEL, Faroux			E
PORTIE (MICHEL'S wife)			E
SAVIGNON			E
VALEE, Auguste			E
BON CORPS, Jean			E
OLLIER (OLIVIER?), Pierre			E

MAY 23, 1718

LIST OF EMPLOYEES OF THE COMPANY OF
THE WEST, CONCESSIONARIES AND THEIR
PEOPLE, OFFICERS, TROOPS, PRISONERS
AND OTHERS EMBARKED ON THE DUCHESSE
DE NOAILLES CAPTAINED BY DE LA SALLE
AND BOUND FOR LOUISIANA

Name	From	Comments

EMPLOYEES OF THE COMPANY OF THE WEST

The LE GAC Party

Name	From	Comments
LE GAC, M.	Nantes	Director
LAMBEZELET, François	Brest	
CESSIN, François	Brest	
LAURENT, Laurent	Landoiré	
DUFRESNE, Jean	St. Malo	
SAUVAGE, Sieur		Clerk
FERAROIS, Sieur		Clerk
SIMON, Sieur		Clerk

PRIVATE PASSENGERS

Name	From	Comments
MARLOT DE VERVILLE, Sieur	Paris	
LUSSARD, Nicolas		Servant
DUSOUCHET, Sieur & Madame	Nantes	

CONCESSIONARIES AND THEIR PEOPLE

The de la HOUSSAYE Party

Name	From	Comments
HOUSSAYE, Charles Scourion de la Montigny		Concessionary
DAUMOIS, Marthe	Metz	HOUSSAYE'S wife
VIENNE, Hector Scourion de	Montigny	
BERTIER, Mariane de		VIENNE'S wife
VILLERS, Nicolas de	St. Quentin	Deserted at the Cape
GUYON, Claude	Nogent	
TISSERANT, Louis Gabriel	Paris	
TISSERANT, C. Gabrielle	Paris	
DUVAL, C. Alexandre		
LE FEVRE, Jean Baptiste		
BINGAU, Catherine		LE FEVRE'S wife
PASQUIER, Antoine	Versailles	
COURIERE, Benoist de la	Nancy	
BULLON, Antoine	Compiègne	
PERON, Jean Baptiste	Valmartin	

Name	From	Comments

CONCESSIONARIES AND THEIR PEOPLE

The de la HOUSSAYE Party (cont.)

Name	From	Comments
ROBERT, Antoine	Paris	
BLANCHARD, Paul	Beauvais	
MAILLEMAIN, Claude	Peronne	
ROQ, Jean Baptiste	Maubeuge	
GRACE, Louis	Versailles	
LE BEAUPIN, Jean		
L'AMIRAL, Marie Henriette		May be the wife of LE BEAUPIN
VAUTIER, Pierre	Bordeaux	
FROMAGE, J.	Guise	
LE MAITRE, Jacques	Mitrey	
MARSAUT, Nicolas	Beauvais	
DAUGY, Jean		
GAUTIER, Bernard	Angers	
BARRIE, Nicolas	Montmirel	
LA FERRIERE, François	Mans	
MARRE, Mathias de la	Chateaudon	
LAMAURY, Pierre	Paris	
BIDAULT, Pierre Simon	Paris	
SAUNIER, François	Paris	
CHEMIN, Guillaume de	Linarot	
DUHAMEL, Charles	Chenil	
RIVOIR, François	Barré	
VIOLETTE, Jean	Montdidier	
BATISE, Jean	Nevileroy	
AGUEREUX (AGEREUX?), Claude	Compiègne	
LINEREUX, Thomas	Compiègne	
LE COQ, Pierre	Lisbon	
NAVARRE, Nicolas	Fontainebleau	
DALEINE, Louis	Rebouville	
FETON, Thomas	Angers	
PATIN, Claude	Beauvais	
LANGEVIN, Pierre	Angers	
MARCHAND, Guillaume	Gennes	
LE FEVRE, Justinien	Nogent	
VILLEROY, Louis de	Beauvais	
CAPON, Michel	Paris	Deserted at the Cape
VILARS, Ferdinand	Besançon	
VACHON, Claude	Troyes	
MARQUETS, Nicolas des	Pontoise	
LE NOIR, Michel	Rouen	
PAYEN, Jean Baptiste	Tours	
QUENETEL, André	Rouen	
LE CONTE (COMTE?), Joseph	Bayeux	
LE TUILLIER, Jacques	Pontaudonner	

Name	From	Comments

CONCESSIONARIES AND THEIR PEOPLE

The de la HOUSSAYE Party (cont.)

Name	From	Comments
NEVEU, Barthelemy	Paris	
DEZELEUX, Aubin	Chartres	Died August 18
JOLY, Charles	Rouen	
MARTIN, Yvonne	La Rochelle	
PIEL, Jeanne	Falaise	
PIEL, Catherine	Falaise	
CHEVALIER, Marie	Paris	
BRONZY, Marianne		
WABE, Romaine	Montdidier	
THEVENARD, Marie	La Rochelle	
HAROND (GARON?), Catherine	La Jarine	
GIRARD, Marie	La Rochelle	
LE SUEUR, Jeanne Françoise	Muran	
MOLINEAU, Marianne	Nantes	
TROUVE, Louise	La Rochelle	
COTTAR, Thomas	La Rochelle	
GIRARD, Jacques	Limoges	
BOURNIE, Marie	La Rochelle	

The LEGRAS Party

Name	From	Comments
LEGRAS, Estienne	Rouen	
MARE, Jacques	St. Romain	
PAUL, Jacques	Gosselin	
FRONTIN, Louis	Isle de Ré	

PASSENGERS EMBARKED AT LE HAVRE

Name	From	Comments
CADOT (CADET?) Paulin	Paris	Embarked by "lettre de cachet"
BOUDIN, Jacques		Soldier taken at Le Havre
VROCHON, Marie Therese		Wife of CRESPEAU, soldier in the colony.

OFFICERS

Name	From	Comments
RICHEBOURG, M. de		Commander
NOUETTE DE GRANDVAL, M.		
LOLBMIERE, M. de		
CHEVALIER, M.		
SAINT REMY, M. de		
L'ARDIERE, M.		

Name	From	Comments

OFFICERS

M. de RICHEBOURG'S People

JASSEMIN, Mathieu	Meulant	
MARTIN, Roze	Nantes	
SAZERNE, Margueritte	La Rochelle	

M. de GRANDVAL'S People

NEVILLE, J.	Dézois in Champagne	
LE VEILLE	Rochefort	
GILBERT, Geneviève	Nantes	

SERGEANTS

LA FRANCE		His wife and daughter are with him.
DUPUY		His wife and son are with him.
BESSAN		
DEVREUGE		

SOLDIERS

LE DUC		
DESFORGES, Nicolas		
POLAIS, Pierre		
LE FEVRE, Vincent		
MARTIN, Richard		
GEORGE, André		
CONARD, André		
TARNOIS, Pierre		
PARMARIN, Louis		
HENRY		
GIGUET, Joseph		
LEBEL, Henry		
DUBIE		His wife and his son are with him.
RAVIEZ, Paul Louis		
BREUVET, Jean Baptiste		
SALLE, Pierre		
DUPRE, François		
LA CROIX, Pierre		
DESMOULIN, Simon		
DUMAY, Gabriel		
BOULLE, François		
MORIS, Guillaume		
BERLA, Jean		
GUIGNON, Maurice		His wife is with him.
BAUDION, François		

Name	From	Comments

SOLDIERS (cont.)

BOURMIEAUX, Cristophle
COUTTEREAU, Charles
VAVASSEUR, Pierre
VIMOR, Jean
BUREAU
VOISIN, Jean
BEAUFORT, Claude
COUR, Gilles de la
LATY, Joseph
BEAUFILS, Jacques
ANDRE, Jean
ST. AMAND, Ferageau de
BALMON, Jean François
BAGUELIN, Pierre   His wife is with him.
ABRAHAM, Louise
PERIN, Augustin
CORNEVILLE, Nicolas
BERGEAIST, François
HUBERT, Jean
LATY, Joseph
BEAUPIN, Simon
CHEUX, Claude   His wife is with him.
BODOUIN, Jacques
ROUSSEL, Daniel
BEAUMONT, Louis
SANS FACON

PRISONERS

DESAUDREST, Pierre
ROUFRE, Guillaume   called SANS FACON
ROUSSEL, Jean   called LA VIGNE
BUY, Jean Isaac   called ST. JEAN
SEIL, Augustin Grand
MICHEL, Charles   called LA VERDURE
LE BEL, Jacques   called LEBEL
BAUDIN, Louis   called POITEVIN
BROSSE, Remond   called BERNE
SON FILS, François   called ST. FRANCOIS
MARMIN, André   called L'ESPERANCE
PETIT, Jacques   called LE GRAND
ANTOINE, Jean   called ST. JEAN
LE BEAU, Augustin   called LE BEAU
VERDIER, Theodore   called LE VERT
VELU, Nicolas   called LE FORT

MAY 23, 1718

LIST OF EMPLOYEES OF THE COMPANY OF
THE WEST, CONCESSIONARIES AND THEIR
PEOPLE, OFFICIERS, TROOPS, PRISONERS
AND OTHERS EMBARKED ON THE VICTOIRE
COMMANDED BY M. DEROSSET AND BOUND
FOR LOUISIANA.

Name	From	Comments

EMPLOYEES OF THE COMPANY OF THE WEST

Name	From	Comments
DUVERGE, Sieur		Clerk
JUS, SIEUR		Clerk
NOLIN, Sieur		Clerk
LEVASSEUR, Sieur		Clerk
BEAUPRE, Sieur		Clerk
LANDE, Sieur de la		Clerk
FLATTIER, Sieur		Clerk (Surgeon?)
PIGEON, Sieur		Clerk

CONCESSIONARIES AND THEIR PEOPLE

The BEIGNOT Party

Name	From
BEIGNOT DE CHANTOUR, M.	Paris
BEIGNOT DE VALLEMONT, M.	Paris
ROY, Nicolas	Brevil
LOMONIER, Louis	Isle de Ré
GENDRE, André	Isle de Ré
LE CORONIER, Pierre	St. Michel
SEQUIN (SEGUIN?), Louise Marthe	Canada
LEIGNAY, Simon	Montpourvoir
BLANCHARD, René	St. Pierre
LE BAUD, Nicolas	St. Sulpice

The VAUTIER Party

Name	From
VAUTIER, M.	Niort
BAUSSET, Jean	Frontenay
BARE, Jacques	Niort
MARLOT, Jean	St. Pezeur

The de la HARPE Party

Name	From
HARPE, M. de la	St. Malo
BAUMAN, M. de	St. Malo
POTIER, M. de	St. Malo
MASTET, M.	Dinan
LE BLANC, de la Croix	St. Malo

Name	From	Comments

CONCESSIONARIES AND THEIR PEOPLE

The de la Harpe Party (cont.)

Name	From	Comments
LAVOS, de	Dinan	
RIVAGE, du	St. Malo	
BOURGAUD	St. Malo	
LA FILOCHE	Rennes	
SERIGNAT	Paris	
MASTET, Maurice	Dinan	
PORTE NOIRE, de la	St. Malo	
CHAIS, de la	St. Malo	
HOUSAIS, de la	St. Malo	
FLEURY	Morlaix	
COUPART, Jean	St. Malo	
BERNARD, Bolloy	St. Malo	
SERVAIS	St. Malo	
BINARD, François	St. Malo	
POULIGUIN, Jean	St. Malo	
MARSON, François	St. Malo	
LE CLERC	St. Malo	
ROUSSEL	Dinan	
RONDIT	Dol	
DUMESNIL	Dol	
LA CROIX	Balois	
GUERQUSET (QUERQUSET?) de	Rennes	
DUQUESNOIS	St. Malo	
SAMSON	St. Malo	
CHAMPAGNE	St. Malo	
DAIN (DAIS?)	St. Malo	
FILLE, Suson	St. Malo	
FILLE, Fauchon	Nantes	
ALMAZOR	St. Malo	
GODEFROY	St. Malo	
JOSEPH	St. Malo	
JEAN BATISTE	St. Malo	
JASMIN	St. Malo	
Batiste	St. Malo	

The PERIER Party

Name	From	Comments
PERIER, M.	Paris	Chief Engineer
BROUTIN, François	Bassée in Flanders	
DESAUNET, Jacques	Ninge in Alsace	
CREUX, Charles de	Paris	
GUILLERME, Julien	Belle Isle	
VINCENT, Pierre	St. Mexant	

CONCESSIONARIES AND THEIR PEOPLE

The LEVEQUE Party

Name	From	Comments
LEVEQUE, Sieur	Angers	
PRE, Magdelaine	Angers	Sieur LEVEQUE'S wife
LEVEQUE, Michel	Chateaubriant	
LEVEQUE, François	La Rochelle	
LEVEQUE, Jean	La Rochelle	
LEVEQUE, Magdelaine	La Rochelle	
LEVEQUE, Maurice	La Rochelle	
LEVEQUE, Thomas	La Rochelle	

The DUFOUR Party

Name	From	Comments
DUFOUR, Joseph	Canton of Bern	
FOURNIER, Catherine	La Rochelle	Joseph Dufour's wife
DUFOUR, Joseph	La Rochelle	Joseph Dufour's son
MASSIOT, Gabriel	La Rochelle	
PINAUD, Mathurin	Brittany	
FAVREAU, Jean	Saintonge	
BOYER, Jean	La Rochelle	

The DUHAMEL Party

Name	From	Comments
DUHAMEL, Richard	La Rochelle	
GILYON, Estienne (father)	Isle de Ré	
GILYON, Estienne (son)	Isle de Ré	
LOMONIER, Louis	Isle de Ré	
ERBER, Jean	Isle de Ré	

OFFICERS

Name	From	Comments
DAVRIT, M.		Commander of the troops aboard ship
BERNEVAL, M. de		Madame BERNEVAL accompanied him
MELIQUE, M. de		
NOYAN, M. de		
DUMESNIL DE CHAMPIGNY, M.		
L'ISLE, M. de		Mademoiselle L'ISLE accompanied him

M. DAVRIT'S People

Name	From	Comments
MEYLAN, Jean de	Grenoble	
DESCOTTE, Pierre	Paris	
TURPIN, Magdelaine de	La Rochelle	

Name	From	Comments

OFFICERS (cont.)

M. de MELIQUE'S People

Name	From	Comments
BIENVENU, Philippe	Port Louis	
BIENVENU, Antoine	Port Louis	Son of Philippe BIENVENU
SOLO, Pierre Henry	Nantes	
GAUTRON, Charles	La Rochelle	
COUSTEAUX, Estienne	Isle de Ré	
BALANGE, Simon	Isle de Ré	
FLAMAND, Jacques	Isle de Ré	
DOYRON, André	Isle de Ré	
BEUNE, Jean de	Paris	
CATHERINE	La Rochélle	
L'ALLEMAND, Jean	Angers	

SERGEANTS

DUVERNAY
PEYRECAVE
SOULAS

SOLDIERS

LA VIGNE
VILLAIN Blanq
PLEAU, Toussaint
ANTOINE, Noël
CARE, Pierre
BOISMARTIN, Antoine
NINET, Denis
JOURDAIN, Louis
LE BRETON, Jacques
CONTANT, Joseph
DUBERNAY, René
SABOURDIN, René
BOURDIN, Pierre
LE ROY, Charles
VIELLON, Jacques
BOYER
MEIPECQ
RABIN
AIZE, Jean
BERGE, Jean
RONDAUT, Jean
MARIE, Antoine
CHEVALIER, Germain
RAUDOLT, Jean
LA BICHE, Louis

Name	From	Comments

SOLDIERS (cont.)

AUGERON, Joseph
PIOU, Joseph
LE PREVOTS, Jean
QUE, Nicolas — His wife is with him.
HUGOTS, Louis
ROBIN, Theodore — His wife, Blanche, is with him.
GACONIT, Pierre
GUIBERT, Hierosme
PICHAU, André
MICHEL, Charles
CADET, Reverain
ROLLAND, Jean
TREVILLON, Chery de
QUZIS, Jean
VALENTIN, Jacques
GILBERT, Antoine
DUTOR, Jacques
CADICQ, François
DESCHAMPS
GALIBERT, Jean Jacques
TIERRY, Pierre
DESTRUMIL, Cezar
LA CROIX
HILLEBERT, Claude
DEJEAN, Jean
ALLISON, Estienne
FERAND, Jean
COUTURIER, Louis
DUPRE, Clares
CLERICE, Noël François
GABELLION, Thomas
BROUET, Louis
FLEURER, Jean
BRAQUET, Jean Batiste
VIELLE, Gilbert
ANGIE, Baptiste
FAISANT, Picot — Performing a sergeant's duties
GOSEZY, Remond
CARIERE, François

PRISONERS

ST. HILAIRE, Jean — called BEL AIR
FOURNIER, Jean — called BEAUSOLEIL

Name	From	Comments

PRISONERS (cont.)

Name	From	Comments
MOREAU, Estienne		called JOLICOEUR
SABLIN, Antoine		called SANS SOUCY
GILBERT, Jacques		called LA LIBERTE
VILLENEUVE		
ROZE, Jean		
LA VIGNE		
SOURD, Antoine		
VILARD (VITARD?) Robin		called LA RIVIERE
PIGNOLLE, Nicaise		called LA VIOLETTE
GOSSELLY, Jean Baptiste		
DUCLOS, François		
PANELLE, Jean Baptiste		
SIVALLON, Jean		
CEVRIT, Jean Baptiste		
NEUTRON (NEUTON?) Augustin		called LA JEUNESSE
BRETON, Altingourt		

NOVEMBER 15, 1718

LIST OF EMPLOYEES OF THE COMPANY OF THE
WEST, MINERS, SOLDIERS, TOBACCO WORKERS,
CONCESSIONARIES AND THEIR PEOPLE AND
OTHERS EMBARKED ON THE COMTE DE TOULOUSE
COMMANDED BY THE CHEVALIER DE GRIEU BOUND
FOR LOUISIANA.

Name	From	Comments
LARCEBAULT, M.		Director General of the Company
GORDON, Sieur		Captain of Infantry
SIMON, Sieur		Clerk
FERRAROIS, Sieur		Clerk
RENAUDIERE, Sieur		Clerk. His wife is with him.
LOUSTAUD, Sieur		Clerk

MINERS

LETOILE, Sieur		Brigadier
OLLIVIER, Sieur		Sous-Brigadier. His wife is with him.
MARC		Sergeant
LA PLUME		Corporal
FRANCOEUR		
BONCOEUR, De		
LA GRANDEUR		
LA BRANCHE		
LEPINE		
GERARD		
ST. JEAN		
LA SOUDE		
CHEVALIER		
Four wives of miners		
Three children of miners		
POULETET, Jean		Garçon des mineurs

SOLDIERS

SAINT SAUVEUR		Sergeant
SAINT JULIEN		Sergeant
BALCON		Cadet
MALO		Cadet
SOCIONDO		Cadet
LA GIRARDIERE		Cadet. His wife is with him.
LARAGONOIS, Jean		
BAUDOUIN, André		
BLONDELOT		Cadet
DARNAUD, Antoine		
DARNAUD, Jacques		
BEAULIEU		

Name	From	Comments

SOLDIERS (cont.)

CAGNEREL
GUERY, Joseph
ST. MARTIN
LE PREUX, Nicolas
LE CROSNIER, François
RINAUD, Jean
ST. MARTIN   His wife is with him.
LA PENSEE
DANIEL, Ollivier
ST. LOUIS   His wife and daughter are
                                                               with him.
ST. JEAN   His wife is with him.
SIMON, Jean
LA FONTAINE
CHERET, Edmé
FARCINE, François
MAUDUISSON, Laurent
LE CROSNIER, Jean François
RAMEE, Pierre
BELLAVOINE
TROISSARD, Yvon
DU PLESSIX
LA FARGE
RENOUD, Jean
DESBOIS
NERISSON, Pierre
GRANDJEAN, Jean
DESCHAMPS
CROSNIER
MOREAU, Jacques
ST. GEORGES, Joseph de
LE GRAND, Augustin
JOIE, Jean Etienne Philipe de la
SURGE, Bernard   called DARGENCOURT
CHEVENET, Pierre
GODER, Nicolas   M. LARCEBAULT'S Servant
LOCAR, Nicolas   M. LARCEBAULT'S Servant
AMANVILLE   M. GORDON's Servant
JAUSON, Jacques   M. GORDON'S Servant

TOBACCO WORKERS
MONTPLAISIR, M. de   Inspector
BAUJON, Sieur   Overseer
DESCARAIT (DESCARAIL?), Antoine
RICARD, Pierre
JALS (JATER?), Pierre
BESSE, Bertrand

Name	From	Comments

TOBACCO WORKERS (cont.)

GIBERT, Pierre
SISSAC, Abraham
DUMICHEL, Jean
CHANDOUC (CHANDRUE?), Pierre
AUDIBERT, Pierre
FOUILLOUSE (FOUILLOUTE?), Jean
OISSON, Pierre
GUIRAUD, Jean
POURCHARESSE, Jean
LA ROGUE, Jacques
CAPDAN, Pierre
SEGAS, Jean
LAVAL, Pierre
BROUGUET, Jean

CONCESSIONARIES FOR THE DE LAIRE PARTNERSHIP

Name	From	Comments
DUFOUR, Sieur	Courcelles	
TANUS		Brewer
BUC, Michel du		Tenant farmer

CONCESSIONARIES AND THEIR PEOPLE

Name	From	Comments
BAULNE, Sieur de		Concessionary
BAULNE, Madame de		
DUPLESSIS, Chevalier		
BOIRON, Sieur		
BOIRON, Mademoiselle		
DEMOUY, Sieur		The older son
DEMOUY, Sieur		The younger son
DEMOUY, Mademoiselle		
LAVERGE, Sieur de		
MOREL, Sieur		M. de BAULNE'S secretary
SIGY, Sieur		Clerk
BONVALET, Louis		Cook
BONVALET, Jean		
ALLARD, Cristine		
POIREE		Gunsmith
SONNIS		Cooper
SABUREAU		Shoe-maker
PELLERIN, Sieur		Concessionary
PELLERIN, Madame		
PELLERIN		The son of Sieur PELLERIN
GUEZO, Pierre		Nephew of the PELLERINS
SOILEAU, Noël		Nephew of the PELLERINS
BOURBON, Louis		called ESSEMENT. His wife is with him.

Name	From	Comments

CONCESSIONARIES AND THEIR PEOPLE (cont.)

The PELLERIN Party (cont.)

GUILLETTE, Annette		Servant
MARIE		Free Negro servant
ARGERE, Marguerite		Servant

The LANTHEAUME and DU BREUIL Party

LANTHEAUME, Sieur		Concessionary
DU BREUIL, Sieur		Concessionary
DU BREUIL, Madame		Two Du Breuil children
GOMBAUD (GOMBAULT?), Marie	La Rochelle	Servant
FRANCOISE	La Rochelle	Servant
COLTIVE, Dauphin	Paris	Carpenter
RAVAUX, Jacques	Mezières	Carpenter
DIORE, Jacques	Salle	Cooper
DAVID, Jacob	Rochefoucault	Shoe-maker
MOREAU, Jacques François	Paris	Carpenter
DAVID, Romain	Rochefoucault	Tailor
CAUDELON, Bernard	Sousac	Laborer[1]
LE FEBVRE	Corbie, near Amiens	Laborer
COURONNAY (COURONNERY?), François	Near Lizieux	Laborer
GAULE, Jacques de	Chalons	Laborer
PIRRAM, (PIVAIN?), Jean	Joué, near Poitiers	Laborer

ADDENDUM

SAUVAGE, Sieur Edmond		Came aboard ship after the present roll was taken
TANUS		Bound for the de Laire concession deserted before the ship sailed.

[1]Although this occupation is simply listed throughout this work as "laborer," the person was more often than not a farm laborer. In time some of these people came to own farms and would then be more properly referred to as farmers.

1719

LIST OF PRIVATE PASSENGERS AND GIRLS
EMBARKED ON THE MUTINE COMMANDED BY
M. DE MARLONNE AND BOUND FOR LOUISIANA

Name	From	Comments

PRIVATE PASSENGERS

CAILLOT, Jacques François
L'ANGLOIS, Dominique Baulentin
SAUVAGE, Louis   L'ANGLOIS' valet
PHILIPPE, Alexis
LAUGROTTE (LANGROTTE?), Denise Marguerite Wife of Alexis PHILIPPE

GIRLS SENT FROM PARIS BY ORDER OF THE KING

MORISSE, Marie
NERON, Marie Antoinette
BRION, Anne
DOYAR, Marie   Called LA LOUP
PELLETIER, Françoise
FREDEVEAU, Marie Antoinette
DINAN, Françoise Nicolle
LA NOIX, Marie   Called CARLIER
BRIERE, Marie
BUFFET, Nicole
BOITARD, Marie Anne   Called GRANDMAISON
MARTIN, Marie Simonne
SARRA, Marguerite
CORROY, Jeanne
DESPLACES, Genevieve
BENOIST, Marie Anne
BRAY, Marie Anne de   Called BOUCHER
FLY, Jolaine
POIULLOT, Jeanne   Called ROCHEFORT
FILBERT, Marie Jeanne
ROUSELLE, Marie Therese   Called LYONNOISE
PESEY, Marie
JOLLY, Charlotte
MORISSE, Anne
BOYARD, Catherine
BRIET, Judith
BOUTIN, Marie Anne
TENON, Marie Therese
ROYEN, Honnoré
CHARTIER, Marie   Called MALLET
ROLLAND, Anne Françoise

Name	From	Comments

GIRLS SENT FROM PARIS (cont.)

LEFORT, Marie Anne
AUTOMNE, Marie Anne
ESVAULT, Justin
LE TELLIER, Marie
VERMANSAL, Marie Anne
BOURGUIGNET, Marie
LONGUEVILLE, Jeanne
SARRAZIN, Claude   Called MARSELLE
DINAN, Marie Anne
CHARPIN or CREPIN, Jeanne
LE COMPTE, Marie
VIVIER, Claude
BRUNELLE, Louise
MAHOUL, Jeanne
DESBAUX, Madeleine
DIELLE, Anne Madeleine
SAUSSET, Françoise
MOUGIN, Marie
REFFE, Angélique   Called FILDIE
METROT, Marie
POTON, Marie   Called D'AUTEVILLE
CERCEUIL, Nicolle
LE COMPTE, Marie Therese
BERTHELOT, Anne
SALLOT, Marguerite
NE, Françoise
FILLASSIER, Marie Anne   Called PRINTEMPS
ROBOUAN, Marie Anne
BOIRON, Marie Madeleine
DIMENCHE, Marie
RAFFLON, Marie
FLASSIN, Catherine
FOURCHET, Marie Anne
BROSSARD, Marie Anne
DANDIN, Marie
OUFROY, Charlotte
YVAIRE, Suzanne
VALENCIENNE, Anne Therese
LÉMAIRE, Marie Agnes
TABOURET, Marie
MELUN, Anne   Called FLORENTIN
BASSINET, Louise
BETTEMONT, Genevieve
BOURN, Marie Madeleine
PORTEFILLET, Genevieve
ROBERT, Marie
HUREE, Claude

Name	From	Comments

GIRLS SENT FROM PARIS (cont.)

GUERIN (QUERIN?), Marie
MOULLE, Marie
SURRIN, Claude
GRENE, Marie
BOGNY, Marguerite
ROT, Marguerite
FONTENELLE, Louise
DESVAUX, Françoise
BARON, Marie
DURIVEAU, Charlotte
CANU, Jeanne Toinette
FODESTAL, Françoise   Called CHARMENT
BOIRON, Marie Anne
MOREAU, Marguerite   Called BAILLY
BOULEY, Suzanne

GIRLS SENT FROM LE HAVRE

CHEVALLIER, Suzanne
DESCHAMPS, Marie

JANUARY 26, 1719

LIST OF OFFICERS, WORKERS FOR THE
COMPANY, GIRLS FROM THE POORHOUSE OF
LA ROCHELLE, SOLDIERS AND OTHERS EM-
BARKED ON THE <u>MARECHAL DE VILLARS</u>
COMMANDED BY M. MESCHIN BOUND FOR
LOUISIANA FROM LA ROCHELLE.

Name	From	Comments

OFFICERS AND OTHERS

SERIGNY, M. de		Probably Bienville's brother
SERIGNY DE LOIRE, M.		
MESNIER, M.		Garde de la Marine
DEVIN, Sieur		
JAURON, Sieur Estienne		Chemist. Put ashore.
BRUNET		M. Serigny's Servant
L'ESPAGNOL, François		M. Serigny's Servant
LE NORMAND		M. Serigny's Servant
LA PLANTE		M. Serigny's Servant

WORKERS FOR THE COMPANY

ARLU, Jean (father)		Master builder
ARLU, Jean (son)		
BAZILLE, Catherine		Wife of Jean ARLU (father)
ARLU, Marie Marguerite		
ARLU, Marianne		
ARLU, Jeanne		
BLANCHET, Pierre	La Rochelle	Ship-carpenter
ROBIE, Jean		Cooper

<u>Workers who have completed their service with the Company and who wish
to establish themselves in Louisiana.</u>

FIEVRE, Estienne	Grosse Oeuvre	Carpenter
DUBOIS, Jacques		Carpenter
BOITEAU, Mansuet	Brouage	Cooper
COURSIER, Jacques	Rochefort	Sail-maker
DE ROSIERS		Cooper

GIRLS FROM THE POORHOUSE OF LA ROCHELLE

COGNOVE, Louise		Age 23. At the poorhouse since birth.
JOUSSEAU, Therese		Age 24. Legitimate. At poorhouse since age 8.
SUBILEAU, Catherine		Age 23. Legitimate. At poorhouse since age 7.

Name	From	Comments

GIRLS FROM THE POORHOUSE OF LA ROCHELLE (cont.)

Name	From	Comments
CERCLET, Suzanne	La Rochelle	Age 24. At poorhouse since age 11
CERCLET, Madelaine	La Rochelle	Age 23. Sister of Suzanne. At poorhouse since age 10.
TEVENARD, Charlotte	La Rochelle	Age 21. Legitimate. At poorhouse since age 10.
DOMINIQUE, Marianne	La Rochelle	Age 19. Legitimate. At poorhouse since age 14.
AIMEE, Catherine	La Rochelle	Age 24. Legitimate. At poorhouse since age 4.
GUILLOTTE, Marie	St. Rogatien	Age 15. Legitimate. At poorhouse since age 10.
FOUCHARD, Suzane		Age 14. At poorhouse since infancy.
PAIN, Marguerite	La Rochelle	Age 15. Legitimate. At poorhouse since age 5.
CHARBONNET, Marie	La Rochelle	Age 14. Legitimate. At poorhouse since age 1.
CHAIGNE, Madelaine	La Rochelle	Age 14. Legitimate. At poorhouse since age 9.
VALONNE, Jeanne	La Rochelle	Age 15. Legitimate. At poorhouse since age 7.
RICHOU, Marie	La Rochelle	Age 15. Legitimate. At poorhouse since age 6 months.
GUIRMOTTE, Jeanne	La Rochelle	Age 27. At poorhouse since age 10.
CORMIEL, Therese	La Rochelle	Age 19. At poorhouse since age 6.
ANDRE, Marie	La Rochelle	Age 19. At poorhouse since age 10.
MALHERBE, Marguerite	La Rochelle	Age 14. At poorhouse since age 7.
BOURGEOIS, Marie	La Rochelle	Age 22. At poorhouse since age 10.

SOLDIERS

Sargeants

DAMERVAL		
DU RONCIER		His wife is with him.

Corporal

D'AUTERIVE

Cadet

D'AQUIN, Antoine

Name	From	Comments

SOLDIERS (cont.)

Cadets (cont.)

JARROSSON, Joseph
LA MANIERE, Joseph de

Troops

MARTIN, Jean
PIOU, Joseph
GERAULT, François
VINCENDRE, Charles
NERODEAU, Nicolas
GEOGROY, Sigibert
DORE, Martin
DAUPHIN, Pierre
THOMAS, Louis
COGNAC, Pierre
CLAUDE, René
MAILLIN, René
MORICEAU, Joseph
REMBAULT
MARTEL, Jacques
DUPIN, Antoine
HERAULT, Jean
POITIER
GEAIN, François
BRAYER, Jacques
LE PAGE, Jacques
LE FLOT, Jacques
LE LONG, Jean
CHARDET, Guillaume
JAMONEAU, François
GALLAIN
GRANDJEAN
BARTHELEMY
LA CROIX
LAURENT, François
TOUSSEAU, Jean
BONVALET, jean
COUSSEAU, Antoine
PAQUIER, Claude
SINET, Laurent
DAUPHAGNE, Evrard   Ill. Discharged because he is
                                           unable to serve.

BONNET, Guillaume
DUMESNIL, Charles

Name	From	Comments

SOLDIERS (cont.)

Troops (cont.)

SAVETIER, Jacques		
DEMAREST, Antoine		
HAUTEBREUILLE, François Ancelet de		Cadet
BERTIN, Pierre		

SOLDIERS ORDERED BY THE COURT TO SERVE THIRTY-SIX MONTHS IN LOUISIANA

TRANCHARDIERE, Alexandre
SERON, Charles Camille
LE CLERC, Patrice
CORPS, François de
LAPOTAIRE, Nicolas
LEBEL, Jacques
DEVAUX, Pierre
GOUPIN, Charles
COFFINEAU, Pierre
CHANDRON, Pierre
PENDRY

JANUARY 26, 1719

LIST OF CONCESSIONARIES AND THEIR PEOPLE,
SOLDIERS, AND PRIVATE PASSENGERS EMBARKED
ON THE PHILIPPE COMMANDED BY M. DIHOURSE
BOUND FOR LOUISIANA FROM LA ROCHELLE

Name	From	Comments
SAUVAGE, Sieur Patrice		Enseigne d'Infanterie
BEAULIEU, Sieur de		Enseigne Réformé
		These two men returned ashore and embarked on the Dauphine

CONCESSIONARIES AND THEIR PEOPLE

The SERNONVILLE and CANEL Party

SERNONVILLE, Sieur de		
SERNONVILLE, Madame de		
CANEL, Sieur de		
CANEL, Madame de		
BELLEGARDE, Sieur de		
GIRARD, François	Mezieres sur Meuse	
PRESSON, François	Verdun	
FREMON, Henry	Mezieres	
DAUVERGNE, Martin	Champeau in Brie	
FLAUDIERS, Louis de	Corbie	
LA FORCE, Anne		Wife of Louis de FLAUDIERS
GAGET, Antoine	Verdun	
FLANDRE, Firmin de	Corbie	
GIROS, Jean	Chabannes in Poitou	
GAILLAT, François de	Paris	
SAMSON, Guy	Douville in Beauce	
LEVE, Louis Estienne	Paris	
LE COMTE, Pierre	Dorton in Franche Comté	
HUPE, François	Paris	
CHEVALIER, Claude	Lyon	
PAYEN, François	Peronne in Picardy	
MARCELLES, Nicolas	Arras	
LA FONTAINE, Jean	Fougère in Brittany	
L'HOMME, Nicolas	Chartres in Beauce	
AUTRUSSEAU, Jean	La Rochelle	
MAUDUISSON, Pierre	Beaugency	
LEMOINE, Marie	Alvert in Saintonge	

The OLIVIER Party

OLIVIER, Sieur		
BRU, Louis de	Paris	Clerk
ROUSSEAU, Marie	St. Jean d'Angely	Governess

Name	From	Comments

CONCESSIONARIES AND THEIR PEOPLE (cont.)

The OLIVIER Party (cont.)

Name	From	Comments
LEMOINE, Pierre	St. Mexant, bishopric of Mans	
MENARD, Jean	Boutteville, near Angouleme	
BRUTIER, Pierre	Ruffé, near Angoulem	
CAMES, Charles Antoine de	Paris	
JOLIVET, Jean	Paris	
DAMIENS, Guillaume	Paris	Surgeon
MORIN, Jean	Chateaubriant in Brittany	
ALAY, Martin	Chezeau in Touraine	
MUNIER, Jacques	Paris	
BOYER, Marc	La Rochelle	
BOUER (BONER?), Pierre	La Rochelle	

The BEAUCOUDRE Party

Name	From	Comments
BEAUCOUDRE, Sieur		Concessionary
LE CLERC, Marianne	Paris	Governess
DUBOIS, Louis Pierre	Paris	Clerk. Deserted
LE COMTE, Jacques	Poitiers	Deserted
MASSE, Maturin	Mareuil in Poitou	
BIDAT, Pierre	Mans	Called FRANCEUR. Deserted
BARRAIL, Antoine	Nantes	Deserted
RIEUX, Jean du	Saumur	Deserted
MILAIN, Jean	Angers	Sent home
SIGUINOZ, Martin	Ste. Marie, bishopric of Nantes	
VANNIER, Pierre	Lavale	Called SANSSOUCY. Sent home.
LEVAL, Jean	Angers	Sent home.
DEMANZ, Gabriel	Bouillez	
BROUSSEZ, Gilles	Plelan	
DANIAU, Philippe		His wife is with him.
TRUGUE, Michel		
MILAIN, Gabriel		

The BROSSARD Party

Name	From	Comments
BROSSARD, Sieur	Lyon	
BROSSARD, Mathieu		Sieur BROSSARD's nephew.
BROSSARD, Madame		Sieur BROSSARD's sister-in-law
MACHOU, Sieur	Paris	
GRANDIN, Madame	Paris	
FAUCON, Madame	Paris	

Name	From	Comments

CONCESSIONARIES AND THEIR PEOPLE (cont.)

The BROSSARD Party (cont.)

Name	From	Comments
PREVON, Noël	Lyon	
DUCLOS, Mathieu	Lyon	
RIVIERE, François	Lyon	
BERNOLDY, Louis		
CHAGNEAU, Catherine	Rompray	
CHAGNEAU, Marie	Rompray	
CHAGNEAU, Madelaine	Rompray	
CHAGNEAU, Jean	Rompray	
TACHON, Marie		
SABOUREAU, Jean	Dampierre	
CHAGNEAU, Estienne		
CHAGNEAU, François		
POIRIER, Claude	Beaugency	
CHALESSIN, Marie	Lyon	
BESSAC, Michel	Saintes	
BOUCHARD, Jean		
TACHON, Jean	Saintes	
TACHON, Louis		

The MAZY Party

Name	From	Comments
MAZY, Sieur		
LA MAITRE, Sieur		
MARTINOZ, Louis	Tours	His wife is with him.
MARTINOZ, Louis		Son of Louis MARTINOZ
CHAILLOUX, Therese	La Rochelle	
BRISARD, Louis	Tours	
LAMOUREUX, François	Paris	
ALLEVIN, François	Corbie	
HERISSE, Jacques	Tours	
BOIS, Jacques de	Metz	
ALLAIN, François	Tours	
DENIS, Antoine	Paris	
LA GOUBLAYE, Antoine	Fontainebleau	
JARRIAS, Gregoire		
JARRIAS, René		
L'HOSPITEL, Jean		
DREUX, Mathurin		

SOLDIERS

Sargeant

Name	From	Comments
SILVESTRES		
BOUTIER		Called DE LANGLE

Name	From	Comments

SOLDIERS (cont.)

Cadets

DU VERNAY
DU ROUVROY
PROTEST
CEZILLE (the elder)
CEZILLE (the younger)

Troops

CRAFT
ALORGE
ROUSSEL (the elder)
ROUSSEL (the younger)
LEVASSEUR (the elder)
LEVASSEUR (the younger)
DUVERGER   His wife is with him.
MARCHAND, Hiacinte   His wife is with him.
PAGOT, Louis   His wife is with him.
MERAULT, Ponce   His wife is with him.
LA ROCHE, Durand   His wife is with him.
SIMON, Benjamin
BRASSARD, Estienne   Called LIMAGE
EMERY, Jean Baptiste
LE CONTE, Jean Thomas
COMPAGNON, Charles
ST. PRIX
GUERDON
LA VILLE, Henry
LANGEVIN, Pierre
LA LANCETTE   His wife is with him.
MAZAYE, Paul

SOLDIERS EMBARKED AT BAYONNE BY ORDER OF THE COURT

DEVAUX, Jean Pierre
FILLATREAU, Pierre
CHOLA, Joseph
MISERE, Antoine
DEVOS, Pierre Henry
BRISEBOIS, Louis Theodore
BERTET, Claude
BARDET (BERTET?), Martin
DEUR, Antoine Joseph
GUERIE (GUERIN?), Antoine

Name	From	Comments

PRIVATE PASSENGERS

DUMONT, Sieur
BATTEON
MARSELAT

CATERRAT

LE BEL, Pierre

Carpenter for the de LAIRE concession
Stone-cutter for the de LAIRE concession
Going to the MASSY concession

MARCH 17, 1719

LIST OF WORKERS FOR THE COMPANY, PRI-
VATE PASSENGERS, OFFICERS, SOLDIERS,
AND PRISONERS SENT FROM LYON EMBARKED
ON THE <u>DAUPHINE</u> COMMANDED BY M. DE LA
FEUILLEE AND BOUND FOR LOUISIANA FROM
LA ROCHELLE

Name	From	Comments

WORKERS FOR THE COMPANY

TILLION, Jean	Maraux	Cooper
AUCHET, Jean Claude	Tours	Laborer
CAVANIER, Paul	Carcassone	Lock-smith or metal worker
REQUIENT, Charles	Poitiers	Lock-smith or metal worker
LEMAITRE, Pierre	Huzarches	Gardener

PRIVATE PASSENGERS

The LE BRET Party

LE BRET, Sieur Louis	
LE ROY, Elizabeth	Wife of Louis LE BRET
LE BRET, Elizabeth	Their child
LE BRET, Thereze	Their child
LE BRET, Louise	Their child
LE BRET, Perrine	Their child
LE BRET, Renée	Their child
LE BRET, Marianne Thereze	Their child
LE BRET, Louis	Their child
LE BRET, Jeanne	Their child

The TOUSSAINT Party

TOUSSAINT, Catherine	Wife of Lo VINCONNEAU who is already in Louisiana
VINCONNEAU, Marie	Their child
ROUSSILANDE, Isabelle	
ROY, Suzanne	

The LE JARD Party

LE JARD, Pierre	Metal worker and edge-tool maker
A servant	
LE JARD, Louis	Age 18
LE JARD, Antoine	Age 13
LE JARD, Marie	

Name	From	Comments

PRIVATE PASSENGERS (cont.)

The LE JARD Party (cont.)

ARNAUD, Pierre	La Rochelle	Baker
ANET, Jean		For M. Legoux's concession

SOLDIERS

Officer

SAUVAGE, Sieur Patrice

Sargeant

LE VILLAIN, Jacques	Alençon	Sieur de BEAUMESNIL

Cadet

JOUBART, Sieur

Troops

CARTIER, Jacques	Chateauroux	Age 38
LEZIEUX, René	Angoumois	Age 23
LE COURT, René	Niort	Age 18
HERMIES (HERIAS?) Lamotte	Rennes	Age 27
FUYER, Pierre	Angers	Age 19
HENAULT, Jean	La Fond	Age 28
ROBIN, Jean	Charente	Age 17
DUHAMEL, Francois Nicolas	Paris	Age 22
LE COCQ, Jean	Contances	Age 28
SIMONNET, Pierre	St. Messan	Age 19
EVENAN, Ollivier	Brittany	Age 21
MESTAYER, Claude	Pontiny in Brittany	Age 32
BRUNET, Jean	Saumur	Age 29
CASMIER, Charles	Preuilly in Touraine	Age 22
HENRY, Pierre	Montauban	Age 24
HOCART, Pierre	Tours	Age 28
DE BILLIEUX, Courbinet	Vitré in Brittany	Age 27
JOUBART	Paris	Age 23

Name	From	Comments

PRISONERS SENT FROM LYON

Name	From	Comments
VALENTIN, Claude Audin	St. Didier in Vellay	Age 35
GUINAU, Etienne	Morvan in Lyonnois	Age 22. Called COUCOU
MERCIER, Gerard	Bonne in Burgundy	Age 23
PRIEUR, Jean	Interville in Champagne	Age 35
HAFAY, Fleury	St. Germy in Forest	Age 17
DARBET, François	Lyon	Age 20
ROUANE, Jacques	Mortagne in La Perche	Age 25
RAMBAULT, François	Bussau in Dauphiné	Age 22
LAVENOT, Jean	Cap in Dauphiné	Age 22
DURAND, Antoine	Lyon	Age 23
GUAY (GAY?), Jean	Bresle, diocese of Lyon	Age 18
PAPY, Jean Baptiste		
LECHEVIN, François		Called VILLEFRANCHE
DESTOURETTES	La Rochelle	Age 26
LE CLERC, Joseph		Called SANSOUCY. This man is listed as Joseph Clery on another list of passengers for the Dauphiné

MARCH 21, 1719

LIST OF CONCESSIONARIES AND THEIR
PEOPLE, PRIVATE PASSENGERS, SOLDIERS
EXILES, AND OTHERS EMBARKED ON THE
ST. LOUIS COMMANDED BY M. DU COULOM-
BIER BOUND FOR LOUISIANA FROM LA
ROCHELLE

Name	From	Comments

CONCESSIONARIES AND THEIR PEOPLE

Name	From	Comments
CAUTILLON (CANTILLON?), Sieur		Concessionary
RUAN (RUAU?), Pierre		
TIXIER, Pierre		
SOUBRONE, Denis		
LEYNE, Guillaume		
HUSSY, Thomas		
BROAT, Jeanne		Wife of Thomas HUSSY
JOURDAN, Guillaume		
LA NOSSE, Jean Mathieu		
COURSY, Jean		
COURBIER, Simon		
COURCEL, Louis		
CORNELLY, Jean		
BARAULT, Anne		Wife of Jean CORNELLY
OWEN, Jean		
SMITH, Jean		
DARBY, Jonathan		Clerk
DARLING, Jean		Clerk
COOK, Robert,	Ireland	
BIDET, Jean		Wheelwright
BONNET, Estienne		Carpenter
JULLIEN, Jean		Baker
BERTIN, Elie		Baker and cook
CROZILIER (CROZIMIER?), Nicolas		Laborer
FORET, Michel		Cooper
COURTABLEAU, Jacques		Cooper
PARANT, Jacques		Laborer
LAISNE (TESNE?), Charles		Valet
MOUGON, Pierre		Sugar-refiner
BULLETON (BALLETON?), Cristophe		Miner
PARONNEAU, Ollivier		Farrier
DUPAIN, Charles		Laborer
ROTUREAU, Honoré		Carpenter
LARTANT (LARTAULT?), Pierre Sebastien		Tailor
DESSAUT, Jean		Barber
AUTRESEAU, Jacques		Carpenter

Name	From	Comments

CONCESSIONARIES AND THEIR PEOPLE

The CAUTILLON Party (cont.)

RAUCON, Jean		Tailor
BERTIN, Marie		Servant
BARBIER, Jacques		Carpenter
LEGAS, Simon		Laborer

The CAUSSEPAIN Party

CAUSSEPAIN, Sieur François		Concessionary
CAUSSEPAIN, Pierre		
VENDUL, Charlotte		Wife of François CAUSSEPAIN
CAUSSEPAIN, Marie		
FONTAINE, Madelaine		Servant

PRIVATE PASSENGERS

COUTURIER, Madame		
MARTIN, Marie		Madame COUTURIER's servant

SOLDIERS

Sargeant

ROUVROY, Luc du	Peronne	Age 38

Cadets

ROUSSELET, Vincent Michel	St. Jean d'Angely	Age 18
ROUSSELET, Joseph	St. Jean d'Angely	Age 16

Troops

LE GENDRE, Simon	Passy, near Paris	Age 38
JOUNEAU, André	La Chaume	Age 23
FOUQUET, Simon	Bellecourt	
MICHEAU, Jean	Dejas in Poitou	Age 18
FOUQUEROLLE, Philippe	Clermont in Picardy	Age 19. His wife is with him.
HUBERT, Jean	Rennes	Age 34

EXILED BY "LETTRE DE CACHET"

BALLAY (DALLAY?), Sieur		Surgeon

Name	From	Comments

DESERTERS AND OTHERS EXILED BY ORDER OF THE COURT

Name	From	Comments
ALBERT	Troyes in Champagne	Age 28. Called RENCONTRE
ANDRE, Paul	Franche Comté	Age 24. Called LA JOYE
FRESINET, Pierre	Grognier in Languedoc	Age 37. Called CHATEAU-NEUF
PICARD	Uzes in Languedoc	Age 28
BARRY, Jean	Pinormiaud in Gascony	Age 33. Called LA GRAN-DEUR
CAMUSAT, Pierre	Troyes in Champagne	Age 25. Called CHAMPAGNE
POUPART, François	Beaumont in Maine	Age 37. Called RENCONTRE
ARCUS, Charles	Clermont in Auvergne	Age 19. Called BEAUSOLEIL
ACHARD, Jean Louis	St. Paul Deverns in Provençe	Age 20. Called ST. PAUL
POMART, Joseph	Chalons on the Seine	Age 20. Called ST. LAURENT
JOUVENT, Joseph	Lyon	Age 20. Called ST. JOSEPH
CATINOIS, François	Franche Comté	Age 20
NICOLAS, Claude	Franche Comté	Age 19
EVRARD, Jean Baptiste	Besançon	Age 28
LAVIGNE	Rouen	Age 21
TRANCHEMONTAGNE	Perigord	Age 30
PRINTEMPS	Besselier in Poitou	Age 30
LA VARETTE	St. Antony	Age 22

MAY 28, 1719

LIST OF COMPANY EMPLOYEES, CONCES-
SIONARIES, PRIVATE PASSENGERS, SOL-
DIERS, DESERTERS, TOBACCO SMUGGLERS,
ILLICIT SALT DEALERS, EXILES, VAGA-
BONDS AND OTHERS EMBARKED ON THE
UNION COMMANDED BY M. DE LA MANSELIERE
GRAVE BOUND FOR LOUISIANA

Name	From	Comments

COMPANY EMPLOYEES

Name	From	Comments
VILLARDEAU, M. de		Director General
MARLOT, Sieur		Bookkeeper
BARD, Jean		Valet
BRETECHE, Antoine		Gunner
BOIRION, Sieur		Owner of a felucca. His wife is with him.
VIEUS, Jean		Carpenter. Called CARPENTRAS

CONCESSIONARIES AND THEIR PEOPLE

Name	From	Comments
RENAUD, M.		Concessionary
CATTON		
OZIAS		
RENDY, du		
BRESSE, de la		
PUGEOL		
LALLEMAND		
THORE, Bernard		
RIEROIT, Ignace		
BASTIEN, François		
PEPIN, Joseph		
TROQUELET, Pierre		
DENIS, Antoine		
JACQUEMIN, Simon		
CHARLIER, Joseph		
STIN, Gregoire		
PETRARD, Jean Jacques		
PLANTE, Pierre de la		
LA MONTAGNE, Jean		
LE FEVRE, Jean Bapte		
DUMONT, Nicolas		
POUILLARD, Jean		
FINE, Hubert		
GAUTIER, Joseph		
ROCROIS, Laurent		
FROGNEUX, Lievains		
BEQUET, François		

Name	From	Comments

CONCESSIONARIES AND THEIR PEOPLE (cont.)

BAURESSON (BAUDESON?), Nicolas
NAMUR, Philippe
BLAMPIN, Léonard
CATHERINE, Joseph
DARMUSEAU, Nicolas
TIERSE, Hubert de
RENIER, Barthelemy
FAUSSIER, Joseph
LE GRAND, Louis
BISSERET, Remis
BOISSIEUX, Joseph
MORAGE, Joseph
BRITEL (BITEL?), Guilleaume
COQUILLARD, Jacques
TISSON, Pierre
DELAGARDE, Jean
PREVOST, Antoine
PREVOST, Jeanne — Wife of Antoine PREVOST
PREVOST, Elizbeth — Elizabeth and Annette PRE-
PREVOST, Annette — VOST are daughters of Antoine PREVOST

LE DOUX, Gabrielle — A girl
MANAYE, Jean Jacques de
THORE, Wife of Sieur — Their daughter is with them.

The PONTVAL Party

PONTVAL, Sieur Jacques de — Concessionary
PONTVAL, Sieur Claude de
FRUSQUELAY, Joseph de — Worker
FRUSQUELAY, Jean de — Worker
LAVENANT, Jean — Worker
SAUMON, Marin — Worker
MARTIN, Thomas — Worker
GAUDIN, René — Worker
LE GALLAY, Jean — Worker
CHEVALIER, François — Worker
GERARD, Jean — Worker

PRIVATE PASSENGERS

COUTURIER, Sieur
GAUDIN, Jeanne — Wife of Sieur COUTURIER
COUTURIER, Jeanne — Daughter of Sieur COUTURIER
DESJEAN, Pierre — Going to M. Diron
RENAUD, Sieur
VERTEUIL, Sieur François — Beaumasson
VERTEUIL, Jean — Son of Sieur VERTEUIL
DESCREUSET, Sieur

Name	From	Comments

SOLDIERS

Officers

Name	From	Comments
CARRIER, Sieur	Nancray	Captain
BEAUCHAMP, Sieur de		Lieutenant
DEGUA, Sieur		Lieutenant
SORTEVAL, Sieur de		Lieutenant. His wife is with him.
LIGOET (?), Sieur		Sub-lieutenant
DES SAUTIER, Sieur		Sub-lieutenant
COUSTILLAN, Sieur de		Sub-lieutenant

Cadets

Name	From	Comments
NOQUET (LOQUET?), Sieur	Paris	Age 24
SANDRA	Paris	Age 19
MICHEL	Paris	Age 19
DARBONNE	Paris	Age 20
DUFOUR	Bordeaux	Age 29
MAURICET	Chareux in Poitou	Age 28
DES SAUTIER	La Rochelle	Age 17
RENEUX	Paris	Age 21

Sargeant

Name	From	Comments
LIVET, Jacques	Lyon	Age 30

Troops

Name	From	Comments
SAINTON, Pierre Charles	Chatellerault in Poitou	Age 20
SAINTON, François Augustin	(same)	Age 18
HEROUX, Pierre	Bellefort in Alsace	Age 22
AMIET, Vincent François	Avanton, near Poitiers	Age 20
JAMIN, Pierre	Paris	Age 24
BRINGUAN, Nicolas	Paris	Age 32
CHERON, Robert	Rouen	Age 29
LA VERGNE, Jean	Chastelvent	Age 19
USQUAIN, Georges	Douzy in Burgundy	Age 17
LOUVY, Jean Louis	Paris	Age 20
SALOMON, Louis	Mans	Age 31
LE CAPITAINE, Adrien	Normandy	Age 25
PAQUET, Jacques	Riom in Auvergne	Age 30
BARBEAU, Guillaume	Normandy	Age 30
CHEVRIER, Jacques	Paris	Age 23

Name	From	Comments

SOLDIERS (cont.)

Troops (cont.)

BARBEAU, Guillaume	Normandy	Age 30.
CHEVRIE, Jacques	Paris	Age 23
GOBET, Pierre	Marsomain in Switzerland	Age 30
MARTEAU, Philippe	Paris	Age 27
PERICHOU, François	Rennes	Age 25
CROLIES, Charles	Bourbonnois	Age 24
PATREU, François	St. Brieux in Brittany	Age 30
GOUIN, Claude	Angers	Age 41
ROBIN, Nicolas	St. Jean la Chaisse	Age 23

EXILED BY ORDER OF THE KING

PRAROMAND, Sieur	Switzerland	
NOLLAND, Sieur	Ireland	
BALIGNAUD, Sieur de	St. Quentin	
JOURDAN, Sieur	Paris	
TOUSSAINT, Nicolas	Lorraine	Age 30. Called LA BONTE
DUVAL, Claude	Rouen	Age 24. Called SANS SOUCY

DESERTERS

GEOFFROY, Hyacinthe	St. Veray	Age 20. Called PROVENCAL
CLAUDE, Joachim	Daix	Age 25. Called SANS FACON
STOCLY (STICLY?), Gaspard	Moré in Switzerland	Age 28
GEORGE, Jean	Montpellier	Age 29. Called BATAILLON
BOHLES (BOTHLES?), Joseph Augustin		
ENGLER (HINGLER?), Gaspard	Agry in Switzerland	Age 30
JARDINIER, Nicolas		
POZAT (POSSAG?), François	Fribourg	Age 35
BIDEAU, Pierre	St. Gaultier	Age 28. Called ST JACQUES
CHESY, Maurice	Switzerland	Age 20
LEONARD, Pierre	Monberon	Age 30. Called ST. MICHEL
CREUSE (COUZE?), Jean de la	Saone	Age 22. Called COUTOIS
LORAIN (LORIN?), Jacques	Avignon	Age 20. Called TARASCON
TERASSE, Louis Vincent	Poitiers	Age 25. Called POITEVIN
PETIT, Claude Antoine	Vaudray	Age 25. Called VAUDRE
GUISSE, Paquet de	Canada	age 22. Called SANSOUCY
GRANDIN, Barthelemy	Montbasson	Age 30. Called ST. LOUIS
DESPACE, Jean	Liège	Age 25. Called BEAUSEJOUR

Name	From	Comments
ALMESSE (ALMENE?), Jean	London	Age 35. Called LANGLOIS
MEDIEU, Antoine	Morias	Age 30. Called BELLE FLEURS
JEUNE, Jacques	Maubeuge	Age 28. Called BAGUETTE
STARUSQUY, Vincelle	Ireland	Age 35
BEAUREPAS, Zacharie	Ireland	Age 25
BEURET, Jean Guillaume	Solier	Age 22
GABRIEL, Antoine	St. Clemens	Age 40. Called LA FOREST
SILAR, Gaspard	Switzerland	Age 30
VALTRE, Gerault	Switzerland	Age 24
FORTIER, Claude	Paris	Age 28. Called SANS REGRET
RASPASSER, Martin	Switzerland	Age 34
JOSSE, François Antoine	Switzerland	Age 28
RENAUD (RENAULT?), Jean	Selon	Age 24. Called SANS REGRET
AUBERT, Noël	Paris	Age 28
THIBAUD, Pierre François	Flanders	Age 23. Called SANS QUARTIER
DAUGES, Louis	Lyon	Age 23. Called LA SONDE
SALLE, François de	Omberson	Age 30
GRANDIN, Michel	Mortin	Age 22. Called ST. AMANT
BRINDONNEAU, René	Chaussé	Age 23
PASQUIER, André	Paris	Age 27. Called BEAULIEU
LAISNE, Simon	Rouen	Age 25
SALOUIN, Mathieu	Switzerland	Age 26. Called LA PRUDENCE

TOBACCO SMUGGLERS

Name	From	Comments
VOISIN, Pierre	St. Pierre de More	Age 30. Called MONTREUIL
BOUTEAU, Pierre	Reims	Age 40

ILLICIT SALT DEALERS

Name	From	Comments
GUILLAUME, Claude	Laon	Age 18
GUILLAUME, Jean	Laon	Age 17
MAGUY (MAQUY?), Pierre	Flers	Age 40

VAGABONDS SENT FROM PARIS AND RENNES

Name	From	Comments
CHERCHERY, Jean	Rennes	Age 21
BELAMY, Charles	Couttances	Age 19
CASSE (CAZE?), Germain	St. Godin	Age 26
LAUNAY, Jean	Mans	Age 22
PAQUIOT, Urbain	Bertenet	Age 15
AUTIN, René	La Milleraye	Age 20
SAUSSIE, François	Rennes	Age 18
CHESNAY, Jean	La Fleche	Age 18
ARREAU, Pierre	Cormery	Age 17
DEMARS, Thomas	La Flèche	Age 19
GUERARD, Pierre	Caen	Age 26

Name	From	Comments

VAGABONDS SENT FROM PARIS AND RENNES (cont.)

Name	From	Comments
VALLET, Nicolas	Rennes	Age 17
GUILLOY, Jean	Leval	Age 18
FERRAND, Jean Baptiste	Sens	Age 22. Called DE MELECOEUR
VERRIER (VENIER?), Jean	Paris	Age 40
JEUSSE, Robert	Paris	Age 20
LA COUR, Charles	Paris	Age 18
MENARD, Simon	Paris	Age 25
LAMERON, Jacques	Garin	Age 22
VERNAY, Jean	Beaume	Age 22
TOUSSIGNER, Estienne	Paris	Age 25
BELLAR (BLAR?), Louis	Douay	Age 22
DAMPIERRE, Guillaume	Beauvais	Age 25
CHARLES, Jean	Ste. Marie	Age 30
SENOUCHE, Pierre	Lyon	Age 27

MAY 27, 1719

LIST OF COMPANY EMPLOYEES, CONCESSION-
ARIES AND THEIR PEOPLE, PRIVAGE PASSEN-
GERS, OFFICERS, TROOPS, EXILES, DESER-
TERS, VAGABONDS AND OTHERS EMBARKED ON
THE MARIE COMMANDED BY M. JAPYE BOUND
FOR LOUISIANA FROM LA ROCHELLE

Name	From	Comments

EMPLOYEES OF THE COMPANY OF THE WEST

Name	From	Comments
BORDIER, Claude		Mason
SOEUR (SAUR?), Louis de la		Sailor
FILATREAU, Thoynon		Wife of Louis de la SOEUR
MAGON, André		
BONNET, Mathurin		Wife of André MAGON
COURTEZ, Louis		
FREBOURG, Jean Baptiste		
ST. QUENTIN, Samuel		

CONCESSIONARIES AND THEIR PEOPLE

Name	From	Comments
CAZE, Sieur François Nicolas		Concessionary
CAZE, Sieur Jacques		
MASCARY, Pierre		
BECHET, François		
BECHET, Marie		Daughter of François BECHET(?)
BECHET, GUILLAUME		His wife is with him.
BECHET, Jean		Age 4 years. Jean, Genevieve
BECHET, Genevieve		and probably Marie BECHET are children of Guillaume BECHET
CAUPIN, Antoine		

The VALDETERRE Party

Name	From	Comments
VALDETERRE, M.		Captain, Concessionary
MARECHAL, François		
VERRIER, Pierre		
BERGE, Louis		
LA HAYE, Louis de		
FRET, Marie		Wife of Louis de LA HAYE
BOYNEAU, Laurent		
TEZE, François		

People for the DE LAIRE Concession

Name	From	Comments
BRULE, Jean		
JACOB, Robert		
POULIN, Genevieve		Wife of Robert JACOB

Name	From	Comments

PRIVATE PASSENGERS

Name	From	Comments
DUVAL, La Demoiselle		
DUVAL, La Demoiselle Charlotte		Daughter of La demoiselle DUVAL
LE PINET (L'EPINAY?), Marie Louise Elizabeth		
LE PINET (L'EPINAY?), Marie Charlotte		Daughter of M.L.E. LE PINET
PIGEAUD, Jacques		Rope-maker
PIGEAUD, Pierre		Pierre, François, and Louis
PIGEAUD, François		PIGEAUD are the sons of
PIGEAUD, Louis		Jacques PIGEAUD
MEROC, René Etienne	Saumur	
MONNILLE, Louis		
BOUTARD, Sieur		
FALCON, Antoine		

SOLDIERS

Officers

Name	From	Comments
VALDETERRE, M. de		Captain
SAINTRAY DE BIRAGUE, M. de		Lieutenant
MARCHAND DE COURCEL, M.		Lieutenant
DUMONT DE MONTYGUY, M.		Sub-lieutenant
MAHNET, Sieur		Sub-lieutenant
ANDRIOT, Sieur		Sub-lieutenant
FLAMING, Sieur		Ensign

Cadets

Name	From	Comments
SOYEZ, Sieur François	Brie	Age 17
BONTEMS, Charles	St. Cloud	Age 18

Sargeants

Name	From	Comments
GUERIN	Paris	Age 40
GARNIER	Blois	Age 28
GIBERTY	Luxembourg	Age 27

Corporal

Name	From	Comments
VINCENT	Paris	Age 38

Troops

Name	From	Comments
GENTIL, Jean	Rochefort	Age 19
VITARD, Edmé	Auxerre in Burgundy	Age 30

Name	From	Comments

SOLDIERS (cont.)

Troops (cont.)

Name	From	Comments
BUSSY, Jean	Saisiere, Eveché de Laon	Age 20
DIETTE, Charles	Disouduy en Berry	Age 21
BEAUVAIS, Jean	Bourg on the Garonne	Age 17
VOLLARD (VOLART?) Chas.	Grisy in Normandy	Age 29
MECHIN, Michel	Cognac	Age 20
LE DE (LEDET), François	St. Brieux in Brittany	Age 19
LA HAYE, Barthelemy de	Paris	Age 19
LA MOTTE, Pierre	Vienne in Bourbonnois	Age 21
SORET, Pierre	Richelieu in Poitou	Age 22
MARQUET, Jean	Chateauneuf in Normandy	Age 18
BALET, François	Amber in Auvergne	Age 22
BELLERET, Nicolas	Burgundy	Age 26
MICHEL, Rogues	Paris	Age 26
DUMONT, Louis	Chalons in Burgundy	Age 38
CLAUTIER, Jean	Paté in Chartres	Age 27
MAINNARD, Christophe	Curzon in Poitou	Age 20
DUPAIN, Louis	Saine in Poitou	Age 18
PARILS (PAVILS?), Pierre	Rheims in Champagne	Age 16
FLERIEUX, Nicolas	Langres in Champagne	Age 21
LE ROY, Pierre	Rheims in Champagne	Age 18
LA HAYE, Robert de	Chateauthiery	Age 21
JOLLIN, Jean	Niort	Age 26
MARCHAND, Jean	Rennes in Brittany	Age 20
BENOIST, Claude	St. Martin La Fosse	Age 35
DUMONT, François	Chalons in Burgundy	age 29
LA MARCHE, Louis	Monfort in Maine	Age 22
BIBERON, Jacques Michel		
GUERIN, Jacques		
GAULTIER, René	St. Hilaire in Normandy	Age 18
GENTIL, François	Serie, near Orléans	Age 25
BOILEDIEU, Louis Raymond	Sivray in Poitou	Age 35
DENIS, Milan	Chaguy in Burgundy	Age 30
BOQUET, Jean Baptiste	Chartre in Bosse	Age 22
MICHELET, Louis	Lance in Picardy	Age 21

DESERTERS AND OTHERS SENT BY ORDER OF THE KING

Name	From	Comments
BEAU, Michel	Piege	Age 30
CHARPENTIER, François	Justinie	Age 22
LAURENDICQ, Pierre	Chernuche	Age 21. Called CHEVALIER
LAURENDICQ, Françoise		Daughter of Pierre LAURENDICQ
COQUERELLE, Marie Fran-çoise		Wife of Pierre LAURENDICQ
BONGER, Jean Pierre	Venise	Age 20
ST. AMANT, Benoist Monder	Chapeauoine	Age 22
LE TOURNEUR, Pierre	Poissy	Age 35
STERLING, Philippe	Alost	Age 27
BREAU, Jean Baptiste	Auchange	Age 30

Name	From	Comments

DESERTERS AND OTHERS SENT BY ORDER OF THE KING (cont.)

Name	From	Comments
BEGON, Jacques		
PASQUIER	Mans	Age 22
HOBREMAN, Panerasse	Boylac	Age 26
NOORWEGH, Thomas	London	Age 24. Called NOORT
BOYD, Jean	England	Age 22. Died of illness in port
LONGCHAMPS, François	Orléans	Age 24
VIGUERON, Jean François	Joguy	Age 30. Called LA VIO-LETTE
HIGUET, Daniel	Ireland	Age 30
L'ARBRE, Marguerite de		Wife of Daniel HIGUET
HIGUET, Catherine		Daughter of Daniel HIGUET
JARRY, Jean Baptiste	Paris	Age 21
LAGRANGE, Jean Sauson de	Noyars	Age 26
COLET, Marie Ferdinande		Wife of LAGRANGE
SAUSON, Isabelle		Daughter of LAGRANGE
MOREAU, Ambroise	Jardeton	Age 30
PAUL, Jeanne		Wife of MOREAU
LE BRETON, Nicolas	Lauderneau in Brittany	Age 22
LE BOURGEOIS, Jacques	Paris	Age 45
MAINDET, Gabriel	Merin	Age 30
LA GAUBERTIERE, Jean François de	Paris	Age 45
SALMON, Jacques	Saumur	Age 26
MASSON, Pierre	- - -	- - -
GAULTIER, Michel	Rouen	Age 30
HOUSSET, Jean	Chambly	Age 35. Called RINGAL
PARTOIS, Jeanne		Wife of Jean HOUSSET
GALLE, Louis	Liège	Age 35
NICOLE, Catherine		Wife of Louis GALLE

TOBACCO SMUGGLERS

Name	From	Comments
REGES, Dominique	Rennes	AGe 30. Called LA MOTTE
GEMBRY, Louis Buttin de	Courtray	Age 30
BALLE (BOLLE?), Ignace de	St. Paul de Leon	Age 30
LA VILLETTE, Antoine Gerre de	Paris	Age 23
BUFET, François	Jossy	Age 30
STELLY, Simon	Ambrassin	Age 35
ST. FROULY, Albert de	Pitersene	Age 26
CALLAY, Jacques	Moulin	Age 21
BOYER, Marie		A girl aged 20 years
LADNER, Cristian	Switzerland	Age 20
BARGAU, Pierre	Florence	Age 30
PETROUCHY, Pierre	Leonce	Age 25
SAUSOT, Sieur Julien	Angoulême	Age 28

Name	From	Comments

BY ORDER OF THE KING (lettre de Cachet)

| CHAVANNES, Sieur de | Paris | Age 35 |
| RENAULT, Jacques | Rouen | Age 16 |

AUGUST 16, 1719

LIST OF OFFICERS, SOLDIERS, TOBACCO
SMUGGLERS, ILLICIT SALT DEALERS, DE-
SERTERS, VAGABONDS AND OTHERS EMBARKED
ON THE MARECHAL D'ESTREES COMMANDED BY
M. GERVAIS DE LA GODELLE BOUND FOR
LOUISIANA FROM LA ROCHELLE.

Name	From	Comments

SOLDIERS

Officers

COURBELLE, M.		Lieutenant of Infantry
SIMARRE, M.		Ensign
LE GENDRE, M.		Ensign
HABAINS, M.		Officier en Expectative
DUCLOS, M.		Officier en Expectative

Cadets

CHABERT, Sieur	Paris	Age 22
FRIZON, Antoine	Paris	Age 14
GILLOT, François	Paris	Age 15

Troops

MALLET, Jean Baptiste	Rouen	Age 20. Founder by trade
MICOUIN, Michel	Villedieu	Age 24
PERAULT, Noël	Paris, St. Paul Parish	Age 17. Silk worker
GAUDRAY, Claude	Metz	Age 48. Gardener
HENAULT, Pierre	Angers	Age 29. Tapestry-worker
MAILLARD, Jean B. Charles	Amiens	Age 17 1/2.
COURBEC, Nicolas	Trepagny	Age 39
MARTIN, André	Chatillon in Berry	Age 28. Tailor
HUS, Jean Baptiste	Eloye, Bishopric of Avranche	Age 17
CADIOU, François	Auray	Age 17
ROCHEREAU, Urbain	Saumur	Age 22. Laborer
NEDELEC, Simon	Landerneau in Brittany	Age 24
HURAULT, Jean	Melun in Brie	Age 28
BAILLET, Amedée Gaston	Brest	Age 21
BERTRAND, Natalis	Geraudan	Age 29 Gardener
ROBIN, Charles	Legere in Marche	Age 24
TALVAR, George	Dol in Brittany	Age 18
JOLLY, François	Nantes	Age 28

Name	From	Comments

TOBACCO SMUGGLERS

Name	From	Comments
LE COINT, Jean Claude	Lefont in Franche Comté	Age 15
SPEGRAND, Jacques	Quetin Dauphiné	Age 36
PUSSIN, Antoine	L'Isle in Flanders	Age 30
CHAPON, René	Autun	Age 18
MAURIX, Pierre	Marsominge in Bresse	Age 28
MARTEL, Nicolas	Dijon	Age 15
LA SORTE, Etienne	Bourg IN Bresse	Age 35
COMTE, Pierre	Lyon	Age 26. Silversmith by trade
VILLET, Jacques	Lyon	Age 21
BERTRAND, Jacques	St. Pierre Dumans	Age 40
BRUNETEAU, François	Sables d'Olonne	Age 35. Laborer
VIALET, Jacques	Begorre	Age 34. Hemp-dresser
ROSSEL, Joachim	Beaumont	Age 56
PAILLARD, Pierre	Vestal	Age 30. Tailor
BOUCHET, André	La Botiere	Age 36. Tailor
GAONDET, Michel	Gamestre	Age 35. Hemp-dresser
CORREOUX, Alexandre	L'Autragne	Age 22. Paper-maker
BIOT, Jacques	Begorre	Age 55
RAYMOND, Joseph	Piolin	Age 27. Surgeon
GAY, Pierre	Chateau Roux	Age 20
PAYEN, Jean	Granot	Age 58
CARPENTIER, Pierre	Poulerville	Age 12
FOURNIER, Paul	St. Neux	Age 12
HYVALLE, Thomas	Corsey	Age 10
BARDET, Paul	Vieux Rouin	Age 30
ROLLAND, Jacques	Unbay in Artois	Age 18
OUAILLY, Jean	Belquin in Artois	Age 70
NAUDIN, Jean	Paris	Age 45
RAQUIN, Rennes		Wife of Jean NAUDIN
PACOT, Antoine	Dijon	Age 35
PACOT, Françoise		Sister of Antoine PACOT
BERLEMON, Barthelemy	Sart	Age 42
MORICE, Marguerite		Wife of Barthelemy BERLEMON
BERLEMON, Marguerite		Daughter of Barthelemy BERLEMON
PADOL, Jean	Dain	Age 18
DALAVIER, Denis	Capin	Age 17
MINARD, Louis	Dauphin	Age 15
DANEL, Louis	Dauphin in Artois	Age 16
LAUNOIS, Pierre	Remy	Age 38
LUCAS, Simon	Thomar in Normandy	Age 50. Cook. Called LAMONTAGNE
DERVILLE, Antoine	Montigny in Picardy	Age 28. Called LACROIX
DELMAZ, Jean	Dalby Cange	Age 40
DURAND, Jean	Landisats in Normandy	Age 34.
CHARPENTIER, Marie		Wife of Jean DURAND
CHEMINET, Blaise	St. Agnal	Age 40. Laborer
PETIT, Henry	Belame	Age 50. Mason
VERDUN, Denis	Chalon in Farne	Age 40. Laborer
VALLET, Joseph	Champlieux	Age 30. Laborer
RIVET, Jacques	St. Nizier sous Charlieux	Age 24. Laborer

Name	From	Comments

TOBACCO SMUGGLERS (cont.)

Name	From	Comments
FORSINE, Jean Baptiste	Rome	Age 40. Tailor. Called ROMAIN
ANSELME, Claude	Roma in Bresse	Age 40. Laborer
DARFIN, Claude	Mont Louet	Age 20. Laborer
GONARD, Philbert	Villefranche	Age 19. Laborer
MONET, Jean Baptiste	Bourg St. Christophe	Age 40. Laborer
NIMOND, Jean	Poul in Beaujolois	Age 29. Laborer
TIERS, Claude	Port Dauton in Dauphiné	Age 35. Laborer
LUSTIER, Jean Pierre	Velin	Age 28. Laborer
DUBOIS, Michel	St. Bonnet in Dauphiné	Age 30. Laborer
CHANAT, Jean	Autrague in Languedoc	Age 24. Laborer
FERATIER, Pierre	Sensinet Luchon	Age 26. Laborer
VARENNE, François	Valence	Age 40. Laborer
MOULIN, Pierre	Givodan	Age 35. Laborer
RIOUX, Claude	Gennister	Age 22. Laborer
COUR, Mathieu de	St. Froc	Age 35. Laborer
BRION, Vidalle	Retourna	Age 35. Laborer
BARNIER, Vincent	Chabrillan	Age 25. Laborer
SUSSIS, Jean	Tellier	Age 42. Laborer. Called PHILBERT
BAUDOT, Philbert	St. Ouin near Paris	Age 42. Laborer
COURTINE, Antoine		
LYONNARD, Jean		

ILLICIT SALT DEALERS

Name	From	Comments
CRETIEN, Julien	L'Isle in Flanders	Age 22. Tiler
BAQUET, Françoise		Wife of Julien CRETIEN
PREVOST, Adrien	Honnecourt	Age 24. Laborer
MARIEZ, Charles	Jean Court	Age 17. Laborer
MONTULET, Martin	Sousman Lemoine in Liège	Age 36. Nail-maker
LE BAY, Adrien	Plomion	Age 30. Laborer
MORNON, Claude	La Roully	Age 45. Laborer
POUCHON, Mathias	Licourt	Age 35. Laborer
OUARNIER, Philippe	Izengerenelle	Age 40. Laborer
LE ROY, Victor	Licourt	Age 19. Laborer
MOY, François	Izon in Berry	Age 36. Laborer
CULLIER, Louis	St. Jean d'Angely	Age 27. Mason
SENECHAL, Claude	Couin	Age 35. Tailor
COLLAS, Elizabeth		Wife of Claude SENECHAL
SENECHAL, Marie Jeanne		Daughter of Claude SENECHAL
GLATIGNY, Antoine	Plomion	Age 25. Sawyer
LEGRAND, Nicolas	L'Ecaille	Age 26. Laborer

Name	From	Comments

ILLICIT SALT DEALERS (cont.)

Name	From	Comments
RIVET, Jacques	Grigny	Age 24. Laborer
FAUBLE, Nicolas	Picardy	Age 38. Tile-maker
BOULANGER, Charles	Bouyeville	Age 30. Butcher
PIERRE, Jean	Paris	Age 20. Mason. Called PETIT JEAN
ESLOIR, Martin	Troville	Age 20. Laborer
AUBERT, Pierre	Crissé	Age 55. Mason
BESOIN, Gabriel	Bousset near Pailly	Age 44. Laborer, Called LE CHAT
VOLLET, Jacques	La Chapelle Blanche	Age 35. Tile-maker

DESERTERS

Name	From	Comments
DOET (DORT?), Pierre	Calais	Age 24. Called GRANVILLE
ROMAIN, Romain	Tour	Age 26. Called ST. GERMAIN
RENAULT, Jean	Lyon	Age 28. Called SANS REGRET

VAGABONDS FROM ORLEANS

Name	From	Comments
BERENGER, Nicolas	St. Laurent de Lin in Anjou	Age 47
BATISIER, Claude Emanuel	Paris	Age 20. Called DUMENIL

VAGABONDS FROM RENNES

Name	From	Comments
MENOUX, Pierre	Sens	Age 33
MERCIER, George	Valence	Age 36
FLEURY, Jeanne		Wife of George MERCIER
MERCIER, Jean		Son of George MERCIER
MERCIER, Madeleine		Daughter of George MERCIER
MERCIER, Jeanne		Daughter of George MERCIER

VAGABONDS FROM LYON

Name	From	Comments
LAFOND, François	Sencier	Age 33. Shoemaker
MIQUEL, Jean	Sencier	Age 21. Silk-worker
PICHON, Aimé	Lyon	Age 17. Silk-worker
RAYMOND, Jean	Lyon	Age 40. Founder
SEYTY, Jacques	Lyon	Age 16. Shoe-maker
RADEAU, Nicolas	Lyon	Age 40
COURSON, Pierre	Bordeaux	Age 17. Button-maker

LIBERTINES

Name	From	Comments
MOREAU, Sébastien	Paris	Age 20. Tailor
CHARBONNIER	Paris	Age 28. Surgeon. Called LA FEUILLADE

Name	From	Comments

LIBERTINES (cont.)

DESLANDES, Jacques	Versailles	Age 29
REGNAULT, Nicolas	Corbeille	Age 30
ALOT, François	Chartres in Bosse	Age 20
JERYGNY, Jean Baptiste	Paris	Age 20. Tapestry-maker

EXILED FROM BAYONNE BY ORDER OF M. DE BERWICK

LE CLERC, Jean	Paris	Age 27
ROULE, Thomas de	Ironne in Spain	Age 63
BERONDE, Antoine	Ironne in Spain	Age 60

AUGUST 16, 1719

LIST OF COMPANY EMPLOYEES, CONCESSION-
ARIES, PRIVATE PASSENGERS, TOBACCO
SMUGGLERS, ILLICIT SALT DEALERS, VAGA-
BONDS, DESERTERS AND OTHERS EMBARKED
ON THE DEUX FRERES COMMANDED BY M.
FERRET BOUND FOR LOUISIANA FROM LA
ROCHELLE

Name	From	Comments

COMPANY EMPLOYEES

BONNET, Mathurin		Carpenter
BONNET, François		
BONNET, Nicolas		

CONCESSIONARIES AND THEIR PEOPLE

TOURNEVILLE, M. le Chevalier de		Concessionary
PIGEON, Adrien		Worker
ROBIN, Charles		Worker
MILET, Jacques		Worker
MARAS, Jean		Worker
PESSON, Jacques		Worker
AUDREBAN, Marie		Servant

The VILLEMONT Party

VILLEMONT, M. de		Concessionary
VILLEMONT, Madame de		Wife of M. de VILLEMONT
VILLEMONT, Jeanne		Daughter of M. de VILLEMONT
MILLEMONT, Marianne		Daughter of M. de VILLEMONT
LIGNAULT, Eustache de		Worker
NINGERS, Alphonse		Worker
CHARVAN (CHARVAU?), Mathurin		Worker
MORISSET, Charles Antoine		Worker
CHAIGNEAU, Jacques		Worker
GIRARDE, Marie		Servant
BROUTIER, Anne		Servant
MANIE, Judick		Servant
VRIGNAULT, Anne		Servant
DAVID, Jean Baptiste		Worker
GEDEON, Henry		Worker
TABARE, Jean		Worker

The CHANTREAU Party

CHANTREAU DE BEAUMONT, M. François		Concessionary
AUBRY, Catherine		Wife of M. CHANTREAU DE BEAU-MONT

Name	From	Comments

CONCESSIONARIES AND THEIR PEOPLE (cont.)

The CHANTREAU Party (cont.)

CHANTREAU, Magdeleine   Daughter of M. CHANTREAU
CHANTREAU, François   Son of M. CHANTREAU
CHANTREAU, Marie Michel   Son of M. CHANTREAU
CHANTREAU, Antoine   Son of M. CHANTREAU
HURAULT, Charles   M. CHANTREAU's brother-in-law
NAMBLARD, Pierre   Servant
NANTES, Pierre de   Servant
CROCHET, Nicolas   Servant

PRIVATE PASSENGERS

DUMAS, Pierre   Tailor
DEMAIN, Marie   Wife of Pierre DUMAS
ST. CLIVIER, Sieur
LOUE, Sieur   Tailor
FERMIGNAC, Marie   Wife of GUERIN, a sergeant
who sailed on the _Marie_
LA RIEUX, Jean   Son of Marie FERMIGNAC
LA RIEUX, Marie   Daughter of Marie FERMIGNAC
BERARD, Jacques
DESERT, Isabelle   Wife of Jacques BERARD. She
has not yet boarded ship.

SOLDIERS

Officers

CHAPPE, M. de   Captain of Infantry
RECLOT, M. de   Officier en expectative
LAFON, M.   Officier en expectative

Sargeant

DELMAS, Pierre   (Note: From CHAPPE through
LANGLOIS it is noted that
these men had not yet boarded
ship.)

CADETS

LANGLOIS, Sieur Bonaventure
MOEUVE, Sieur de
ST. JUST, Sieur de
MASSON, Sieur Richard
COMMERIE, Sieur de la
HUGOT, Sieur
BAUDOUIN, Sieur

Name	From	Comments

SOLDIERS (cont.)

Troops

AUFRET, Alexandre
PAILLARD, Pierre
PEZE, Jacques Philippe
POYER, Nicolas
CONDAMINE, Jean Baptiste de
LEMAITRE, Jean Baptiste
CONTANT, Jacques
NORMANDIN, Jacques
ROLLAND, Guillaume
SIMON, Martial
MARCHAND, Charles
BRIAN, Alain
TOSTAIN, Pierre
PAYSAN, Pierre
HOUSSAYE, Joseph
BARBOTTE, Jacques Joseph
PONCIN (POUCIN?), Pierre
LENAUD, Jacques
PAREN, Jean
ROY, François
LOSSERANDS, François
GUIGNARD, Jacques
ACHARD, Pierre
MONIER, Laurent
PELTIER, Pierre
BAYARD, Dominique
HARNAULT, Jacques
COURTINEAU, Mathieu

TOBACCO SMUGGLERS

DUCRET, Pierre
MALBOS, Louis
MARSSEAU, Louis
CARTIER, Margueritte   Wife of Louis MALBOS
LIEPART, Claude
MONSIEUR, François
BRISSY, Jean Baptiste
LANGLOIS, André

ILLICIT SALT DEALERS

CHETINOT (CHETIVOT?), Claude
CHAPELLE, Claude
MANEZ (MAVEZ?), Claude

Name	From	Comments

ILLICIT SALT DEALERS (cont.)

BRIAN, Charles
DEMARLY, Charles
MORIN, Pierre   Called CLAIRE FONTAINE
JERBOZ, Jean
MINORET, Jean Baptiste
LEFEVRE, Jean
ROYON, Jean   Called CORVILLE
SAVOURET, Jean
BIGORD, Jean
DUMOULIN, Jean
DERTIN, Jacques
BRET, Jacques de
LEVASSEUR, Jacques   Called Vaudeville
CARY, Jacques
VASSEUR, Jacques
BATAILLE, Nicolas François
MONCEL (MOUCEL?), Nicolas
BILEUX, Nicolas
CABULOT, André
LENOIR, André
MIANEZ, Antoine
CAMUS, Antoine
DUSAUSSOIR, Antoine
TELLIER, Michel
TREQUENOT, Michel
CONDOT, François
BOTEL, François
AMOND, François
BOUVARD, Pierre
HUPIN, Pierre   Called HUBERT
SELLIER, Pierre
CONNYOT, Pierre   Called PETIT JEAN
DEVOCHEL, Louis
LA LOIX, Louis
D'ESPAGNE, Louis
BOUCLET, Thomas
CARET, Urbain
DIEU, Guillaume
BOULLE, Germain
OUAILLIER, Nicolas
DURU, Roland
LE TRILLARD, Jeanne   Wife of Roland DURU
LE ROY, Antoine
FRESSON, Jean
MERLE, Jean
TROLET, Jean

Name	From	Comments

ILLICIT SALT DEALERS (cont.)

COURT, François
TROLET, Antoine
BERTIN, François
HAUTOIS, François
VALET, Etienne
LE ROY, Jean

VAGABONDS FROM ORLEANS

VALENCIE, Jean
BROUERE, Denis
DENIS, Jacques
DUFEU, Benoist
TOUSSARD, Louis
TOUZET, Nicolas   Called RICHARD

VAGABONDS FROM LYON

JOULEUR, François
MICHON, Marguerite   Wife of François JOULEUR
FALQUET, Etienne
HODIEU, Etienne
METZ, Charles de
DESCOMPTES, Julien
RIVIERE, Jean

LIBERTINES

FOUQUET, Jean
MAILLARD, Pierre
GRANGEMONT, Sieur   By special order of the king.

DESERTER

BLANCARD, Blaise   Called ST. BLAIZE

WOMEN AND GIRLS EXILED FOR FRAUD

LE DOUX, Nicole
AVRIL, Marie
GRILLON, Marie
TACY, Jeanne
DURAND, Louise
LENFANT, Jeanne
BORDEAU, Marie
BRISSON, Magdeleine
MICHEL, Marie

Name	From	Comments

WOMEN AND GIRLS EXILED FOR FRAUD (cont.)

CEMTURIER (CENTURIER?), Marie
BAGUELOT, Françoise
NAMOND, Anne
FERRET, Françoise
VIGNERON, Blanche
GOGUET, Marie Jeanne
HERODE, Marie Ficlon
AMIOT, Marie Claire
GRIZE, Marie Anne
FRESSIN, Françoise
ARNAUDE, Jeanne

WOMEN EXILED FROM ROCHEFORT

PERCHE (PORCHE?), Marie Anne
LEFEVRE, Jeanne
LAFONTAINE, Marie
HABY, Catherine
HOUDART, Catherine
LAFLEUR, Babet
BRUNETTE, Marie Louise   Called VALENTIN
PARIS, Marie
IGNOHET, Marie
VALLET, Marguerite
COUTELIER DE PERTY, Marie Françoise de
GENNET, Tiennette
VIGNERON, Jeanne
CHAUVALLON, Germaine
DUCLAUD, Marie
AIGREMONT, Marie Jeanne d'

SEPTEMBER 12, 1719

LIST OF CONCESSIONARIES AND THEIR PEO-
PLE, WORKERS FOR THE COMPANY, PRIVATE
PASSENGERS, SOLDIERS, ILLICIT SALT
DEALERS, TOBACCO SMUGGLERS, VAGABONDS
DESERTERS, AND OTHERS EMBARKED ON THE
DUC DE NOAILLES COMMANDED BY MONSIEUR
COUTTANT DEPARTING FROM THE ROADSTEAD
OF CHEF DE BAYE BOUND FOR LOUISIANA

Name	From	Comments

CONCESSIONARIES AND THEIR PEOPLE

Those destined for the DARTAGUIETTE Concession

BABAQUI, Sieur		
SOROATTE, Sieur		
D'HOSPITEL, Sieur		
RESSENDIER, Sieur		Surgeon
DEGRAT, Pierre		A child

The BAIL DE BEAUPRE Party

BAIL DE BEAUPRE, M.		Concessionary
BAIL DE BEAUPRE, Madame		
MARCHAND, Marie		Chambermaid
LA PORTE, Anne de		Chambermaid

WORKERS FOR THE COMPANY

VIGNE, Jean de		
VIGNE, Jeanne de		Wife of Jean de VIGNE
VIGNE, Pierre de		Child of Jean de VIGNE
VIGNE, Jean de		Child of Jean de VIGNE
AUSIOT (ANSIOT?), Nicolas		
OPURTEMS (?), Jacques		
FOSSE, Jean		
PARABERT, Jean		
BRENIER, Jean		
LAVEINE, Nicolas		
DORANGE, Mathieu		
LANGLOIS, Antoine		
MONTUIS, Simon		
MONTUIS, Marie		Wife of Simon MONTUIS
MONTUIS, Joseph		Child of Simon MONTUIS
MONTUIS, Jacob		Child of Simon MONTUIS
MONTUIS, Jeanne		Child of Simon MONTUIS

Name	From	Comments

WORKERS FOR THE COMPANY (cont.)

LE MIRE, Louis
GAMBIER, Michel
BRUNEL, Jean
HAURY (HANRY?), Gilles

PRIVATE PASSENGERS

PINON, Sieur	Tours	
TOUT DOUCE, Marguerite		Sent from Paris

SOLDIERS

Officers

CARON, M.		Captain of Infantry
DETCHEPARRE, M.		Lieutenant
LONGUEVAL, M. de		Lieutenant
BASSEE, M. de		Lieutenant
COURTEN, M.		Sub-Lieutenant
VILLECOURT, M. de		Sub-Lieutenant
CHARREAU, M.?		Sub-Lieutenant
LAMBERT, Le Chevalier		
DUQUARTIER, M.		Ensign
FRANCHOMINE, M.		Ensign
ST. ESTEBEN, M. de		Ensign

Cadets

TILLOY, Sieur Claude	Paris	Age 21
JORDAN, Sieur Claude	Valence	Age 19
MALLER, Jean Baptiste	Paris	Age 18

Sargeant

LA ROCHE, Jacques	Chalons in Champagne	Age 43

Troops

DUFLOS, Pierre Antoine	Tournay in Flanders	Age 30
LE GUERNE, Guy	Carliax in Brittany	Age 24
MERCIER, Claude	Paris	Age 17
CREVECOEUR, Elzear Fleix de	St. Omer	Age 36
DRUET, Luc	Nancy	Age 17
ROUSSEL, Claude	Corby in Picardy	Age 44

Name	From	Comments

SOLDIERS (cont.)

Troops (cont.)

Name	From	Comments
GOUET, Denis	Paris, parish of St. Germain de Lauxerrois	Age 20
VOYSIN, Pierre	Paris, parish of St. Sauveur	Age 24
BEZUCHET, Pierre	Paris, parish of St. Sulpice	Age 17
MOREAU, François	Chateau Signon in Guernois	Age 33.
BILLECAULT, François	Auzerre in Burgundy	Age 37
GOUET, Jacques	Clermont in Auvergne	Age 26
ROCHER, René du	Poitiers	Age 16 1/2
LEMOINE, Florent	Saumur	Age 18
DUVAL, Charles	Villedieu in Normandy	Age 24
DUBOIS, François	Bayonne, parish of St. Louis	Age 20
OZANNE, Louis	La Tardière, bishopric of La Rochelle	Age 20
DUPRE, Jean	Rochefort	Age 15
PERDON, Agatte Ange	Saumur	Age 45
MAINGUENEAU, François	Paris	Age 21
MAILLARD, Jean	Brest in Brittany	Age 22
LAMARZELLE, Jean de	Libourne	Age 40
BREAU (BRAU?), Nicolas	Nevers	Age 26
FREMENTIER, Jean François	Rennes	Age 45
LE ROY, Etienne	La Fleche in Anjou	Age 30

PERSONS EXILED BY ORDER OF THE KING

Illicit Salt Dealers

Name	From	Comments
BRUNET, Jean	Angers	Age 19
CALET, Charles	Versan in Bourbonnois	Age 35
GIRAULT, François	Rilly	Age 30. Called BONNEMENS
LINGER, René	Martizet	Age 45
GENTIL, Jacques	Martizet	Age 41
PERIN, Louis	Reont in Poitou	Age 42
JARDIN, Alexis du	Reignol	Age 21
CHAPELLE, Guillaume	Ste. Marie du Bois	Age 48
MALSIEU (MALFIEU?), Pierre	Charbain	Age 42
ROCHE, Louis de	Neville in Normandy	Age 26
RIDEL, Claude	Paris	Age 33
FROCOUR, Jean	Amiens	Age 45
DESCHAMPS, Joseph	Lamboy	Age 40. Called LA ROSE

Name	From	Comments

PERSONS EXILED BY ORDER OF THE KING (cont.)

Illicit Salt Dealers (cont.)

Name	From	Comments
GLAINE, Claude	Dauphiné	Age 24
DUPRE, Jean	Serreport	Age 13
FAMECHON, Louis Nicolas	Dinque	Age 15
MASSUEL, Louis	Hotion	Age 30
BOUCHET, Jacques	La Salle Guenant	Age 42
DAUPHIN, François	Teout in Poitou	Age 32
PALLIER, Nicolas	Seré in Touraine	Age 45
BAUDET, François	Chapelle Blanche	Age 48. Called BASTILLON
BLANCHARD, Louis	Arles	Age 15
VERDURE, Adrien	Cette Outtre	Age 50
GOTTEFRIN, Jean	Corbie, near Amiens	Age 50
ASSAY, Louis	Montrichard in Touraine	Age 50. Called MANCHET
AUBERT, Pierre	Crissé	Age 55
FROGET, Vincent	Marseille	Age 38. Called PIED DE CHAT
MARLY, Jean de	Laudoussy la Ville	Age 43
BLOCHET, Louis	Verlay	Age 33
TRINQUAR, Jean Baptiste	Cavullan	Age 15
DUPRE, Thomas	Seuerpan	Age 14
ANSAN, Thomas	Coutance	Age 42
VAU, Bernard de	Paris	Age 17
ALLARD, Antoine	Montreuil	Age 20
TESSON, Georges	Metz	Age 34
LAMBERT, Jacques	St. Meuline	Age 34
NOIRON, Jacques	Barenton sur Seine	Age 38
PINCHARD, Michel	Rimar	Age 32
MARLY, Jean de	Mione (?)	Age 35
HAUT, Philippe de	Corby	Age 30. Called ST. OLIVE
DAUVIN, Jean	Neully	Age 37
MOLLARD, Jean Baptiste	Paris	Age 31. Called MONTAL
COUTTANT, François	Tiviere	Age 38

Tobacco Smugglers

Name	From	Comments
MALEZIEUX, Etienne	Dampierre in Champagne	Age 47
D'ESTEL, Nicolas	Metz	Age 24
COLLAIN, Jean	Coublance (Coblenz?)	Age 30
BIAT, Jean	Elbet	Age 28
VASSEUR, Marie		Wife of Jean BIAT
CUSSIN, Pierre	Sarmetieux	Age 33
PASSERAT, Pierre	St. Etienne en Forest	Age 36
GUERNEL, Louis	Rhodon	Age 18
GOTTARD, Jean	Lyon	Age 27
BERSON, Ennemond	Lyon	Age 50
MAURIX, Pierre	Marsoninge in Bresse	Age 30

Name	From	Comments

PERSONS EXILED BY ORDER OF THE KING (cont.)

Tobacco Smugglers (cont.)

Name	From	Comments
JOUMAS (JOUNNAS?), Joseph	Voute de Vautadouce	Age 30
FERRAND, Laurent	Confranchon	Age 50
CHERON, François	Bordeaux	Age 34
ROUSSEL, Louis	L'Angre	Age 16
VEILLON, Benoist Etienne	Lyon	Age 35
DUTARTRE, Claude	Franche Comté	Age 25
SOUBAYGUE, Jean	Dax	Age 34
DETROUILLET, Catherine		Wife of Jean SOUBAYGUE
SOUBAYGUE, Catherine		Child of Jean SOUBAYGUE
SOUBAYGUE, Anne		Child of Jean SOUBAYGUE
BERNARD, Claude	Dax	Age 27. Called CHAMBERY
BERTHELOT, François	Talont	Age 48. Called MARAIS
RAFFIN, Joseph	Cursia	Age 40
FLEURY, Antoine	Bourg in Bresse	Age 32
FENEROLLE, Catherine		Wife of DAMEL
GIRAUDE, Marie		Wife of Claude BERNARD

VAGABONDS SENT FROM ORLEANS

Name	From	Comments
THOMAS, Silvain	Meule	Age 35
FAUSSET, Pierre	Pussy in Brie	Age 23
BRANCHET, Michel	St. Benoist sur Loire	Age 54
PEPIN, André	La Trinité in Normandy	Age 25
JEAN, René	Paris	Age 52
BARBIER (BOUBIER?) Pierre	St. Germain la Valle	Age 19

DESERTERS SENT FROM BAYONNE BY ORDER OF M. DE BERWICK

Name	From	Comments
GIRARD, Nicolas	Calais	Age 30
LA ROQUE, Joachim	Lyon	Age 36

EXILED WOMEN

GAFFER, Françoise
HARDY, Marie

JANUARY 4, 1720 TO JANUARY 24, 1721

LIST OF PERSONS WHO EMBARKED ON THE
L'AURORE, DRIADE, AND AVENTURIER
BOUND FOR LOUISIANA.

Name	From	Comments

THE AURORE

Name	From	Comments
LE BLANC, Sieur		Captain of Infantry
COUSTEAU, Sieur Pierre		Inspector of silk workers
DIDIER, Gaspard		Cooper
DIDIER, Jacques		Turner
ALBERT, Françoise		
JAY, Ysabeau		
SEIGNEURET, Genevieve		
BRET, Louise		
GRISON, Claudine		

THE DRIADE

Name	From	Comments
PELERIN, Sieur		Ensign
MATAPAN, Issac		Negro
BOUDIN, Marie		Falconer
COLEDO, Rose Limoniere		
PORTE RIEU, Françoise de la		
NEUVILLE, Marie Thereze		
BOTREL, René Anne		

THE AVENTURIER

Name	From	Comments
ST ANNE, Father Mathieu		Missionary
COMTE, Pechon de		Major at the Alibamons
DAUTRIVE, M. Renault		Captain
CLARE, M. de		Lieutenant
DAUREL, M.		Lieutenant
DARSILLY, M.		Sub-lieutenant
ROULLET, Sieur Regis du		Ensign
LARDY, Sieur		Ensign
SUPUIS, Sieur		Cadet
LE VACHON, Marie		
MICHEL, Jacques		Volunteer
PLUVAIR, Nicolas		Volunteer
BRESSILLON, Charles		Volunteer
CHOUQUET, Michel		
CHOUQUET, Jean		

Name	From	Comments
AUBRY, Charles		Volunteer
BANNOT, Nicolas		Volunteer
MALINGRE, Bernard		Volunteer
MIGAU, Philippe		Volunteer
BAJEUIL, Clement		Volunteer
FOUCHET, Nicolas		Soldier

(Note: The exact date of sailing for these three ships does not appear with this list. They did, however, sail between January 4, 1720 and January 24, 1721.)

JANUARY 4, 1720 TO JANUARY 24, 1721

LIST OF COMPANY OFFICIALS, WORKERS FOR
M. DE LA TOUR, SOLDIERS AND OTHERS EM-
BARKED ON THE DROMADAIRE COMMANDED BY
M. DE ST. MARC BOUND FOR LOUISIANA.§

Name	From	Comments

COMPANY OFFICIALS

Name	From	Comments
LA TOUR, M. de		Engineer in Chief
LEBLOND, M.		Brother of M. DE LA TOUR
BOISPINEL, M.		Brother of M. DE LA TOUR
DEVERGE, M.		Draughtsman
MARCHAND, M.		Volunteer
BISSARD, M.		Captain of a company
JUIF, M.		Almoner
BAILLY, M.		Surgeon
(9 domestics, not named)		
(A sargeant, not named)		

WORKERS FOR M. DE LA TOUR

Name	From	Comments
GUILLOUX, François	Tour	Silk worker
ARNY, Charles	Tour	Laborer
LOUIZON, Louis		Turner
GOMBEAU, Jean		Laborer
TAUDON, François		- - -
LA CAILLE, Simon		Carpenter
OBLICHON, Charles		Metal worker
SERENE, Michel		Carpenter. Wife and one child.
GOURU, Jean François		Gunsmith
DUFLOT, Pierre		Carpenter
LESTONNER, Charles		Mason
PARAIN, Louis		Linen worker

SOLDIERS

ST. LOUIS
ST. GERMAIN
SANS REMISSION
ST. JEAN
LA LIBARDIERE
LE PRINCE
BRUNET, Louis
COLLIN
LA CHASSE
POUSSES, Louis des
POLLY, Claude
COQUELIN
DUBUISSON
VERRARD
LISIMOIRE

Name	From	Comments

SOLDIERS (cont.)

FROMAL, Jean
GILLET, Jean
PICARD
COUTOIS
PHILIBERT
ST. LOUIS
ROUSSEAU, François
TALLON, Simon
GIGOT, Corentin
D'HERVY, Alexandre
PICART
DUMAT, Jean
SOREOT, Gervais
PETRU, Pierre

§ The exact date of departure of the DROMADAIRE is not known. It probably left France in August or September, 1720. It arrived at Old Biloxi about the middle of December, 1720. M. DE LA TOUR complained, after arriving in Louisiana, of Captain St. Marc's treatment of the passengers. St. Marc was subsequently relieved of duty.

JANUARY 4, 1720 TO JANUARY 24, 1721

LIST OF GERMAN FAMILIES EMBARKED ON
THE GARONNE COMMANDED BY M. BURAT
BOUND FOR LOUISIANA. §

Name	From	Comments
BILLIC, Cristophe		Provost. Wife & 2 children.
FRANC, Conrad		Wife.
JOUNG, Claude		Wife and three children.
WERSLE, DOURTH		5 children are with him.
MOOF, André		Wife.
TOURY, DIETHERIC		Wife and one child.
KUSTER, Mathieu		Wife.
JEANSIER, Jean		Wife and two children.
GUSTAUER, Sebastien		Wife and one child.
HERMAN, Jean Martin		Wife and four children.
BOUCHARD, Widow of François	Leopoldas	
MENUE, Jean Henry	Leopoldas	Wife and four children
PARISIEN, Thomas	Leopoldas	Wife and four children
AVERMAN, Melchor	Augsbourg	Wife and one child
STEYDLER, Ubric	Augsbourg	Wife and one child
CHMID, Bartholomé	Augsbourg	Wife and one child
CLEGEL, Thomas	Augsbourg	Wife and one child
KICK, Widow of Thomas	Augsbourg	Three children are with her.
LOCH, George Adam	Augsbourg	Wife and one child
KATEMBERGER, Ernst	Augsbourg	Wife.
WICKENHAUZER, Jean George	Augsbourg	Wife and one child.
MULBACH, Jacques	Augsbourg	Three children are with him.
TRICHEL, Adam	Augsbourg	Wife and three children
LOCH, George André	Augsbourg	Wife and one child
BERNSTELER, Baltazard	Freibourg	Wife and one child
WEINAR, Jean George	Freibourg	Wife and two children
TINSLER, Jean George	Freibourg	
RONIH, Bernard	Freibourg	Wife and five children
TRAEGER, André	Friderichsort	Wife and one child. This man may have been mayor of Friderichsort.
EGSMAN, Simon	Friderichsort	Wife and one child
HYLL, Herman	Friderichsort	
GRADY, Michel	Friderichsort	Wife.
KAILLER, Joseph	Friderichsort	Wife and two children
WACHLLER, Leonard	Friderichsort	Wife and two children
DEZEL, Jean Ernst	Friderichsort	Wife.
EBENHO, Jacques	Friderichsort	Wife and three children
CHAUB, Jean Pierre	Friderichsort	Wife and three children
ROUCLE, Michel	Friderichsort	Wife and two children

§ The exact date for the departure of the GARONNE is not known.

Name	From	Comments

GERMAN FAMILIES (cont.)

Name	From	Comments
BOUCHBAUM, Magnus	Friderichsort	Wife.
WINCHKLER, Joseph	Friderichsort	Wife.
STEGMAYER, Adam	Friderichsort	Wife and two children
KAMMERER, Fredéry	Friderichsort	Wife and four children
CHORR, Jean George	Friderichsort	Wife.
REINCHARDT, Joseph	Friderichsort	Wife and two children
RICARD, Joseph	Friderichsort	Wife.
RICARD, Antoine	Friderichsort	Wife.
OSNER, Michel	Friderichsort	Wife and one child
LITTER, Ernetz	Friderichsort	Wife and two children

The following families
were probably from
Friderichsort, but that
is not known for a cer-
tainty.

Name	Comments
HEYSELER, Ignaty	Wife and two children
GUZINGUER, Joseph	Wife and two children
CHAFF, Jacques	Wife and six children
TRAGER, Jean Martin	Wife.
GAUB, Martin	Wife.
MEYIER, Laurent	Wife.
RAPP, Thomas	Wife and one child.
BLUM, Jean Guillaume	Wife.
MULLER, Jean Duborld	Wife and five children
LEHRER, Christian	Wife and two children
CHNEYDER, Jean Reinhard	Wife and two children

JANUARY 4, 1720 TO JANUARY 24, 1721

LIST OF PRIVATE PASSENGERS AND GERMAN
FAMILIES EMBARKED ON THE CHARENTE
COMMANDED BY M. MIRAMBAULT BOUND FOR
LOUISIANA. §

Name	From	Comments

PRIVATE PASSENGERS

DE LORME, Madame		Her mother is with her.
MASELARY, M.		A servant is with him
JOUBERT, M.		His wife is with him. 2 child-ren

GERMAN FAMILIES

KERC, Jean von	Neukirchen	Wife and four children.
BILLETO, Jean Baptiste	Neukirchen	Wife and four children
CHILLEMAND, Henry	Neukirchen	Wife.
ADAM, Dieterick	Neukirchen	Wife and four children
CHOMB, George	Neukirchen	Wife.
ZINGLER, Jean	Neukirchen	Wife and three children
MEYER, Michel	Neukirchen	Wife and six children
KEYDEL, Widow of Jean Adam	Neukirchen	
ROTSH, Cristophe	Neukirchen	Wife and two children
KOUN, Jacques	Neukirchen	Wife and six children
KESTEMACHER, Estienne	Neukirchen	Wife and two children
GREILENER, Michel	Neukirchen	Wife and one child
WEISS, Michel	Neukirchen	Wife.
COUMMERCER, Etienne	Neukirchen	Wife.
DODERER, Jean George	Neukirchen	Wife.
MOOZER, Martin	Neukirchen	Wife and two children
VANDRIE, Philippe	Neukirchen	
CHOUMP, Widow of	Neukirchen	Two children
CHELER, Michel	Neukirchen	Wife and one child
METZQUER, Jean Michel	Freudenuel	Wife.
WOLFEG, Toussain	Freudenuel	
LECHER, Mathieu	Frendenuel	Wife and three children
HESS, Veit	Frendenuel	Two children
GASSNER, Bernard	Frendenuel	Wife and two children
MEUCLER, Pierre	Frendenuel	Wife.
RUBEL, François	Frendenuel	Wife and five children
KECK, François	Frendenuel	Wife and two children
FICHER, André	Frendenuel	Wife and two children
REEM, Joseph	Frendenuel	Wife and one child

§ The exact date for the departure of the CHARENTE is not known.

Name	From	Comments

GERMAN FAMILIES (cont.)

Name	From	Comments
FROLICH, Jean	Frendenuel	Wife.
RAOUS, Mathieu	Frendenuel	Wife and 3 children
FOAGT, Jean	Frendenuel	Wife and two children
GLANTZ, Simon	Frendenuel	Wife and three children
GLANTZ, Jean	Frendenuel	Wife and four children
JEUGER, Christoph	Frendenuel	Wife and two children
RILLER, Joseph	Frendenuel	Wife and six children
KALLCHMID, Simon	Frendenuel	Wife and two children
ENTICH, Michel	Frendenuel	Wife and three children
RUBLER, Pierre	Frendenuel	Wife and two children
EMMELE, Jean Michel	Frendenuel	Wife and one child
VETZ, Simon	Frendenuel	Wife and three children
FELLEZ, Christian	Frendenuel	Wife and one child
RETHEL, Jean Loup	Frendenuel	Wife.
ETLIN, Widow of André	Frendenuel	
RUTHLE, Eberhard	Frendenuel	Wife and three children
VOURSTER, Simon	Frendenuel	Wife and one child
KALTDAUR, Pierre	Sintzheim	Wife and one child
MOUZER (MOOZER?), Martin	Sintzheim	
FEUGLE, Joseph	Sintzheim	Wife.
RUPRECH, Philippe	Sintzheim	Wife.
EFFRICH, Jean George	Sintzheim	Wife.
ALTER, Jean	Sintzheim	Wife.
WOLF, Pierre	Freudembourg	Wife, and four children
WOLF, Jean	Freudembourg	Wife and three children
MANGELINAN, Charles	Freudembourg	Wife and one child
KNOCHEL, George	Freudembourg	Wife.
HELZER, Jean	Freudembourg	Wife and three children
HILPERS, Adam	Freudembourg	Wife.
HELLEBRAND, Jean	Freudembourg	Wife and four children
HOUBERT, Michel	Freudembourg	Wife and two children
SPEZ, Widow of Mathieu	Brettheim	Two children
HENGEL (HEUGEL?), Jacques	Brettheim	Wife and three children
BRANDEMBERGER, Jean	Brettheim	Wife.
ACCREMAN, Ulric	Brettheim	Wife and one child
STALDEMEYER, Marc	Brettheim	Two children
BINTNAGLE, Children of Jean	Freibourg	Two children
FOGINON, Jean George	Freibourg	Wife.

JUNE 9, 1720

LIST OF SOLDIERS OF THE COMPANY OF
THE INDIES EMBARKED ON THE LEGERE
COMMANDED BY SIEUR KLASIOU DE QUEL-
FELEC BOUND FOR LOUISIANA FROM LA
ROCHELLE.

Name	From	Comments
LENEE, Charles	Chinon in Tourenne	Age 17
MESSAN, Pierre Jean	St. Messan	Age 35
PISENAS, Joseph	Autun	Age 22
PEYRAU, Gabriel	Rançon in Basse Marche	Age 17. Surgeon
ARTOYSOUL, Joseph	Carcassone	Age 23. Shoe-maker.
LA CHAPELLE, François	Bourg de la Borne near Limogès	Age 18. Mason

JUNE 1, 1720

LIST OF SOLDIERS AND PERSONS FOR THE
DARTAGUIETTE CONCESSION EMBARKED ON
THE PROFOND COMMANDED BY M. DU GERNEUR
BOUND FOR LOUISIANA FROM LA ROCHELLE.§

Name	From	Comments

SOLDIERS

Cadets

LA CUREE, Pierre Peronde	Issouduy	Age 23
ROBILLARD DE BEAUREPAIRE, Thomas Bernard	Caen	Age 20

Sargeant

MARECHAL, Claude	Moulins in Bourbonois	Age 39

Troops

FERTEL, François	Corby in Picardy	Age 18
MAGDELEINE, Julien	Rennes in Brittany	Age 20
GAU, Louis	Tours	Age 17
BORGNE, Pierre	Troyes in Champagne	Age 26
ROUSSEL, Jean	Vannes in Brittany	Age 15
VAUGOIS, Pierre	Rennes in Brittany	Age 18
MENARD, Louis	Longueville in Poitou	Age 35
EUGUENAIN, Etienne	Maçon	Age 16
LA ROCHE, Antoine	Maçon	Age 20
POUSSINE, Pierre	Monbart in Burgundy	Age 14
LEGROS, Antoine	Moulin	Age 20
OHIER, Nicolas	Abbeville	Age 22
THIBAULT, Nicolas	Clermont in Auvergne	Age 16
REY (ROY?), Claude	Cié in Charolais	Age 40
CONMOLET, Jean Baptiste	Cayla in Languedoc	Age 20
BENARD, Jacques	Angers	Age 36
GRIMAL, Antoine	Aurliac in Auvergne	Age 30
PERRON, Claude	St. Etienne de Riz	Age 20
RIGOLET, Nicolas	Lyon	Age 16
CALLET, Pierre	Lyon	Age 20
THOMAS, Henry	Chalons	Age 21
DUPAIN, Jean Louis	Bourg in Bresse	Age 18
SIMONET, Jean	Chateau Regnault in Tourenne	Age 21
PARRIOU, Claude	Marsonnat in Bresse	Age 25
BRULE, Aymé	Marsonnat in Bresse	Age 23

§ June 1, 1720 is not the departure date for the Profond. It
probably left France about the middle of June, 1720.

Name	From	Comments

PERSONS FOR THE DARTAGUIETTE CONCESSION

VAQUIER
MARON
ROUX, Jacques
MARTINOT, Pierre
REGAN, Blaize
GAUSSERAN, Etienne
MAURY, Pierre
SUDRY, Jean
MALTY, Louis
GIRO, Jean
GALTIER, Jacques
MORISSON, Robert
SCHIR, Jean
GIBILY, Joseph
GUISIER, François
CASTAN, Joseph
SEGUIR, Michel
TOURNOIR, Jacques
COLSON, Nicolas
ESSARTIER, Jean
RISPO, Jean
TINEL, Antoine
BORT, Antoine
BELLAIR, Jean
BENIER, Rémond
RAGES, Jean
GOBERT, François
LEPINE, François
VALES, Pierre
AUDIN, Claudine
DALENTIN, Margueritte

JUNE 10, 1720

LIST OF OFFICERS AND WORKERS FOR THE
LAW CONCESSION EMBARKED ON THE PROFOND
COMMANDED BY M. DU GERNEUR BOUND FOR
LOUISIANA FROM LA ROCHELLE.

Name	Name

OFFICERS

LE SAIN
MAXIMIEN
NAVARRE
LABRO
MAROLLE
LABRO (fils)
PITACHE
SERCILLEZ
LEDREUX
GRALLAIN
LINCHE
MERIC
NADAL
BERAT
LE COMTE
GARATTE

WORKERS

ALLAIN, Guillaume	DUPERIT, Charles
BATAILLE, Jacques	SEGUIN, Ives
GAMOT, Louis	PERIER, Guillaume
LE MION, Jean	GRANGE, Guillaume
FAVIER, Nicolas	GAY, Jean
AUDIER, Jean	VALTAN, Alexandre
RAPAN, Guerre	ACHET, Jean
SEAU, Jean du	COSTAN, Guillaume
JARAINNE, François	BERTELEMY, Arenaud
MAZEAS, Jean	GUEGAN, Yves
CONNART, Gilles	VAILLANT, Louis
GALLE, Jean	COULLEAU, Jean
LE COR, Jean	GISQUART, Louis
GARABET, Dominiques	LE BOIRT, Jean
PREJEAN, Philipe	SEIGNART, Jean
FOUQUET, François	BOURGADE, Antoine
CORELLAS, Manuel	MADEE, Guillaume
MAUDET (MANDET?), Arenaud	BERNARD, André

Name	Name

WORKERS FOR THE LAW CONCESSION (cont.)

MARIE, Joseph
BOUCHER, Simon
DUSERT, Etienne
FARGUE, Jean
DALBERT, Jean
LA CROIX, Thomas
BALISTRE, Jacques
PECHEREAU, Pierre
BERDER, François
BERGEREAU, jean
VERGEANS, François
LE QUERE, Jean
AUDRAIN, Yves
LIONNARD, Louis
HUARD, François
TARTIF, Jean
GULINE, Jacques
VIGOUREUX, Pierre
LEDUC, Guinolet
JAILLET, François
SEVERRE, Jacques
DOS, Jean
HOURS, Jean
COTENCEAUX, Lorant
AURY, Nicolas
RICHAL, Allain
GENOUY, François
HAIS, Mathurin
DESCASOR, François
MOREAUX, Joseph
LANCLOS, Jean de
BOURDON, François
MARQUANT, Isme
HONNART, Louis
FOURQUADE, Jean
GUILLIEN, Pierre
MAILLEUX, Pierre
RESERE, Jean
MICHEL, Jacques

NOGUIEZ, Bartelemy
SALOMON, Pol
FOY, Nicolas
MEUNIER, Simon
MEVEL, François
POISONNET, Sebastien
FORSAN, Thomas
FOCHET, Jean
DARELON, Jacques
LE ROU, Jacques
LE CORE, Michel
TOURMAIN, Pierre
GUENAN, Gabriel
BOUCHER, Louis
DELOMBRE, Jacques
SALOMON, François
LE MOIN, Michel
ALTINGO
GENOUI (GENONI?), René
GUE, Allain de
DEJEAN, Guillaume
HONNART, Jean Baptiste
VINCENT, Jacques
DROUILLON, Louis
TABARY, Etienne
PICOU, Charrles
GUION, Jacques
LUSEAUX, Etienne
CANTERELLE, Jacques
DORIDEAU, Pierre
TESIER, André
BIENVENU, Isac
DALBERT, Pierre
ABIVAIN, Simon
LARDREAUX, Thomas
GASTIER, Nicolas
COSTE, Jean
PEGNAN, Claude

WIVES AND CHILDREN

BLANCHE, Marie
AUGINE, Marie Anne
AURY, Marie
MOREAUX, Jeanne
NIVAIT, Madelenne
MEILLAN, Marie Françoise

LE MEUDE, Jeanne
CONGUART, Marie
LE LIEVRE, Jeanne
POUPON, Jeanne
PICOU, Catherine
DAMOURETTE, Jeanne

Name	Name

WIVES AND CHILDREN (cont.)

SELLIER, Marie	CROUET, Catherinne
LA HAIS, Claude	STER, Suzanne
SARAS, Dominique	SAILLAR, Elizabet
HAIRE, Elizabete de	QUERAMOILLE, Marie
MOREAUX, July	BOURDON, Marie
MOREAUX, Anne	BOURDON, Françoise
BIENVENU, Jeanne	BOURDON, Madelainne
MARQUANT, Theresse	HOMART, Elizabet
	HOMART, Adrienne

BOYS

AURY, Nicolas	PICOU, Urbain
CHANLUSSEAU, Antoine	MOREAU, JOSEPH
LANCO, Joseph	MOREAU, Vincent
FRANCOIS, Jean	MOREAUX, Jean
TESIER, Jean	BOURDON, Louis
TESIER, Andiol	BIENVENU, François
CANTRELLE, Jean	BIENVENU, Guillaume
MARQUAND, Hugue	BIENVENU, Daniel
	BIENVENU, Jean

DOMESTICS

SIDANNER, Challes	BERGERAC, Jean
GARY, Louis	PERON, Thomas
CASTENAUVE, Joseph	

JUNE 26, 1720

LIST OF PASSENGERS EMBARKED ON THE
ALEXANDRE BOUND FOR LOUISIANA FROM
LORIENT.

Name	Comments
DELORMES, M.	Director General in Louisiana. Commissoned November 10, 1720
MAGUIRE, M. de	Captain of Infanterie. Commissioned March 23, 1720
VARENNES, Sieur de	Sub-lieutenant. Commissioned March 23, 1720
ETIENNE, Sieur	Storekeeper. Commissioned February 17, 1720
FREBOUL, Sieur	Storekeeper. Commissioned April 6, 1720
VERCHANT, Sieur	Bookkeeper. Commissioned April 6, 1720
DES ESSARTS, Sieur	Clerk. Commissioned April 6, 1720
LEBOIS, Sieur	Clerk. Commissioned April 6, 1720
ESMAR, Sieur	Inspector General and Secretary to M. Diron. Agreement of April 15, 1720
MACARTY, Sieur de	Lieutenant. Agreement of April 30, 1720
VIEUSSENS, Sieur	Doctor. Agreement of January 15, 1720
ROYER, Sieur	Surgeon Major. Agreement of April 15, 1720
CHAMPIGNEUL, Sieur de	Sargeant
RUARC, Sieur	Volunteer
JU, Sieur	Volunteer

Three servants for M. DELORMES

PERSONS FOR THE LE BLANC CONCESSION

Name	Comments
BROUTIN, M.	Captain (Réformé). In charge of Le Blanc's troops.
NORVILLE, Sieur	Clerk for Le Blanc's troops.
VELAR, Philipe François	Carpenter
DUPLECHIN, Joseph	Carpenter
CALAIRE, Jean François	Carpenter
TOURNET, Claude	Caulker
BAVILLIN, Pierre	Edge-tool maker
BOTION, Claude	Edge-tool maker
LIERMONT, Michel	Nail maker
LE CORNET, Joseph	Sawyer
REVIRE, André	Sawyer
PETIT, Pierre	Sawyer
DEFLEUR, François	Sawyer
Three women and two children	

JULY 15, 1720

LIST OF PERSONS FOR THE LAW CONCES-
SION, OFFICERS AND TROOPS EMBARKED
ON THE MARIE COMMANDED BY M. DE
PONTLO BOUND FOR LOUISIANA FROM THE
ROADSTEAD OF CHEF DE BAYE.

Name	From	Comments

FOR THE LAW CONCESSION

LEVENS, M.		Assistant Director
MEYNARD, Sieur		Overseer

FOR THE CONCESSION OF M. LAW AND THE DUKE DE GUICHE

MARIN		Inspector of Tobacco Workers

TOBACCO WORKERS

MORAND, François	Caramb, County of Avignon
BOURE, Jean	Montdragon in Provençe
DUMAS, Sebastien	Montdragon in Provençe
BOURE, Joseph	Montdragon in Provençe
MARRE, Paul Louis	Montdragon in Provençe
BOYER, François	Montdragon in Provençe
FABRE, Charles	Montdragon in Provençe
FEUILLE, Jean	Montdragon in Provençe
GUAY, Joseph	Bays in Vivaretz
BERNARD, Louis	Montdragon in Provençe
BRUN, François	Montdragon in Provençe
CLAUZONNIERE, François	Montdragon in Provençe
MANQUIT, Charles	Capaluy, County of Avignon
BRUNEL, Pierre	Bouleme, County of Avignon
DUFOUR, Joseph	Montdragon in Provençe
CHARRIER, Joseph	Montdragon in Provençe
HONDRACQ, Marc Antoine	St. Andiol in Vivaretz
ROLAND, Hierome	La Garde Pariot, County of Avignon
TRON, Pierre	St. Alexandre in Languedoc
FUMAT, Jean	Montdragon in Provençe
VERNET, Jean	Lapalüe, County of Avignon
FLANDRIN, Jean	Lapalüe, County of Avignon
SARIGNON, Jacques	Mornan, County of Avignon
TEILLIERE, André	Tirange in Forest
CHARASSE, François	Niascossene, County of Avignon
MANNE, François	Serignan, County of Avignon
ROBERT, Jacques	Lapalüe, County of Avignon
RICORD, Pierre	M. LEVEN's servant

Name	From	Comments

WIVES OF THE TOBACCO WORKERS

MIARDE, Louise
TRORADE, Anne
MIAR, Roze
RICHARDELLE, Isabeau
PINET, Isabeau
TAFFANELLE, Jeanne
GAUDIBERT, Marguerite
VIALLENCE, Victoire
BOURUE, Anne
MAZERTE, Roze
TAVERNADE, Jeanne
FERVEQUE, Marie
SESGRANGES, Marguerite   Mother of Jean FLANDRIN
PERRONNE, Antoinnette
RUIRDE, Isabeau
ROUSSELLE, Françoise
BARNUINE, Jeanne
JAMBONNE, Suzanne

SONS AND DAUGHTERS OF THE TOBACCO WORKERS

Name	From	Comments
ROBERT, Jeanne		Daughter of Jacques ROBERT
MORAND, Gabriel		Son of François MORAND
MORAND, Fabriel		Daughter (?) of François MORAND
MORAND, Catherine		Daughter of François MORAND
CLAUSSONNIERE, Catherine		Daughter of François CLAUZONNIERE
MANNE, George		Son of François MANNE
MANNE, François		Son of François MANNE
MANNE, Joseph		Son of François MANNE
MANNE, Therese		Daughter of François MANNE
MANNE, Françoise		Daughter of François MANNE
BOYER, Madelein		Daughter of François BOYER
FABRE, Antoine		Son of Charles FABRE
FABRE, Jacques		Son of Charles FABRE
CHARASSE, Clair		Son of François CHARASSE
CHARASSE, Jean		Son of François CHARASSE
CHARASSE, Baptiste		Son of François CHARASSE
CHARASSE, Marianne		Daughter of François Charasse
CHARASSE, Dominique		Daughter of François CHARASSE
VERNET, Roze		Daughter of Jean VERNET
FLANDRIN, Claude		Son of Jean FLANDRIN

Name	From	Comments

SONS AND DAUGHTERS OF THE TOBACCO WORKERS (cont.)

Name	From	Comments
SARIGNON, François		Son of Jacques SARIGNON
DUMAS, Guillaume		Son of Sebastien DUMAS
DUMAS, Marianne		Daughter of Sebastien DUMAS
FEUILLE, Jean		Son of Jean FEUILLE
MANQUIT, Françoise		Daughter of Charles MANQUIT
MANQUIT, Jean Martin		Son of Charles MANQUIT
BRUN, Jacques		Son of François BRUN
BRUN, Anne		Daughter of François BRUN

SOLDIERS

Officers

Name	From	Comments
ST. BOEURE DE MONMORT, M. de		Captain of Infantry
BANES, M.		Major at New Orleans
MONMERQUE, M. de		Lieutenant of Infantry
RABOUL, M.		Lieutenant of Infantry
MOUY, M. de		Sub-lieutenant
THIERY DE CHASSIN, M.		Sub-lieutenant
MAILLARD, M.		Sub-lieutenant
LARDY, M.		Ensign

CADETS

Name	From	Comments
MEURLY, Daniel de	St. Gal in Switzerland	Age 28
CHAZELLE DE MERGELLE, Nicolas	Paris	Age 40
DURCET DU HAUTBOIS, Jacques	St. Jacques in Bausse	Age 25
L'ISLE, Joseph de	St. Sulpice	Age 15
MAISON NEUVE, François de	Blois	Age 30
RIBERT, Louis	Versailles	Age 17

Sargeants

Name	From	Comments
HEBERT, Louis	Rouen	Age 48
PREVILLE, Jacques	St. Helene in Savoy	Age 28

Troops

Name	From	Comments
BONNEAU, Jacques	Autun	Age 18
LIONSEL, Louis	Coudon in Saintonge	Age 23
DUFOUR, Bernard	Bergerac in Perigord	Age 31
LA TOUCHE, Mathurin de	Plomene, Bishopric of St. Malo	Age 26

Name	From	Comments

SOLDIERS (cont.)

Troops (cont.)

Name	From	Comments
BERNARD, Pierre	Rufay in Poitou	Age 18
LE DELIVRE, Yves Joseph	Carhoux, Bishopric of Grimpert	Age 35
LESDIGUIERE, Louis	Abbeville in Picardy	Age 45
FLEURTET, Pierre	Gergy, near Chalons	Age 18
ST. MIGHEL, Nicolas	St. Germain in Laye	Age 25
DESJARDINS, Jacques	Chomotel	Age 40
LENORMAND, Etienne	Orléans	Age 36
PIERRE, Jean Baptiste	Frainay in Champagne	Age 23
FROIN, Bastien	Mauzé	Age 30
FOUCAUD, René	Niort	Age 40
BOYER, Jean	Ardam in Poitou	Age 25
FOURNIER, Jean	Angoulême	Age 31
POUPART, Philippe	Alençon in Normandy	Age 23
CHANFAILLY, Jean	Alençon in Normandy	Age 23
GARREAU, Pierre	St. André in Poitou	Age 16
VINCONNEAU, Nicolas	Seche in Anjou	Age 15
DURIN, Pierre Mathieu	Marle in Picardy	Age 45
FONTAINE, Claude	St. Germain in Laye	Age 37
HUBERT, Julien	Dol in Brittany	Age 26
DUCROS, Joseph	Toulouse	Age 27
BOUCAUD, Pierre	Richelieu in Poitou	Age 17
GRIVOIS, Jean	Villaire in Picardy	Age 36
MENANTEAU, Jacques	La Gore, near La Rochelle	Age 28
GILLE, François	Clerc in Touraine	Age 36
BAZILLE, François	Auxerre in Burgundy	Age 22
LOPINOT, Louis	Canada	Age 14
BULOIN, René	Flemier, near Angers	Age 22
HERY, René	Angers	Age 16
BASOURDY, Israël	Loudun	Age 45
ARNOULT, Blaize	Paris	Age 21
RENOULEAU, Blaize	St. Martin in Saintonge	Age 22
PICAULT, Nicolas	Orléans	Age 19
GOUANOT, Simon	Giron, near Bordeaux	Age 25
ROULEAU, François	Rennes in Brittany	Age 23
SINAIS, Antoine	Meillen, near Bordeaux	Age 17
METIVIER, Jean	La Chapelle Blanche	Age 21
FULMY, Jean	Belville in Poitou	Age 18
ROUANNE, Antoine Dom. de	Near Lyon	Age 28
DUCOUDRAY, Louis Ysac	Geneva	Age 30
NOVET, Jacques	Bogency	Age 35
FALIGAN, Jean	Argenton Les Eglises____ in Poitou	Age 33

Name	From	Comments

SOLDIERS (cont.)

Troops (cont.)

Name	From	Comments
DIMIER, Jean	Chateauneuf in Augoumois	Age 21
FERRET, François	Rennes in Brittany	Age 20
ARNOULT, Claude	Besançon in Franche Comté	Age 30
JACQUES, Jean	Laugon, near Bordeaux	Age 37
BERTAUDOT, Jacques	Ardam in Poitou	Age 16
ROBERT, Jacques	Sel in Poitou	Age 33
YVONNET, Jean	Chateau Regnault in Tourenne	Age 21
FORT, Jean	St. Douy, near Bordeaux	Age 30
CASSERAND, Jean	Givere in Bearn	Age 20
GODINEAU, Louis	St. Pierre Achain, near Tours	Age 29
ROLLAND, Louis Antoine	Orléans	Age 26
MINCE, Michel	Parish of St. Severin, Bishopric of Blois	Age 20
BOUFANDEAU, Philbert	Barbeziere	Age 17
PIZENAC, Joseph	Autun	Age 20
BODINEAU, Guillaume	Paray	Age 20
FLEUR, Martin	Paray	Age 21
MARCOU, Jean	Parish of St. Victor on the Loire	Age 19
BREDA, Jean Baptiste	Mans	Age 18
CORNET, Claude	Mans	Age 20
DUFOUR, François	Paris	Age 32
BERTRAND, Claude	Grenoble	Age 17
MANDERLIER, Nicolas	St. Jullien	Age 22
THIBAUD, Luc	St. Jullien	Age 18
FRAINE, François	Corby in Picardy	Age 18
LEBLANC, Hubert	St. Brun	Age 25
LA BOISSIERE, François	St. Brun	Age 21
DAVID, Jean	Maçon	Age 18
MAILLE, Pierre	Maçon	Age 20
DARGENTEL, Guillaume	Bourg de la Clayette	Age 18
PERRIN, Claude	Serigny	Age 25
MAIN, Pierre	Chef Bouton in Poitou	Age 40
DURCY, François	Bordeaux	Age 23
SAMSON, Pierre	Abbeville in Picardy	Age 35
GASSAGNE, Pierre	Channac in Languedoc	Age 25

WIVES OF THE SOLDIERS

CHARPENTIER, Marie
PIGNON, Toussaint
MARTINE, Marie
PARENTE, Marie Catherine

Name	From	Comments

WIVES OF THE SOLDIERS (cont.)

GAUTIER, Anne
ANDRELLIER, Marie
GARNIER, Gabriel

CHILDREN OF THE SOLDIERS

ROBERT, Pierre
ROBERT, Jacques
ROBERT, Simon
LESIDGUIERE, Daniel Louis
ST. MICHEL, Nicolas
FOURNIER. Jean

AUGUST 3, 1720

LIST OF MEN AND WOMEN FOR THE CONCES-
SION OF M. DE CHAUMONT EMBARKED ON
THE GIRONDE BOUND FOR LOUISIANA FROM
LORIENT.

Name	From	Comments
ç		

OFFICIALS

Name	From	Comments
REVILLON, M.		Director General of Stores
MORIN		Inspector. His wife is with him.
HAMELE,		Comptroller
RIDE		Engineer
MORAND		Surgeon major
HUQUEVILLE		

WORKERS

Name	From	Comments
GOUDIN, Joseph	Pont du Rhein in Touraine	Age 18. Tailor
HENIQUE, Nicolas	Namur	Age 20. Tailor
BROUSSE, Jean Philippe	Neuf Brisaque in Upper Alsace	Age 30. Cooper
TREMANT, Jeanne	Morzan, Parish of St. Pierre Blanchisseuse	Age 26. Wife of Jean Philippe BROUSSE
CIDAR, Jacques	Nantes	Age 28. Sailor
PERCHA, Guillaumette		Age 30. Washwoman. Their child is with them. She is wife of Jacques CIDAR.
BEQUET, Jean Baptiste	Paris, Parish of St. Sulpice	Age 30. Locksmith.
BAROT, Catherine	Toifou in Poitou	Age 23. Washwoman. Wife of J. B. BEQUET.
CARMOUCHE, Jean	L'Ayrane, Bishopric of Taille	Age 28. Locksmith
ROZEAU, Antoine du	Orléans, Parish of St. Pierre	Age 19. Apprenticed locksmith.
NAMURIAU (NAMURIAN?) Jean	Namur	Age 17. Locksmith.
BOURDY, Jean	Guirande, Parish of St. Aubin	Age 22. Edge-tool maker
BELY, Antoine	Ste. Pazanne	Age 48. Carpenter
ERRAND (ERRAUD?), Jean	St. Eutroppe, Parish of Saintongeois	Age 20. Apprenticed carpenter. Called SAINTON-GECIS

Name	From	Comments
WORKERS (cont.)		
BARBOTTEAU, François	Nantes, Parish of St. Nicolas	Age 20. Apprenticed carpenter
GAUTIER, Pierre	La Roche Brenard, Parish of Neuvillac	Age 23. Apprenticed ship's carpenter.
BRAILLARD, Etienne	Tour, Parish of St. Croix	Age 19. Apprenticed carpenter
DAVID, Laurent	Vannes, Parish of Ersalle	Age 19. Apprenticed ship's Carpenter
CARNEL, Pierre	Londelle, Parish of St. Martin, Bishopric of Avranche	Age 30. Sawyer. His wife and one child are with him.
LE BESCON, Pierre	Ville Neuf Bourbenne, Bishopric of Aurange	Age 48. Sawyer.
AILLERYE, Jean Baptiste	Mormand in Brie, near Laguy	Age 20. Apprenticed carpenter.
RASIE, Guillaume	Mormand in Brie Laguy	Age 18. Apprenticed carpenter.
KEBRIAQUE, François	La Chapelle au Fumet, Bishopric of Daule	Age 40. Gardener
MORDAS, Julien	Reine, Parish of All Saints	Age 28. Gardener
LE MAITRE, Pierre	La Marche, Parish of St. Damien	Age 24. Gardener
DUROUZEAU, Pierre	Orléans, Paris of St. Pierre en Santelet	Age 24. Harness-maker.
DROUIN, Jean Nicolas	Chartres in Bausse	Age 20. Shoemaker
BARBIER, Pierre	Vannes in Brittany, Parish of St. Pater	Age 28. Cultivator
LEFICHANT, Jean	Paris, Parish of St. Nicolas	Age 40. Cultivator
LE MAIRE, Jacques	Paris, Parish of St. Martial	Age 26. Baker
JOLY, Jacques	Chimé, Parish of Ste. Manegonde, Bishopric of Liège	Age 40. Cook and Butcher
LANAE, Joseph	Nantes, Parish of St. Clerment	Age 26. Engagé
LUSARD, Nicolas	Paris, Parish of St. Sulpice	Age 20. The Director's Servant
CUSSY, August	Pontivie in Brittany	Age 16. Engagé
Girls		
MELIER, Jeanne	Nantes, Parish of St.N	Age 18. Linen worker
CHANIOT, Marie	Isle de Noirmoutier	Age 20. Washerwoman
VILLIERS, Margueritte	Nantes, Parish of Esée	Age 20. Servant
BOETE, Marie Jeanne	Morlay, Bishopric of Cornuailles	Age 22. Embroiderer

AUGUST 10, 1720

LIST OF PASSENGERS EMBARKED ON THE
ELEPHANT BOUND FOR LOUISIANA

Name	From	Comments

SOLDIERS

Officers

DILLON, M.		Captain
FABRY, M.		Captain
BAVAREL, M.		Lieutenant
GUILLERMET, M.		Lieutenant
DE LA COMBE		Sub-lieutenant
DE LA SUZE		Sub-Lieutenant

Sargeants

DEMINE
ST. LOUIS
CHANSEY, Joseph
DESNOYER, Laurent
RITTER, Henry

Cadets

DE ROLLA, Sieur
LAGENOIS, Sieur

Sur Pied de Sergent

PHILIPPES, Sieur

Troops

ST. LOUIS
SELAMME, Jacques
LA ROSE
LIONNOIS
LA CROIX
SANS SOUCIE
SANS CHAGRIN
L'ESPERANCE
PIED FERME
VA DE BON COEUR
LALANDE
BELAIR
PARISIEN

Name	From	Comments

SOLDIERS (cont.)

Troops

TRANCHE MONTAGNE
BRISFER
CAMBRAY
BEAUSEJOUR
MEZIERE
LA DEROUTE
A LANCON
SOISSONS
LA GIBERNE
ST. PIERRE
SAN QUARTIER
LA JEUNESSE
BIARNOIS
DRAGON
LA FRANCE
BERRY
LA RAME
L'EVEILLE
DU ROCHER
LA TULLIPPE

2nd Company

LA FLEUR
BELLE ROSE
LA TERREUR
LA PRAIRIE
LA ROSE
LA GUERRE
LA TULLIPE
CASAR
BEAUSOLEIL
SANS SOUCIE
LA GRANDEUR
PREST A BOIRE
FRAPE D'ABORD
SANS QUARTIER
TRANCHE MONTAGNE
PASSE PARTOUT
LA RIGUEUR
AUGUSTE
SAUVE LES MEUBLES
LA FUREUR
LA TAPPAGE

Name	From	Comments

SOLDIERS (cont.)

Troops (cont.)

CHAMPAGNE
LA GIROFFLE
SANS PEUR
LE GAILLARD
LE TRANCHANT
TAPPE DRUE
LA GLOIRE
L'ARDEUR
ST. PAUL
FELIX
L'HARDY
LA PERLE

WIVES

DESJARDINS, Marie Barbe — Wife of CLAUDINS, called ST. LOUIS, AND their children: François, Jacob, Elisabethe, Barbe.

CHARTIOU, Angelique — Wife of DENOYER, a sargeant.

RITTER, Marie Catherine — Wife of Henry RITTER, a sargeant, and their children: Jean Pierre, Louis, Joseph, and Marie Anne

MARIE ANTONNETTE — Wife of a soldier
ROCROY, PERINE — Wife of a soldier
PECHEUX, Anne — Wife of a soldier

LIST OF OTHER PASSENGERS ON BOARD THE ELEPHANT.

HUGOT, Jean — Storekeeper
LESTIEVANT, Jean François — Storekeeper
DELAPERIERE, Sieur — Storekeeper
NEBOUT, Jean — Register of Tobacco
MESNAGE, Malo August — Assistant Storekeeper
CHOLLE, François
LARMUSIAU, Jean Baptiste — Surgeon major

WORKERS

LE BLEU, Paul
PRUD'HOMME, Jean François
CHATEAU, Martin du

Name	From	Comments

WORKERS (cont.)

PARMENTIER, Jacques François
GAUDIN, Joseph
COULON, Joseph
CRIEE, Martin
DENEL, François
BONS, Pierre Alexandre
LE MOINE, Charles François
LANTIER, Gratien
FOY, François
LAFER, Jean
LE DUC, Phillippe
LOISE, Jean Antoine   His wife and two children
                                   are with him. The
                                   children are aged 4 & 7.
VITREQUIN, François   Wife and two children.
                                   Children aged 2 & 4.

LAUTIER, Joseph
DESMARETZ, François   Wife is with him.
LAUTIER, Jean Baptiste   His mother is with him.
MANARD, François   Wife is with him.
MACCONNEAU, Joseph
BARIE, Pierre de
PIERPONT, Hiacinte
RAUDON, Jean
TORS, Jean
ESCASE, Jacques
CHALONNIAUX, François
ROCHE, Nicolas
DELON, Jean
ESPICARD, Pierre
BREAU, Pierre
DAUTIN, Phillippe
CASOLAT, Antoine
LESEYRAC, Calix
LA NOIX, Guilleaume Joseph
HERCHAIN, Nicolas
HOUAGON, Henry
BUIT, Antoine
BODENELLE, Antoine
BLONDELLE, Jean Baptiste
AUDEBARD, François
LE CAT, Jean Nicaise   Wife and two children.
                                   Children aged 2 & 3
TUBOEUF, Joseph   Wife and two children.
                                   Children aged 6 months
                                   and three years.
DU QUAY, François   Wife and 3 children.
                                   Children aged 3,7, & 9.

Name	From	Comments

WORKERS (cont.)

DENIS, Dieu Donné

LE CAT, Jacques — Wife and three children. Children aged 3, 4, and 7 months.

ROCOU, Charles

LASSE, Denis

VICE, Jean (père) — Wife and 1 child, aged 20.

VICE, Nicolas (fils)

DAUPHIN, Jean François (père) — Wife and 1 child, aged 3 1/2 years.

DAUPHIN, Jean François (fils)

DARCHER, Nicolas

NOIZERS, Nicolas

HENEQUIN, Bastien

GENTILLON, Antoine — His wife is with him.

CARON, Estienne — His wife is with him.

FOURNIER, Jean

FORT, Pierre — Wife and one child, aged 9 years.

BODON, Jean Simon

MAISTRE, Toussaint de

TANNEUR, Pierre Lefebvre

ROGON, Jean Baptiste

BARBIER, Barthelemy

ESCASE, Michel

ALEXANDRE, Nicolas

PASQUIER, Jacques — Wife & child, aged 6

VITREQUIN, Nicolas — Wife and child, aged 1

MUNERO, George

COEURS, Henry Haute

LEFEBVRE, Pierre — A miner.

SAUVE, André

LE NOIR, Jean

LE BLANC, Pierre

LAUSIAU, Jean

OURS, Jean Paul — Wife and child, aged 7

PASSE, Jean Baptiste — One child of 11 years

SOLME, Antoine — Wife is with him.

FEU, Pierre

VINCINS, Jean — Wife and two children, aged 14 & 18 years

FRAY, Jean Baptiste

LEBRUN, Henry — Wife and two children, aged 5 & 15 years

COUSIN, Antoine — Two children, aged 7 and 12 years.

Name	Comments

WORKERS (cont.)

DAMBLY, Jean
GALLET, Jean

MARRIED PEOPLE

Name	Comments
DUPLESSIS, M.	Lieutenant. His wife is with him.
HUGOT, M.	Storekeeper
MARTIN, Françoise	Wife of HUGOT. One child, aged 18 mos.
LARMUSIAU. M.	Surgeon major
SEVENIN, Catherine Thereze	Wife of LAMUSIAU. 3 children, aged 3, 10, 17.
LA FLEUR	Soldier
ANGRAN, Marie Anne Toinette	Wife of LA FLEUR
PASSE PARTOUT	Soldier
ROSCOT, Perine	Wife of PASSE PAROUT
LOISE, Jean Antoine	Worker
BAUDOIN, Janneton	Wife of Jean Antoine LOISE
VITREQUIN, Francois	Worker
EXCE, Charlotte	Wife of François VITREQUIN
DESMARETS, François	Worker
LAUTIER, Marie Thereze	Wife of François DESMARETS
LAUTIER, Anne Marie	Mother of Marie Thereze LAUTIER
MANARD, François	Worker
MACRA, Marie Catherine	Wife of François MANARD
LE CAT, Jean Nicaise	Worker
FIEVET, Marie Angelique	Wife of Jean Nicaise LE CAT
TUBEUF, Joseph	Worker
DOUSY, Marie Margueritte	Wife of Joseph TUBEUF
DU QUAY, François	Worker
SAVATTE, Marie Antoinette	Wife of François DU QUAY
LE CAT, Jacques	Worker
BOUTANIN, Marie Barbe	Wife of Jacques LE CAT
VICE, Jean	Worker
VICE, Margueritte	Wife of Jean VICE
DAUPHIN, Jean François	Worker
GIRANDALLE, Jeanne	Wife of Jean François DAUPHIN
DARCHER, Nicolas	Worker
DEASSE, Marion	Wife of Nicolas DARCHER
GENTILLON, Antoine	Worker
FAURE, Jeanne	Wife of Antoine GENTILLON
CARON, Estienne	Worker
BAZY, Marie Anne	Wife of Estienne CARON
FORT, Pierre	Worker
GUICHON, Marie	Wife of Pierre FORT
PASQUIER, Jacques	Worker
VATEL, Marie	Wife of Jacques PASQUIER

Name	Comments

MARKED PEOPLE (cont.)

MARRIED PEOPLE (cont.)

Name	Comments
VITREQUIN, Nicolas	Worker
JOSEPH, Thereze	Wife of Nicolas VITREQUIN
SAUVE, André	Worker
CUILLIERE, Catherine	Wife of André SAUVE
OURS, Jean Paul	Worker
OURS, Marie Salmé	Wife of Jean Paul OURS
SELME, Antoine	Worker
SELME, Anne Marie	Wife of Antoine SELME
VINCINS, Jean	Worker
VINCINS, Anne Marie	Wife of Jean VINCINS
LEBRUN, Henry	Worker
VERPIAC, Marie Joachine de	Wife of Henry LEBRUN
COUSIN, Antoine	(Wife absent)

AUGUST 11, 1720

LIST OF OFFICIALS AND WORKERS FOR THE
CONCESSION OF COUNT DARTAGNAN EMBARKED
ON THE <u>CHAMEAU</u> BOUND FOR LOUISIANA
FROM LORIENT.

Name	Comments

OFFICIALS

DARIGUERRE, M.	Director General
BENAC, M. de	Assistant Director
DE MONTRAL	Storekeeper
LA FRENAYE, M.	Surgeon major. Two daughters are with him. Two sons.
COUSTE, M.	Secretary
VISON, M.	Surgeon

WORKERS

CASUILON	Laborer
TRIBAUD	Laborer
BONNEFOY	Laborer
REFAIT	Carpenter
MARCHAND	Carpenter
DONOND	Carpenter. His wife is with him.
COUTARET, Antoine	carpenter
TURIO	Carpenter
MAZANOT	Miller
FOUCARD	Miller
ANGOT	Edge-tool maker. His wife is with him.
PAPIN	Edge-tool maker.
TEILLE	Cooper
LA TREILLE	Cooper
LA COSTE	Baker. His wife is with him.
CACON	Baker.
PIRE BON	Baker.
IMBERT	Locksmith
TIBAULT	Locksmith. His wife is with him.
JARY	Gardener. His wife and one child are with him.
LE SIOUX	Gardener. His wife is with him.
PREVOST	Wheelwright. His wife is with him.
LE COEUR	Wheelwright. His wife is with him.
POUPARD	Wheelwright.
DESCOLES	Coppersmith
LARASSE	Coppersmith. His wife is with him.
FERANDON	Founder. His wife is with him.
NAVERT	Founder. His wife is with him.

Name	Comments

WORKERS (cont.)

Name	Comments
SONGY	Founder. His wife is with him.
LE TEILLEY	Shoemaker
BOURGOGNE	Shoemaker
MERAND	Shoemaker. His wife is with him.
ROBERJE (?)	Shoemaker.
BORDERY	Mason. His wife is with him.
CRISMAN	Mason
NOURRY	Mason. His wife is with him.
NOUEL	Mason
BOUTEIR	Tiler
GODIN	Tiler
LE MAISTRE	?
DAN	?
GEOFFROY	Tailor
BROCHAT	Tailor
LA HAYE	Sawyer
GUYNARD	Sawyer
LEVESQUE	Cook. His wife and 1 child are with him.
RICHARD	Cook. His wife is with him.
BEAULIEU	Tobacco worker
HUGUES	Tobacco worker. His wife is with him.
SERCORIN	Tobacco worker. His wife is with him.
BRETON	Tobacco worker
RIMBERT	Silk worker
CAVALIE	Silk worker
MONETA	Silk worker
PETIT CORROYEUR	
AUBRY	HOSIER
LE GENDRE	Butcher
DUMAS	Butcher
ST. GERMAIN	Digger. His wife and 1 child are with him.
GUY	Digger
PICOLIE	Digger
CHEVALLIER	Digger. His wife is with him.
HERRULE	Digger.
LAGRANGE	Digger
HARDY	Digger
CURTY	Digger and Laborer
BALERON	Digger
CORBIN	Digger. His wife is with him.
BRITOMAR	Digger
LIONNOIS	Digger. His wife is with him.
COLIN	Digger. His wife is with him.
RESEAUD	Digger. His wife is with him.

Name	Comments
WORKERS (cont.)	
CHABEAU	Digger
ROUX	Digger
RENARD	Digger. His wife is with him.
BERTRAND (frères)	Diggers.
POUCE (PONCE?)	Digger
FAISOLE	Laborer
COSTE	Laborer
CAUTION	Laborer
RICHAUD	Laborer
PEPIN	Laborer
CRESPE	Laborer
MONGES	Laborer
MESNARD	Laborer
SIGAUD	Laborer
COULARET, P.	Laborer
MONGES	Laborer
PIERE	Laborer. His wife and son are with him.
RIDRY	Laborer
NOLOT (?)	Laborer
LAMBART	Laborer
BRETON	Laborer
BELFOND	Gunsmith
BOUSIGNAC	Barber
SAVARY	Barber
CARLET	Barber
LA GRANDEUR	Barber
PATU	Wig-maker. His wife is with his. His son is also listed as a wig-maker.
ROLLAND	Glazier. His wife is with him.
PUJOL	Tile-maker
REGIS	Reaper
COUDER (CONDER?)	Stone cutter
BARUNE	Stone cutter
CHATELVIS	Stone cutter
DAPOIS	Candle maker

AUGUST 11, 1720

LIST OF COMPANY OFFICIALS AND WORKERS
FOR THE CONCESSION OF MARQUIS DANCENIS
EMBARKED ON THE <u>SEINE</u> BOUND FOR LOUISI-
ANA FROM LORIENT.

Name	From	Comments

OFFICIALS

Name	From	Comments
L'EPINAY, M. de		Director General
CORMIER, Sieur du		Assistant Director
DEBAUVE, Sieur		Assistant Director
ROSIER, Sieur de		Assistant Director
BOURGEOIS, Sieur		"Aumosnier"
DORE, Sieur		"Aumosnier"
RICHARD, Sieur		Tobacco Inspector
GENESTE, Sieur		Tobacco Inspector
BOURGEOIS, Sieur		Tobacco Inspector
CHEVAL, Sieur		Tobacco Inspector
ST. JEAN		Surgeon
BROSSET		Surgeon
CHAPOTIN		Cook
FRANCOIS		Cook

WORKERS FOR THE DANCENIS CONCESSION

Name	From	Comments
DAVID, François	Nantes	Carpenter. His wife and 2 children are with him.
LEBAS, Mathurine	Nantes	Carpenter. Wife with him.
AUDRAN, Joseph	Nantes	Mason. Wife with him.
BONNET, Jacques	Nantes	Mason. Wife & 2 children
ARNODEAU, Pierre	Nantes	Mason.
MAURICE, Joseph	Nantes	Mason. Wife and 2 children.
BARBEAU, Jean	Nantes	Brick-maker. Wife.
HARDY, Jean	Nantes	Brick-maker. Wife.
ANGEBEAU, Joseph	Nantes	Carpenter.
VALLERAN, Jacques	Nantes	Carpenter. Wife.
LOYER, François	Nantes	Edge-tool maker. Wife.
VIAU, Thomas	Nantes	Edge-tool maker. Wife.
PROVEL, Nicolas	Nantes	Wheelwright
RACIER, Michel du	Nantes	Harness-maker. Wife & 2 children.
GOUZI, Nicolas	Nantes	Gunsmith. Wife.
DUPRE, Jean Dumoulin	Nantes	Gunsmith. Wife.
LA GORGUE, Jullien	Nantes	Cooper
MALARY, Pierre	Nantes	Cooper

Name	From	Comments

WORKERS FOR THE DANCENIS CONCESSION (cont.)

Name	From	Comments
LAMBERT, François	Nantes	Axe-maker
LA GARENNE, Jean	Nantes	Axe-maker
BOUILLARD, Jullien	Nantes	Miller. Wife.
BOUILLARD, Jean	Nantes	Miller
BOUILLARD (fils)	Nantes	Miller
GUITTON, Guillaume	Nantes	Baker. Wife.
DUBOIS, Joseph	Nantes	Sawyer
PENHALEU, Joseph	Nantes	Sawyer
GUILLEBAUT, Pierre	Nantes	Sawyer. Wife and 1 child.
AGASSE, Yves	Nantes	Sawyer.
JOUET, Louis	Vannes	Laborer. Wife.
LE GALIC, Jacques	Vannes	Laborer
LA COMBLE, Pierre	Vannes	Laborer
LA MOTTE, Jean	Vannes	Laborer
PUPILLE, Arnault	Vannes	Laborer
LE CHAPELAIN, Pierre	Vannes	Laborer
GUERIN, Isac	Vannes	Laborer
TILLE, Fiacre	Vannes	Laborer
LA VIGNE, Etienne	Tonneins	Tobacco grower. Wife and 2 children.
VIC, Barthelemy	Tonneins	Tobacco grower. Wife.
PUJOL, Pierre	Tonneins	Tobacco grower.
GAUTTERON, François	Tonneins	Tobacco grower. Wife
COUSIN, Jean	Tonneins	Tobacco grower. Wife & 1 child.
GAULTIER, Jacques	Uzes	Silk worker.
GARAU, Etienne	Uzes	Silk worker. Wife.
ROUVIER, François	Uzes	Silk worker.
MAZERY (MAROY?), Guillaume	Uzes	Silk worker.
RIELLE (VIEILLE?), François	Uzes	Silk worker. Wife.
CHABRIE, Barthelemy	Uzes	Silk worker.
CARTIER, Antoine	Uzes	Silk worker. Wife.
CORMIER, Isac	Uzes	Silk worker.
FOLECHIER, Jean	Uzes	Silk worker.
LA BESSEDE, Jean	Tonneins	Rope-maker. Wife & 1 child.
CUVILLIER, Jean	Paris	Brewer.
GUIBERT, François	Ancenis	Tailor
GUIBOURG, Jacques	Ancenis	Tailor
RONDE, Michel de	Paris	Shoe-maker. Wife & 2 children
BOULLOT, François	Nantes	Wool-comber.
MONDON, Louis	Nantes	Wool-comber.
BONCOUR, Etienne	Ancenis	Tailor

WORKERS FOR THE CONCESSION OF M. LE BLANC AND THE MARQUIS DASFELD

Name	From	Comments
PERLOT, Antoine		Shoe-maker
GOBAUT, Alexandre		Tailor
BOURGEOIS, Jacques Henry		Lawn cutter

Name	From	Comments

WORKERS FOR THE CONCESSION OF M. LE BLANC AND THE MARQUIS DASFELD (cont.)

Name		Comments
LANGLOIS, Antoine		Shoe-maker
STORNES, Romain		Tailor
LEBON, Joseph		Basket-maker
LE ROUX, Pierre		Founder
BODARD, Jacques		Gunsmith. Wife is with him.
FONTAINE, Maximilien		Excavator
DESJARDINS, Thomas		Mason
MANNEQUIN, André		Brewer
BRIOT, Jean		Shoe-maker
BOURLONS, Louis		Marshal
MENIEN, Forien		Carpenter
JACOB, Joseph		Edge-tool maker
RALTIER, Jean		Excavator. Wife & 3 children.
TABOULET, Pierre		Carpenter
PIERRARD, Henry		Laborer
LEJEUNE, Antoine		Cobbler
LE CAILLON, Joseph		Excavator
FERRET, Nicolas		Tanner. Wife.
DURAND, André		Butcher
GUILLAIN, Robert		Carpenter
ANTOINE		Carpenter
LE GREMOND, Antoine		Metal worker. Wife.
LILET, André du		Edge-tool maker.
DAVID, Joseph		Shoe-maker. Wife.
DUCROS, Jacques		Gardener
GUILLARD, Pierre		Butcher
DUBAT, Jacques Hugues		Mason
FAIZON, Jean Joseph		Tailor
GOBERT, Gilles		Laborer
ENSELME, Jacques		Excavator. Wife & 1 child.
SALO, Jacques		Laborer. Wife.
BERNARD, Charles		Lawn-cutter. Wife & 1 child.
MADELAINE, Marie		Hair-dresser
CALO, Louis Marie		Excavator
FONTAINE, Jean Baptiste		Excavator
LEZON, Pierre François		Carpenter
CARPENTIER, Thomas		Metal founder
CASSEL, Alexis Nicolas		Metal worker
JOBERT, Quintin		Metal worker
PANNEL, François		Metal worker
VANDRE, Nicolas		Metal worker. Wife.
CHARPENTIER, Pierre		Laborer
SANTERAIN, Pitre		Tiler
JAFFRET, René		Metal worker
DONAC (DOUAC?), Dominien		Tobacco grower

Name	From	Comments

WORKERS FOR THE CONCESSION OF M. LE BLANC AND THE MARQUIS DASFELD (cont.)

Name	From	Comments
CHAMBAU (CHAMBAN?), Louis		Excavator
AVIGNON, Mathieu		Gardener
FOURTON, Pierre		Cutler
BOTSSON, Jean		Lawn-cutter. Wife.
CAVANA, François		Shoe-maker
VERNET, Pierre		Excavator. Wife. 1 child.
BON, Jean		Marshal. Wife.
BENARD, René		Baker. Wife.
VICHY, Clement		Laborer. 4 children.
FONTAINE, Pierre François		Tailor. Wife & 2 children.
MINCIAN, François		Metal worker
ROBA (RUBA?), Jacques		Laborer
FALAZEM, Jean		Butcher
VINCENNES, Jean		Silk worker
VINOM, Antoine		Saddler
CREILLY, Jean Baptiste		Grape-grower
MADRON, François		Shoe-maker
RACINE, Claude		Lawn-cutter. Wife.
GOUNET, Claude		Excavator. Wife.
FOUNET, Thomas		Edge-tool maker. Wife.
JOURNIER, Pierre		Nail-maker
CAILLETAY, Thomas		Forrester. Wife.
MILATTE, Jean		Grape-grower. Wife & 3 children
ALDEBERG, Alexandre		Excavator. Wife.
ANDRONNY, Honnoré		Excavator. Wife & 3 children.
LABARELLE, Pierre		Excavator. Wife & 1 child.
GREFFET, Pierre		Tiler
MEUNIER, Martin		Edge-tool maker
PARE, Martin Joseph		Brewer. Wife.
COUVREUR, Pierre		Miner. Wife & 1 child
POLETIES, Pierre		?
BREHO, Jacques		Excavator

AUGUST 11, 1720

LIST OF OFFICIALS AND ENGAGES FOR THE
STE. REINE CONCESSION EMBARKED ON THE
LOIRE BOUND FOR LOUISIANA FROM LORIENT.

Name	Comments
OFFICIALS	
CEARD	Director
HUBAINT	His wife and 1 child are with him.
ADAM	His wife is with him.
DUPLESSIS	His wife is with him.
LABEE DE BRABANT	
FELOT	
VASEGUAN	
DE LONGRAIS	
DE LA RUE	
BOURGEOIS	
RXNION (?)	
CHEVANCE	His wife is with him.
BEAUMONT	
FOURQUIER	
SUGIER	
KNEPPER (?)	
DARGARET	
PIGEON	
MELIZAN	
ENGAGES	
TIERCE, Jean Charles	Baker
LION, Michel	Miller
RENESSE, Etienne	Laborer
LAURENS, Simon	Laborer
DE LATTE, Antoine Joseph	Laborer. His wife is with him.
LAMBREMONT, Philippe	Nail-maker
ROULLY, Joseph	Laborer
LE NEUVE, Antoine	Shoemaker
TARRARE, Joseph	Linen worker
ROUSSEAU, Henry	Laborer. His wife and 2 children are with him.
VESOUE, Nicolas	Gardener. Called BOURGUIGNON
LE DUC, Jacques	Brewer. Called SALPIN"
COCHE, Philippe	Laborer
REYNNE, Etienne	(Clapteur). His wife and one child are with him.

Name	Comments

ENGAGES (cont.)

Name	Comments
BRULO, Pierre	Sawyer. His wife is with him.
VINCENT, Jean François	Laborer
BIENMENOT, Aldxandre	Brewer
TELLIER, Jean Bonnaventure	Shoemaker
RENAULT, Jean François	Marshal
BINEUR, Jacques	Mason
CAUDERLIER, Jacques Antoine	Laborer
ROCHEFORT, Gilles	Painter
BONNET, Bastien	Founder
MORAGE, Antoine	Laborer
CROSIC, François	Laborer
ROUSSEAUX, Jean Baptiste	Laborer
AFFINEE, Joseph	Carpenter
HENON, Jacques	Laborer
JOANNO, Bartholome	Marshal
LANGLOIS, Gille	Tobacco worker. His sons are with him.
GUICHARD, Thomas	Gardener. His wife and child are with him.
FONTAINE, Jacques	Laborer
BOYAUX, Pierre Joseph	Hatter
TORDEUR, Jean Baptiste	Laborer
CALAIS, Simon François	Laborer
BUCHAIN, Guillaume	Mason
MORIANNEC, Jean	Laborer
BAIZE, Pierre de	Nail-maker
LONGUEVILLE, Jean Louis	Nail-maker
FRIQUET, Jean François	Edge-tool maker
LE DELPHE, Thomas	Laborer. His wife is with him.
MOUSQUET, Remy	Gunsmith
DUBOIS, Antoine	Carpenter. His wife is with him.
LAUNAY, Antoine	Mason
DEMAREST, Gilles	Laborer
VARDANOIR, Pierre	Shoemaker
LE JEUNE, Nicolas	Laborer
BADOT, Guillaume	Nail-maker
HUBERT, Jean	Laborer. His wife is with him.
BAYART, Vincent	Laborer
AUDNOT (AUDUOT?), Jean	Laborer
RICCARD, Louis	Boatman
FASCIAUX, Antoine	Laborer
BOUBLED, Theodore	Carpenter
BONNIES (BOUNIES?), Guillaume	Baker
STURBOIS, Jean François	Cutler
HAUSSY, Pierre	Laborer. His wife is with him, also one child.

Name	Comments

ENGAGES (cont.)

Name	Comments
HEDON, Michel	Laborer
GRAUX, Albert	Laborer
ESCORIES, Jean Baptiste	Laborer
FILLIEUX, Endrien	Metal worker
LE COMPTE, François	Laborer
RONFLETTE, Albert Joseph	Miller
TROYES, Antoine	Refreshment-room keeper
MULQUANT, Jean	Land clearer
LAMBOTTE, Hubert	Iron founder
DENOIR, Quentin	Cooper
CASTAIGNE, Nicolas	Land clearer
POISSON, Louis	Land clearer
THEVELIN, Joseph	Land clearer
LE GRAND, Albert	Shoemaker
MORIANNE, Joseph	Carpenter
BARBIER, Thomas	Laborer
TALMA, Nicolas	Laborer
GAILLIC, Guillaume	Land clearer
RADOT, Pierre	Brick-maker
GAFFIAUX, Antoine	Laborer
WILLOT, Guillaume	Laborer
HUBINT, Ferdinand Armand	Land clearer
LEBON, Jacques Amant	Nail-maker
VINIER, Guillaume	Edge-tool maker
BOUCHER, Jacques Pailla	Butcher
MAIGNOT, Jacques	Tailor
DESHAYES, François Joseph	Shoemaker
LE GRAND, Nicolas	Harness-maker
ANNANTIAUX, Antoine	Carpenter
PENNASSE, Evrard	Boatman. His wife is with him.
PENNASSE, Jean Lambert	Boatman
PIQUERY, Pierre	Baker
TENREC, François	Mason
D'ESTREES, Jacques	Shoemaker
DE CUIRE, Albert	Miner. His son and daughter are with him.
POUCEAU, Jean Baptiste	Miner. His son is with him.
MAZURE, Jean Baptiste	Mason
DECOURE, Michel	Stone mason
MAUFROY, Guillaume	Potter
BARBIOT, Philippe	Sawyer
DAUZAIN, Bartholomee	Mason
LE GROS, Gille Ignace	Stone mason
SALMON, François	Land clearer
DYART, Gabrielle	Wheelwright
HENAIN, Hippolite	Brick-maker. Called COLSON
MOTTE, Antoine	Cutler

Name	Comments

ENGAGES (cont.)

SALBANIAC, Jacques — ?
ALLARD, Jean Gregoire — Shoemaker
CAMBIERT, Pierre — Carpenter

WORKERS

FOSSES, Jean Joseph — Apprenticed butcher
LE CLERC, Pierre — Mason. His wife and 2 children are with him.

BOUILLIE, Jean Baptiste — Seaman
PLATTIAU, Jean Baptiste — Brick-maker
EVRARD, André Joseph — Laborer
DAUBLIN, Valentin Joseph — Edge-tool maker
MIAUX, Andres — Metal worker
AVOTE, Gille — Gunsmith. His wife and 1 child are with him.

MORLIERS, Pierre — ?
PENASSE, Jeorge — Boatman
HENAULT, Philippe — Land clearer
DUMONT, Jean Philippe — Cutler
VANDEVORT, Antoine — Gardener
VERCHEM, Theodore — Mason
MARTAUX, Nicolas François — Carpenter
Etienne, Hubert — Carpenter
BRION, Pierre — Coppersmith
BIENNE, Joachim de — Tailor
DAUBLIN, Jean François — ?
MARECHAL, Norbert Joseph — Metal worker
DAUPHIN, Jean — Gunsmith
MATHIEU, Joseph — Shoemaker
DUBOIS, Louis — Carpenter. His wife is with him.
DORGEOT, François — Mason. His wife is with him.
CORDIER, Jean Baptiste — Carpenter
LE PILLIES, Pierre Joseph — Tailor
QUENTIN, Antoine — Baker
MATHIEUX, Thomas — Sawyer
BAILLE, Leandre — Carpenter
FAUDE, Mathieu — Gardener. His wife and one child are with him.

MAINGAN, Pierre — Gardener. Called JOLLICOEUR. His wife is with him.

LOISE, Jean Joachim — Turner
BOULANGER, Charles — Clothier
FONDEUR, François — Brandy distiller
DECOUX, Jacques — Cooper

Name	Comments

WORKERS (cont.)

Name	Comments
ROBILLARD, Louis	Shoemaker. His wife is with him.
DUBOIS, Jean	? Called LA JOYE
LOUIS, Antoine	Carpenter
DROUILLARD, François	Shoemaker
GENUT, Jean	Sawyer
PRUDHOMME, François	Baker. His wife is with him.
MICHEL, Guillaume	Miller
LACEUIL, Joseph	Mason. His wife is with him.
PIQUERY, Louis	Cutler
MAUTIER (NANTIER?), Martin	Carpenter
TRENAULT, Jean	Lantern-maker
SPINOSA, Nicolas	Turner
COUET, George	Painter
SALAVILLE, Antoine	Carpenter
MARSIN, Charles Joseph	Tailor
RENEO, René	Edge-tool maker
BAILLIF, Guillaume	Metal worker
FLEURY, Pierre	Butcher
METINIES (?), Jacques	Gardener
NOES, Pierre	Carpenter. His wife is with him.
BENOGUES, Henry	Tailor
LE DUC, Mathieu Joseph	Shoemaker
JUSTANCON, Estienne	Carpenter
BUZART, Charles	Seaman
CHAISNE, François	Laborer

ADDITIONAL ENGAGES

Name	Comments
CARLO, Jean	Laborer
ROSSIGNOL, Antoine	Seaman
MARTIN, Pierre	Gardener
PIERRE, Jean	Seaman
CUISINIER, Dubourg	Cook
BRICE, François	Gardener
CHEVALLIER	(Boy)
FRADE (PADE?)	(Girl)
VILLENEUVE	Servant
BAGORY, Michel Duclos	Seaman
HESRY, Pierre	Seaman
MENARD, René	Baker

AUGUST 20, 1720

LIST OF WORKERS FOR THE STE. CATHERINE
CONCESSION EMBARKED ON THE SHIP OF THE
COMPANY OF THE INDIES, THE LOIRE,
BOUND FOR LOUISIANA FROM LORIENT.

Name	Comments

WORKERS

GILLEBERT, Adrien	Master carpenter
GUERIN, Brin	Laborer
AUBARVET (OUBARVET?), Dominiaue	?
LEJEAN, Jerome	Laborer
JOUANNE, Eloy	Edge-tool maker
GERNIGOT, Mathurin	?
CHARETIER, Jullien	Laborer
COULBOUCH, Michel	Clerk
LE BECONTE, Nicolas	Marshal
ACOMET, Vincent	Gardener
LEFRAND (LEGRAND?), Jean	Edge-tool maker
GUILLAUME, GABRIEL Hyacinte	?
BOUDEY, Robert	Mason
HERVEY, Charles	Gardener
DENIS, Jean	Gardener
CHOUIN, Jean Bertrand	Laborer
VOIDY, Michel	Day-laborer
THOMAS, Claude	Carpenter
RAFFRAY, Jean	Day-laborer
BARBON, Simon	Laborer
MENIL, Pierre	Butcher
CORNUK, Joseph	Edge-tool maker
BOURET, Louis	Laborer
THOMAS, François	Tailor
BERNARD, Pierre	Shoemaker
FOLIO, François	Laborer
SAUNEUF, François	Laborer
SAUNEUF, Noël	Called MENUISIER
LE BRETON, Perinne	Laborer
FLAU, Jean	Laborer
GAUTIER, Pierre	The younger
RAIMOND, François	Laborer
DERAND, Olivier	Gardener
MINARD, Jean	Tiler
JAPIO, François	Carpenter's helper for Olivier THOMAZON
THOMAZON, Olivier	Carpenter

Name	Comments

WORKERS (cont.)

Name	Comments
LE CLERC, Gilles	Carpenter
VIOLETTE, Jean	Carpenter
LOYER, Pierre	Valet of M. LABEE DE SARANCE
LE FEVRE, Jacques	Sailor
ST. LO, George	Sailor from St. Malo
AURAY, Pierre François	Shoemaker
CHEVIN, Pierre	Day-laborer
REYBILLARD, Simon	Miller
DORE, Jullien	Maker of stone lanterns
QUEPRET, Simon	Tiler
CUVREU, Jean	Carpenter
PEPIN, Gilles	Bricklayer (or maker)
DUBOIS, Mathurin	Bricklayer (or maker)
GARAUD, Jean	Day-laborer
FERAD, Pierre	Day-laborer
BALLE, Robert	Block-maker
TESSIER, Noël	?
SERIEL, Louis	Apprenticed miller
JOUAN, Jean	Day-laborer
GUYOMARD, François	Day-laborer
GOURMY, François	Miner
RAFFRAY, Noël	Laborer
POQUET, René	Day-laborer
SOLIVERON, Jacques	Rope-maker
JEANNAL, Pierre	Rope-maker
JOUIN, Jacques	Laborer
ROBICHON, Claude	Laborer
ROBIN, Henry	Gardener
COLUT, Jean	Marshal
LA MOTTE, François de	Laborer
LE DANTIER, Louis	Laborer
HAMON, Louis	Wooden shoe maker
DU MONT, Gabriel Corbin	?
DAVRI, Michel	Laborer
GAUTIER, Pierre	Day-laborer
HALAIRE, Mathurin	Marshal
PREVOST, Etienne	Laborer
GODON, Jean	Carpenter
LUCAS, Joseph	?
REGARD, Vincent de	Turner
PIGNARD, Jacques	Reaper
CARAMOND, Lucas	Laborer
ALISE, François	Tiler
LE GOUTE, Claude	?
ANDRE, Jean	Day-laborer
HAMON, Michel	?
LE MOINE, Jean	?

Name	Comments

WORKERS (cont.)

SPAVOT, Bertrand	?
LASSIEY, Jean	Metal worker
FORESTIER, François	?
PICHON, Pierre	?
MOHR, Jean	From Coutance
LE VRETTE, Jullien	Laborer
BROUSSEL, Jean	Mason
LE GLACE, Laurent	Miner
EQUALA, Pierre	Laborer
GOYAU (GOYAN?), Nicolas	Grape grower
DUBORD, Jacques	Wine presser
NEVEUX, Pierre	Laborer
LEBLOND, Jacques	Laborer
ETIENNE, Gilles	Laborer
BOURGER, Jacques	Carpenter
VARRAIN, Jean	Laborer
LE CORS, Alexis	Charcoal burner
PORTIER, Guillaume	Cooper
JOSSIAUME, Gilles	Day-laborer for Jean LE ROUX, Laborer
LE ROUX, Jean	Laborer
DURAND, Martin	Laborer
ROBINET, Simon	Grape grower
GAUTIER, Jean	Laborer
FAUCONNET, Jean	Lace-maker
DUREAU, Jean	Laborer
MOREAU, Jacques	Laborer
PITOU, Jean	Laborer
LAVIE, Nicolas	Laborer
FLEAU, François	Laborer
COUDREY, Pierre	Cooper
LA COUR, Nicolas de	?
QUINTRECK, Jean Joseph de	Shoemaker
LE BRACE, Jean	Miller
GAUCHER, Jean	Baker
GEFFRIN, François Florrian	Marshal
GRAILLARD, Jacques	Laborer
LETAN, Pierre	Laborer
BROUSSEL, Jean	Mason
ANTIQUAIRE, Gregoire	Sailor
GILLEBERT, Simon	Laborer
BEAUFRERE, Antoine	Bellows-maker
FLORIER, Claude	Fountain worker
QUECEPRIO, Louis	Day-laborer in vinyards
BOURSSELIER, Toussaint	Laborer
DUFOUR, Remy	Laborer
TISSERANT, Christophe Humbert	?

Name	Comments

WORKERS (cont.)

Name	Comments
DOGNON, Noël	Laborer
LA CHAU, Claude	Laborer
BRINDEVAS	Grape grower
BOULLERNAIR, Alain	Carpenter
GASPALTIARET, Henry	Gardener
PICCAUDAY, Mathieu	Day-laborer
LE MOINE, Nicolas	Day-laborer
CHANOINE, Claude	?
JOSSE, Etienne	Mason from Nancy
BRAR, Hive	Laborer
BAVAILLAUD, Pierre	Marshal
GOURRIER, Jullien	Stone cutter
ACARD, Jean	Clerk
GILLEBERT, Nicolas	Carpenter
GOUEL, Mathieu	Shoemaker
DESSALE, Maurice	Carpenter
GUEUPEL (QUEUPEL?), Yvon	Tiler
LEFLAN, Pierre	Cook
SAILLAND, Jullien	Tiler
CARLES, Pierre	Wheelwright
CORVEB, Joseph	(Valet of M. DUMANOIR?)
GUILLANCHET, Robert	?
GUERIN, Pierre	?
CHOUEN, Sebastien	Cooper
HELLEIN, Hobein	Day-laborer
SUBLET, Mathurin	Carpenter
DAVID, Pierre	Tailor
GUICHARD, Thomas	Laborer
DUVAL, Guillaume	Carpenter
BONSOIR, Claude	Laborer
SATIBOT, Jean	Shoemaker
DANIEL, Guillaume	Gardener
BRILLIAU, Jullien	Laborer
METTEYER, Jean	Wooden shoe maker
PANNELTIER, Jean (AURAY?)	?
MATHEY, Nicolas	Laborer
BECHERNIN, François	Carpenter
AUZANNE, Jullienne	Gardener
THOMAS, Christophle	Day-laborer
LOYER, Jean	Brewer
LEGARNEY, Pierre	?
SADOU, Jean	Linen worker
HANVIAN (HAUVIAN?), Jullien	Butcher
LAURENT, Simon	Laborer
PINART, Jean	Carpenter
TISSERAND, Louis Moired	?

Name	Comments

WORKERS (cont.)

SAUNIER, Martine	Washerwoman
CHARRETIER, François	Washerwoman
DORE, Jean Baptiste	Founder
DORE, Charles	Coppersmith

WOMEN

BROISE, Jeanne de	Tailoress
VESSAILLE, Germaine	Knitter
ROUSSEL, Marguerite	Dressmaker
COUDREY, Anne	Spinner
LE DARCE, Jeanne	?
CARDINAL, Marie	Baker
CONAUD, Anne	Spinner
DELARUE, Marie	Dressmaker
PERRINE	Cook. Negro
CORLEY, Vincente	Baker
LE REG, Yvonne Marie	Washerwoman
DOLEY, Marie	Baker
DUVAL, Marie	Spinner
CHATRENCY, Françoise	Laborer
FREVAL, Marie	Washerwoman
DORE, Marie	Linen worker
GRAPPALIERE, Perinne	Laborer
JULLIE, Marie	The elder
JULLIE, Marie	The younger
MASSON, Guillemette	Mender
LEFEVRE, Anne	Linen worker
TATIBOT, Louise	(A young girl)
TATIBOT, Jullienne	(An infant)
GOURNIEL, Renotte	From Vannes
DORE, Renée	?
DUREGARD, Nicolas	?

AUGUST 13, 1720

LIST OF OFFICIALS AND WORKERS FOR THE
CONCESSIONS OF MM. MEZIERES AND DES-
MARCHES EMBARKED ON THE GIRONDE BOUND
FOR LOUISIANA FROM LORIENT

Name	Comments

OFFICIALS

MARIE, M.	Director
FRERVILLE, M. de	Director
MONTRERMY, M.	Inspector General
DESAUNAY, M.	Assistant Inspector General
BRIQUET	Storekeeper and Treasurer
MARTIN, M. de	Storekeeper
PENLAER, M.	Assistant Storekeeper
MOTET, M.	Assistant Storekeeper
TRONGUIDY, M.	Ship inspector
MARIE, M. (the younger)	Clerk
DAUSSINANGES, M.	Tobacco inspector
BAUJON, M.	Tobacco Inspector
LE MONIER, M.	"Aumosnier"
LE TURBIL, M.	"Aumosnier"
DUVAL, M.	Major for the miners
DELAGE, M.	Surgeon major

CARPENTERS

LE FORMAL, Philippe	
POPINGIEN, Pierre	
FORMAL, Jean	
MORGAN, Louis	
DANIEL, Marc	
FOULON, Perinne	Wife of Marc DANIEL
DANIEL, François	Son of Marc DANIEL
DANIEL, Marie	Daughter of Marc DANIEL
DANIEL, Catherine	Daughter of Marc DANIEL
DUDAIN, Jean	
CAPITAINE, Jacques	
MACHEGUIERE, Catherine	Wife of Jacques CAPITAINE
CAPITAINE, Marie Frelienne	Daughter of Jacques CAPITAINE
CAPITAINE, Jacques	Son of Jacques CAPITAINE
CAPITAINE, Jean	Son of Jacques CAPITAINE
CAPITAINE, Jeanne	Daughter of Jacques CAPITAINE
CAPITAINE, Marie	Daughter of Jacques CAPITAINE

Name	Comments

CARPENTERS (cont.)

LA MARD, Jean de
LE PORCHE, Lucas
MICHEL, Jullien
LE TEXILES, Jeanne · · Wife of Jullien MICHEL
MICHEL, Marie Daughter of Jullien MICHEL
MICHEL, Guillaume Son of Jullien MICHEL
MICHEL, Philibert Son of Jullien MICHEL
MICHEL, Anne Daughter of Jullien MICHEL
CHARDES, Jean Baptiste
FACIOLY, Antoinette Wife of Jean Baptiste CHARDES

FOUNDERS

CROLA, Joseph
HIOT, Claudine Wife of Joseph CROLA
CROLA, Laurence Sister of Joseph CROLA
CLEREAU, Pierre
MARCHAND, Mathurine Wife of Pierre CLEREAU
MARCHAND, Perinne Sister of Mathurine MARCHAND
LEBELEC, Guillaume
BRIVARD, Margueritte Wife of Guillaume LEBELEC
LEBELEC, René Son of Guillaume LEBELEC
BOTHALAN, Yves
TABAU, Denis
DU DAR, Louis
INQUELLON, François
INQUELLON, François Son of François INQUELLON
GODMELEC, François

MASONS

GAUTIER, François
LA COSTE, Pierre
LA CROIX, Simon
LE PORCH. Guillemette Wife of Simon LA CROIX
LE ROY, Louis Joseph
LE MAHEC, Yves
LE PAPE, Guillaume
LEZEC, Pierre
PEZES, René
BOUNIC, Marie Wife of René PEZES

METAL WORKERS

CARNAREC, Armel
CHARTIER, Michel

Name	Comments

METAL WORKERS (cont.)

NABOUR, Charles
LE ROY, Renné — Wife of Charles NABOUR
NABOUR, Jacques Pierre — Son of Charles NABOUR
NABOUR, Jacques — (Relationship not designated)

BREWERS

LE QUERE, Jacques Louis
SEJOUR, Yves

COOKS

LE GOFF, Ollivier
CHICOT, Reme (René) — Called LA CASTER

TAILORS

ROLLAND, Louis — His wife is with him.
PERON, François — Master tailor
PERON, Joseph
MANET, Noël
DOUTANT, Jeanne — Wife of Noël MANET
MANET, Joseph — Son of Noël MANET

BUTTON MAKERS

LECLUSE, Pierre
Marie Elizabeth — Wife of Pierre LECLUSE

SHOEMAKERS

GAULTIER, Marain
BRUNETTE, Guillemette — Wife of Marain GAULTIER
HUBOT, Jullien
SADONUS, Jean
SANCON, Guillaume

TANNERS

LETOUPAIN, Etienne
HELLEGURAS, Henriette — Wife of Etienne LETOUPAIN
LETOUPAIN, François — Son (?) of Etienne LETOUPAIN

BUTCHER

BRABAN, Yves

Name	Comments

BAKERS

BERS, Joseph
GUILLAUME, Vincente — Wife of Joseph BERS
BERS, Sebastienne — Daughter of Joseph BERS
BERS, Jacques — Son of Joseph BERS
BERS, Perinne — Daughter of Joseph BERS
LA SALLE, Simon

CANDLE MAKER

HAMELAIN, Antoine

COPPERSMITHS

RONDOT, Edouard
RONNELEAU, Guillemette — Wife of Edouard RONDOT
RONNELEAU, Marie Louise — Daughter of Guillemette RONNELEAU
CHRISTAUPH, Nicolas Clement
ERELLE, Margueritte — Wife of Nicolas Clement CHRISTAUPH

WEAVERS

TARTABEAU, Jean
LE VENIE, Claudine — Wife of Jean TARTABEAU
LETOUPAIN, Guillaume
CASTAIN, André

COOPERS

ROYER, Pierre
LA BUSSIERE, Pierre — His wife and his son are with him.

MILLERS

PADER, Pierre
RIOU, Jeanne — Wife of Pierre PADER
GENTIL, François
PERON, Louis
LEBOUDIE, Antoine

LAND-SURVEYORS

LE PORCHE, Jacques
QUANTAIN, Philibert — Wife of Jacques LE PORCHE
LE PROCHE, François — Son of Jacques LE PORCHE
LE PORCHE, Pierre — Son of Jacques LE PORCHE
LE PORCHE, Vincent — Son of Jacques LE PORCHE
LE PORCHE, Marie — Daughter of Jacques LE PORCHE

Name	Comments

LABORERS

Name	Comments
ALIAUME, Jean Baptiste	
CLAMARD, Marc	
DU PRED, Jacques	
RICHARD, Pierre	
COURSAN, André	
LE MANASSE, Michel	
NEDELEC, Claude	
DUFANY, Mathieu	
TARTES, Olives	Wife of Mathieu DUFANY
DUFANY, Jacob	Son of Mathieu DUFANY
CASTEL, Pierre	
MAHE, Jacques Leglas	
LEBAN, Perine	Wife of Jacques Leglas MAHE
JOUAN, Maurice	
QUIERE, Marie	Wife of Maurice JOUAN
QUIERE, Marie	Daughter of Marie QUIERE
DAIN, Jean Le	
ANDRE, Marie	Wife of Jean LE DAIN
MARQUIER, Mathurin	
OCHOU, Jeanne	Wife of Mathurin MARQUIER
COUNNAN, Gregoire	
QUIBY, Guillemette	Wife of Gregoire COUNNAN
DAVID, Jullien	
MATEL, Jullienne	Wife of Jullien DAVID
DAVID, Jullien	Son of Jullien DAVID
DAVID, Fanchon	Daughter of Jullien DAVID
LE FAUCHEUX, Jacques	
LESOL, Marie	Wife of Jacques LE FAUCHEUX
LE FAUCHEUX, Michel	Daughter of Jacques LE FAUCHEUX
LE FAUCHEUX, Anne	Daughter of Jacques LE FAUCHEUX
TANQUION, Louis	
LE CAIGNAC, Marie Rose	Wife of Louis TANQUION
POULAIN, Jean	
PERIVAL, Bernard	
VIVIES, Guillaume	
ALLANOU, Grenelle	Engaged to marry Guillaume VIVIES
FERAN, Jean	
BAPTISTE, Jean	
DESNOM, François	
LARDIC, Perinne	Wife of François DESNOM
ROUGENT, François	
BOUILLAU, Jean	
DERAISON, Marie	Wife of Jean BOUILLAU
CORRANTIN, Dorvain	
ONEF, Marie	Wife of Dorvain CORRANTIN
CORRANTIN, François	Son of Dorvain CORRANTIN
CORRANTIN, Regné	(Son?) of Dorvain CORRANTIN
CORRANTIN, Yves	Son of Dorvain CORRANTIN

Name	Comments

LABORERS (cont.)

LE TREUDIC, Yves
GUILLARMAN, Jean
NINOT, Pierre
LE CORRE, Louis
DAFACEN, Catherine — Wife of Louis LE CORRE
LE CORRE, François Louis — Son of Louis LE CORRE
GIROTON, Jullien Claude
JIGONEUF, Marie — Wife of Jullien Claude GIROTON
TANQUION, Marguerite — (The TANQUIONS may have been some
TANQUION, Marie — relationship (blood or foster)
TANQUION, Louis — to Jullien Claude GIROTON)
TANQUION, Jullien
TRAMPE, Toussaint
LE METAYER, Yves
LE METAYER, Meur — Son of Yves LE METAYER
LAMOUR, Jerome
DELEBAT, Jean
LE PAPE, Jullien
MICHARD, Guerain
PHILIPPE, Antoine
BEDES, Clement
CHARPENTIER, François Alexis
MARMIUION (?), François
JOUAN, Jean
BODION, Françoise — Wife of Jean JOUAN
GOEBEL, Jullien
TORTELET, Caire — Wife of Jullien GOEBEL
LE DAIN, Louis
PICARD, Anne — Wife of Louis LE DAIN
QUERLEAU, François
MALECOSTE, Margueritte — Wife of François QUERLEAU
QUERLEAU, Mathieu — Sons of François QUERLEAU
QUERLEAU, Louis — Daughter of François QUERLEAU
LE TEBOUR, Yves
NICOL, Guillemette — Wife of Yves LE TEBOUR
LE TEBOUR, Jean — Son of Yves LE TEBOUR
ELEGOUARD, Laurans
ELOF, Jullienne — Wife of Laurans ELEGOUARD
ELEGOUARD, Françoise — Daughter of Laurans ELEGOUARD
ELEGOUARD, François — Son of Laurans ELEGOUARD
ELEGDUARD, Catherine — Daughter of Laurans ELEGOUARD
ELEGOUARD, Marie — Daughter of Laurans ELEGOUARD
JARDELER, Alain
ILLIC, Marie — Wife of Alain JARDELER
FISEAU, George
DUBOIS, Joseph
LAGUEU, Françoise — Wife of Joseph DUBOIS
DUBOIS, Joseph — Son of Joseph DUBOIS

Name	Comments

LABORERS (cont.)

Name	Comments
HEON, Jean	
GREVEMBERG, Joannes	
NORIZON, Joseph	
JOSSEAU, Margueritte	Wife (?) of Joseph NORIZON
PAUBEGUIN, Yves	
GILLARMAUX, Louis	
DUPUIS, Nicolas	
POMERAY, Catherine	Wife of Nicolas DUPUIS
GOURU, Paul	
BOURSAU, Guillemette	Wife of Paul GOURU
MARTIN, Pierre	
LE MOINE, Pierre	
BASTIEN, Marie Anne	Wife of Pierre LE MOINE
LE MOINE, Marie Joseph	Son of Pierre LE MOINE
MESSAGE, Pierre	
MICHARD, Regue	
ALLANOT, Marie	Wife of Regue MICARD
ALLANTO, Marie	Daughter of Marie ALLANOT
LIGIEN, Jacquette	Marie ALLANOT's daughter by her first marriage
LIGIEN, Yvonnette	Marie ALLANOT's daughter by her first marriage
LIGIEN, Joseph	Marie ALLANOT's son by her first marriage
CHENOT, Pierre	
CORODIER, Renné	Wife (?) of Pierre CHENOT
CHENOT, Pierre	Son of Pierre CHENOT
CHENOT, Renné	Daughter (?) of Pierre CHENOT
CRAVAIN, Jean	
CADICE, Jacquette	

AUGUST 21, 1720

LIST OF OFFICIALS AND WORKERS FOR THE
CONCESSION OF MM. DEUCHER AND COETLOGON
EMBARKED ON THE SAINT ANDRE BOUND FOR
LOUISIANA FROM LORIENT. §

OFFICIALS

DUMANOIR, M.	Director
LE FAURE	Assistant Director
DU CHENNE	Clerk
LITANT	Clerk
VILLET HEBAULT	Clerk
DES LONGRAIS	Clerk
COUTANT (CONTANT?)	Clerk
DU BUL	Clerk
DE LA RUE	Clerk
DUHAL	"Aumosnier"
ST. HILAIRE	Surgeon major
ALEXANDRE	Assistant surgeon, druggist and botanist

WORKERS

VIOLETTE, Jean	Land-clearer
GRUERE, Mathurin	Land-clearer
DINGUE, Jean	Land-clerarer
PORTIER, Guillaume	Cooper
GAVOL, Bertrand	Cooper
PICODAIS, Mathieu	Cooper
CHANNAN, Laurens	Laborer
OBARET, Dominique	Mason
CHAUVIN, Bertrand	Mason
GAUTIER, Simon	Mason
ALAIRE, Mathurin	Edge-tool maker
LE MARESTIER, Jean	Carpenter
GODON, Jean	Carpenter
BABULAINE, Mars	Carpenter
FROMONT, François	Carpenter
CHENU, Julien	Carpenter
SCUSON, Hilaire	Carpenter
ADAM, Servan	Carpenter
MECHU, François	Carpenter
JOAS, Antoine	Carpenter
JULOUP, François	Carpenter and Rope-maker
JULOUP, Noël	Carpenter
MOUILLE, Pierre	Carpenter
BRIJON, Claude	Carpenter

---

§ There are names appearing on this list that are identical to some
of those names appearing on the passenger list of the LOIRE, dated
August 20, 1720. This is probably more than mere coincidence. The
Company may (for unknown reasons) have shifted some of the Loire's
passengers to the St. André.

Name	Comments
WORKERS (cont.)	
GOUASY, Nicolas	Mason
HUERE, Jean	Gardener
CARAMOUS, Lucas	Gardener
CARON, Paul	Gardener
DUVAL, Julien	Gardener
HAMON, Michel	Gardener
CAMDON, François	Gardener
JACQUET, Toussaint	Gardener
D'AVRIL, Michel	Land-clearer
LA MOTTE, François de	Land-clearer
DENIS, Pierre	Land-clearer
COCHIE, Jean	Edge-tool maker
CHARLIER, Julien	Edge-tool maker
OLIVARON, Jean	Laborer
JENEST, Simon	Laborer
LEGAGNE, Thomas	Laborer
JOUANNE, Jean	Laborer
LE GAGNE, Pierre	Laborer
POLLIER, Mathieu	Tailor & Land-clearer
MOREL, Claude	Laborer
RASTIN, Jean	Laborer
LAMOTTE, Jean	Laborer
GUICHAR, Thomas	Laborer
BUVEL, Louis	Land-clearer
BIERZEL, Jean	Mason and Laborer
QUILLET, Yvon	Mason
THOMAS, François	Mason and Stone cutter
BOUNEL (BONNEL?), Robert	Laborer
GODEFROY	Land-clearer
ROBERT, Julien	Laborer
COUSIN, Louis	Laborer
LE LIEVRE, Julien	Laborer
RAFFRAY, Noël	Laborer
GOUSSET, François	Laborer
CHOLLET, Toussaint	Rope-maker and Land-clearer
LE BON, Yves	Land-clearer
FOUCAUD, François	Laborer
BICHET, Jean	Laborer
POQUEL, Renes	Laborer
LA COUR, Nicolas	Laborer
POLICE, Jean	ᵀand-clearer
THOMAS, Christophe	Laborer
LESEURE, Jacques	?
PAYEN, Gabriel	Laborer
LEBRETON, Ambroise	Laborer

Name	Comments

WORKERS (cont.)

RAIDER, André	Mason
ELIME, Aubín	Laborer
DAUTIE, Louis	Land-clearer
TRICHARD, Joseph	Butcher
LERAY, Pierre	Laborer
RUELLAN, Jacques	Wagon maker
LUCAS, Joseph	Laborer
GERNIGOU, Andre	Mason
BLANCHON, Modeste	Laborer
LEVESQUE, Jean	Mason
CHOEMEL, Maturin	Laborer
LE FRANCOIS, Jean	Marshal
PERINEE, Noël	Metal worker
LEMONNIER, François	Laborer
GAUTIER, Pierre	Laborer
MENUL, Pierre	Laborer
BRARD, Yves	Laborer
BUSSON, Antoine	Laborer
BERCEE, Noël	Laborer
CHALOINE, Claude	Sawyer
LAUNAY, George	Laborer
PICHON, Pierre	Laborer
LE BRETON, Pierre	Laborer
FLOT, Julien	Laborer
TASSIN, Yvon	Laborer
LEMOINE, Nicolas	Laborer
CHAUVIN, Pierre	Laborer
GUILLOCHEL, Robert	Sawyer
FLANC, François	Laborer
DUVAL, Guillaume	Laborer
TAHIER, Jean	Laborer
JASSIER, Jean	Metal worker
SADOS, Nicolas	Laborer
BARBUT, Simon	Laborer
DANDOULE, Jacques	Laborer
LEMOLLE, Guillaume	Carpenter
BOURUEL, Jean	Tailor
OZANNE, Julien	Gardener
JARNIGOU (JARNIGON?), Mathurin	Carpenter
JENEQUIN, Louis	Butcher
FENARD, Louis	Land-clearer
GOURIER, Julien	Mason
MENAGE, Maturin	Tiler and Carpenter
GUIOMAS, François	Laborer
GUENAN, Mares	Laborer
LEQUEUX, Olivier	Laborer

Name	Comments

WORKERS (cont.)

Name	Comments
GIRARD, Jean	Rope-maker
CHAUVIN, Jacques	Laborer
SAUNEUF, François	Carpenter
SAUNEUF, Noël	Carpenter
THOMAS, Olivier	Sawyer
BALE, Robert	Block-maker
DAHER, Gilles	Laborer
LEMOYE, Jean	Carpenter
DUREGARD, Vincent	Laborer
BOUL, Maurice	Tailor
TATIBOUTE, Jean	Roper-maker
CORDONNIER, Louis Jean	Land-clearer
LE BLOND, Jacques	Laborer
PIGNART, Jacques	Sawyer
LOYER, Pierre	Laborer
PLEUM (?), François	Metal worker and wheelwright
GAUVIN, Laurens	Laborer
FORESTIER, François	Metal worker
LAUNAY, Pierre	Laborer
BOULMER, Elin	Carpenter and Planer
FRANCOIS, Jean	Land-clerarer
MOREOL, Jean	Cooper and Carpenter
LOUIS	Laborer
GAUTIER, Jean	Wheelwright
SERCLE, Louis	Carpenter
ANDRE, Jean	Laborer
GOMY (GORNY?), Nicolas	Stitcher
GUETREE, Noël	Mason
LE PRINCE, Pierre	Edge-tool maker
TOINON, Julien	Land-clearer
FLORIENT, François	Marshal
BUNEL, François	Edge-tool maker
PREBERNARD, René	Land-clearer
FOURNIER, Joseph	Land-clearer
SUBLET, Maturin	Cooper
FERRARD, Pierre	Cooper
LE CLERC, Gilles	Sawyer
LE GALLAIS, François	Butcher
LAURENS, Yvon	Laborer
LESLANCHES, Jacques	Laborer
LERUCANT, Julien	Butcher
LE ROUX, Jean	Laborer
GIGARLT (?), François	Baker
LEGLADIT, Guillaume	Gardener
BENARD, René	Baker
CHALON, Yvon	Laborer

Name	Comments
WORKERS (cont.)	
DORE, Julien	Founder
COUVE, Benois	Land-clearer
LECLANCHE, Olivier	Laborer
DENIS, Jean	Gardener
DANIEL, Guillaume	Gardener
DREAN (DREAU?), Olivier	Gardener
LE BRACE, Jean	Miller
MIELLE, Jean François	Land-clearer
FLEURIER, Claude	Land-clearer
GOYAU, Nicolas	Laborer
BOURSEILLIER, Toussaint	Mason
CHERCY, Pierre	Cooper
MERCIER, Estienne	Day-laborer
LAROISSE, Nicolas	Cooper
HUMBERT, Cristof	Laborer
BAVOILOT, Pierre	Marshal
BONNET, Claude	Edge-tool maker
DUFOUR, Renny (?)	Land-clearer
GARNIER, Alexis	Land-clearer
NESOT, Jean Baptiste	Laborer
GUERIN, Benigme	Land-clearer
ROBICHON, Claude	Laborer
MATHEY, Nicolas	Laborer
POTEUR, François	Laborer
BOURNOL, Jean François	Laborer
ROBINEL, Simon	Laborer
GRALLARD, Jacques	Laborer
BEUFRERE, Antoine	Laborer
MOREAU, Jacques	Laborer
JANNEL, Pierre	Laborer
GUERIN, Jean	Laborer
ROBIN, Henry	Laborer
BLANC, Antoine	Laborer
BAPTISTE, Jean	Founder
DORRE, Charles	Founder
BAUCHE, Julien	Land-clearer
ESTIENNE, Giles	Land-clearer
BRISVAL, Jean	Carpenter
LA LOUET, Jacques	Metal worker
GOURNUL (GOUMUL?), François	Mason
PITOIS, Jean	Land-clearer
MIELLE, Claude	Land-clearer
LELANG, Pierre	Land-clearer
MORE, François	Mason
MAISTROL, Estienne	Laborer
DEVARS, Benigme	Day-laborer

Name	Comments

WORKERS (cont.)

TIERROL, Louis	Cooper
VARIN, Jean	Laborer
GILBERT, Simon	Laborer
HUMBERT, George	Tailor
PIOCHEL, Claude	Land-clearer
MAYEUR, Jean	Butcher
CHABANNE, Jean	Mason
JACOB, Nicolas	Laborer
GAUCHER, Jean	Baker
DOIGNON, Novel	Laborer
LAURIER, Nicolas	Laborer
JOURNEE, Henry	Laborer
NOUZOIR, Claude	Laborer
MOREL, Toussaint	Carpenter
FOUCONEL (COUCOUEL?), Jean	Land-clearer
MILLOT, Claude	Land-clearer
JAPIOL, François	Land-clearerr
PREVOST, Estienne	Land-clearer
GUERIN, Pierre	Land-clearer
CLAUY (CLANY?), Claude	?
GARARD, Jean	Land-clearer
DU BOST, Jean	Wheelwright
JANNEL, Thomas	Land-clearer
THOMAS, Claude	Carpenter
ANTOINE, Jean	Carpenter
JOSEPH, Mathieu	Carpenter
JUSTAMON, Estienne	?
TESNAY, Jean	Laborer
CARLE, Jean François	Laborer

22 women and children (not listed)

NOVEMBER 14, 1720

LIST OF OFFICERS, SOLDIERS AND OTHERS
EMBARKED ON THE MUTINE BOUND FOR
LOUISIANA FROM LORIENT

Name	Comments
MERVEILLEUX, François Louis de	Captain
MERVEILLEUX, Jean Pierre de	Ensign
VILLARD, Rodolphe	Surgeon
ANDIC, Pierre	Secretary

PIKEMEN

THOMAS, Pierre
CHEVALLIER, Jean Pierre

DRUMMERS

SALBER, Hans Jacob
DUBOIS, Gaspard
SIMONIN, Georges
BOURY, Estienne

SARGEANTS AND SOLDIERS WHO ARE CARPENTERS BY TRADE

ROCHA, Jean Jacques	Sargeant
FILLAT, Jean	Sargeant
JALLAZ, Jonas	Sargeant
GAUDIN, Jean Baptiste	
BETJEAN, Adam	
VIONNEL (VIOUNEL?), Gabriel	
COLOGNY, Estienne	
GANGUIN (GAUGUIN?) Abraham	
FER, François	
MONTERGEAU, Gabriel	
PRODOIN, Jean Daniel	
FAVRE, Nicolas	
CUJEAN, André	
CHENAU, Jean Michel	
PATRET, Pierre Estienne	
ROSSEL, Jean Jacques	
GUICHET, François	
GROSBESTY, Jacques	
GENET, Jean Pierre	
DESCOSTES, Philibert	
JAILLET, Pierre Jeremie	
MARTIN, Jacob	
CHAIR, Abraham	
BELJEAN, Antoine	

Name	Comments

SARGEANTS AND SOLDIERS WHO ARE CARPENTERS, METAL WORKERS AND OTHER THINGS BY TRADE

Name	Comments
VERNEY, Jacques	Sargeant
MARONZY, Jullien de	Sargeant
EBERSOL, Nicolas	
CHANNE, Nicolas	
BROCARD, Jean François	
BESSON, Charles	
TABOUIN, Jean	
MEIRY, Jean Pierre	Has remained ashore because of illness.
DYVORNE, Moyse	
TAVERNIER, Gedeon	
MARMET, Jean	
VANNA, Pierre	
GRETILLAD, Pierre (father)	
GRETILLAD, Pierre (son)	
VUNDRERALD, Pierre	The younger

SARGEANTS AND SOLDIERS WHO ARE FOUNDERS BY TRADE

Name	Comments
PRANGIN, Pierre	Sargeant
MARTIN, André	
BOULET, Jean Urbain	
GOURDON, André	
WIFFLER, Gaspard	
PERRET, Jean François	
DUBOIS, Samuel	
BOULLET, Jean François	
FARDET, Antoine	
CEZUR, Jean Pierre	
GIRAUD, Louis	
KUESLER, Jacob	

SARGEANTS AND SOLDIERS WHO ARE MASONS BY TRADE

Name	Comments
MACABEY, Jean Francois (father)	Sargeant
BENOIT, Jacques	Sargeant
BRUN, Jean Rodolphe	Sargeant
MONTENDON, Baltazar	
FAVRE, Abraham	
MACABEY, Jean François (son)	
TRUCHET, Jean Marc	
TRUCHET, Antoine	
TRUCHET, Jean Marc (?)	
ROBERT, Gaspard	
GUERRE, Pierre	
POGET, Jean	
CORNU, David	
GAGNARD, François	
COUGNORD, François	
PELLET, Jacob	
FLENTY, Hans	
PARIA, Claude	
LAPIERRE, Jean	

Name	Comments

SARGEANTS AND SOLDIERS WHO ARE MASONS BY TRADE (cont.)

ROBELLA, Georges
GUYOT, Louis
TARDY, François
DUPUYS, Jean Pierre
BOQUET, Nicolas
GARDE, David Joseph
BARBIER, Jean Pierre
CASTELLA, Jean
BONHOSTE, Daniel
EMOUNET (EMONNET?), Olivier
JACQUIER, Jean Georges
KELLER, Joseph
KETTEL, Johannes
BORNET, Abraham
BEAU, Joseph
NETTEMAN, David
TAYAN, Philibert
VANNIER, Pierre
NOVERIAZ, Gabriel
MARQUIS, Estienne
DUNAND, Jean Mermet
DUNON, Jean Morel
GLAIRE, Pierre
BRACHOT, François
STEBLER, Hans
JOLLY, Jean Gabriel
BIEHMAN, Joseph
BIEHMAN, Christophle
LESSER, Pierre de
BOUTEL, François

MARRIED MEN WHO HAVE THEIR WIVES AND CHILDREN WITH THEM

Name	Comments
JENNERET, Abraham Perret	His wife, Suzanne, and daughter, Jeanne are with him.
RUVILLOT, Rodolphe	
JENNERET, Jacob (Daniel?) Perret	The wife of Daniel (Jacob?) Perret Jenneret and daughter, Marie Magdelaine are with him.
BESENSON, Samuel	His wife, Jeanne Barbe, daughter, Margueritte, and son, Claude, are with him.
JACOB, Jean	
PETITIN, Claude	His wife, Jeanne, is with him.
ENOCA, Jean	Wife, Marie Magdelaine, is with him.

Name	Comments

MARRIED MEN WHO HAVE THEIR WIVES AND CHILDREN WITH THEM (cont.)

Name	Comments
HUGUENAIN, Abraham	No mention is made of the family.
BAILLY, Charles	His wife, Margueritte, is with him.
MULLER, Michel	His two sons, Jonas and Michel, are with him.
JACQUET, Jacques François	His wife, Jeanne, and sons, Estienne, André, Jean Guillaume, & Jean Jacques, are with him.
ENNY (EUNY?), Criste	He has remained ashore because of illness. His wife, Peronnelle, and daughters, Michelle and Marion, are with him.
BERNARDIN, Jean	His son and daughter are with him.

OTHER PASSENGERS

Name	Comments
DUROT, M.	Director of M. LE BLANC's concession. His wife is with him.
RICHARD, Jean	Missionary
ALAIR, Sieur	Storekeeper on M. LE BLANC's concession.
LE BRUN, Sieur	Clerk on M. LE BLANC's concession
DARTOISE	M. Diron's servant. His wife is with him.

APRIL 7, 1721

LIST OF PERSONS EMBARKED ON THE VENUS
BOUND FOR LOUISIANA FROM LORIENT

Name	Comments
DU VERGIER, M.	Director General. Ordonnateur of the Colony.
HARPE, M. de la	Commander at St. Bernard Bay
MANCELIERE, M. de la	Going to M. de Mezieres' concession
MOREL. M.	Going to M. de Mezieres' concession
PELAN, Jullien de	Going to M. de Mezieres' concession
DUFRENES, M.	Going to M. de Mezieres' concession
LALOE, M.	Ensign in the colonial army.
LABEYRIE, M.	Clerk
AUBERT, M.	Fortifications Clerk for the Colony.
DAUVILE, Madame	Midwife for the colony. Her husband is with her.
BRETOUX, Sieur	To be employed in the colony.
RAFINEUR, Sieur	To be employed in the colony.

MERVEILLEUX'S COMPANY

BRAND (BRAUD?), Sieur	Captain of the company.
BRAUX, Issac	Sargeant
NETTERNAN, Jean Rodolphe	Sargeant

Solder-Workers of the Company

GAUIN, Jean Claude	
SOQUEL, Abraham	
SOQUEL, Samuel	
BALIE, Charles	
BONEAUX, Daniel	
LEONARD, Jean Baptiste	His wife and 4 children are with him.
HOFERT, Pierre	His wife and 2 children are with him.
CAMUS, Pierre	
BEAUFORT, René	
BRIE, Christophe	His wife and 1 child are with him.
LENEAUX, Nouel	His wife and 1 child are with him.
FAUVRET, Dominique	His wife and 1 child are with him.
GASMAN, François	
BRETIN, Denis	
LE GALON, Julien	

Servants for M. DUVERGIER, M. de la Mancliere, M. de la Harpe and M. Brand
(They are not named)

APRIL 13, 1721

LIST OF GERMANS WHO EMBARKED ON THE
ST. ANDRE BOUND FOR LOUISIANA FROM
LORIENT.

Name   Family

(D) denotes deceased or absent when list was compiled

Name		Family
PRIMOUSE, Jean		Wife and one child
CROSE, Mathurin		Wife and three children
VOLFE, Mathieu		Wife and one child
VOLFE, Jacob		Wife and one child
AIGRE, Jacob		Wife and one child
RALLE, Adam		Wife and three (?) children
MAIRE, Felixe		Wife and five children
AFFER, Jean		Wife and two chidlren
ANISE, Michel		Wife
GEORGE, Jean		Wife and two children
MAIRE, Pierre		Wife
CHOUMER, Jean George		Wife and two children
SELDERAY, Jacob		Wife
SIVAL, Villerme		Wife
VACHER, Jean		Wife and two children
MAISONCE, Henry		Wife and one child
CAUSER, Sel France		Wife and two children
HIPE, Mathurin		Wife and three children
SERCE, Anserique		Wife and two children
CAUSE, Gaspard		Wife and one child
RISE, Joseph		Wife and one child
HELE, George		One child
ALEVANDE, Gaspard	(D)	Wife and two children
COBLE, Jean George de		One child
PAMONSEAUX, Hour		One child
QUERSE, Pierre		Wife and one child
ELINGUE, Gaspard		Wife and two children
BERGUE, Laurens Mil de	(D)	Wife and four children
MESQUER, Jonase	(D)	Wife and five children
ITILLER (?), Jacob		Wife and one child
PROQUE, Antoine		One child
ROTERNER, Jacob	(D)	Wife and three children
ROSETTE, Jean George	(D)	Wife and one child
ANDER, Anseriquer		Wife and two children
EPETTE, Jacob	(D)	One child
CRESPERLOS, Villehm		Wife and one child
SELLER, Jean		One child
GOURY, Nicolas	(D)	Wife and one child
RIQUER, Cristianne	(D)	Wife and one child
SCELLER, Jean George	(D)	Wife and one child

Name		Family
QUERY, Nicolas		Wife and one child
CRYQUER, Condrat		Wife and one child
HERTEMANT, Secriasse	(D)	Wife
HOUBRE, Jean George		Wife and one child
MOUSSER, Martin	(D)	Wife and one child
VINGUER, Jonase		Two children
CHELER, Michel		Wife and one child
ALDER, Jonase		
RAFFAUT, Daniel		Wife and one child
CEQUER, Mathieu		Wife and two children
FORTUNE, Antoine		
MOUSSER, Pierre		
PIPOT		
DURAIN, Magdelaine		A woman with two children

APRIL 23, 1721

LIST OF GERMANS EMBARKED ON THE
DURANCE BOUND FOR LOUISIANA FROM
LORIENT.

Name		Family
	(D) denotes deceased or absent when the list was compiled.	

Name		Family
EMERIQ		Wife and one child
STOT, Madelaine		She is alone
OBRELE, Magdelaine		She is alone
GHLER, Marie		She is alone
ERLE, Jacques		Wife and one child
BOUTH, Jacques		Wife
STIMPHOFLE		Wife
FORSNÉR, Conrat	(D)	Wife and two children
RABLOGET, Jacques		Wife and two children
TILLY, Gaspard	(D)	Three children
LUMINGER, Jean	(D)	Two children
ANTOINE, Albré		
MULER, Joseph		Wife and one child
CHABER, Volf		Five children
RUBERT, Petre	(D)	Two children
ENCRYER, Oullerie		Wife and one child
LIYP, Conrat		Wife and three children
FOREST, Anne Marie		She is alone
FORSTENER		Alone
QUERNER		She has one child with her
VALER, Frid		Wife and three children
VEIDEL, André		Wife and one child
DOUBS, Gaspard		Wife and two children
GUERNER		One child
POUCH		She is alone
FOUGARD, Sebastien		Wife
BERGER, Equels	(D)	Wife
CHOUP, Philippe Adam		Wife and three children
CHERNIC, Vicq		Wife and three children
CAUSER, Jean George		Wife
LIELY, Barbe		She is alone
PETICH, Jean George		Wife
BENIC, Barbe		She has two children with her
MANE, Bernard		Wife and one child
AUSMETIN, Anne Marie		She is alone
SAMBREMAN, Jean George		One child
RITTRE, George		Wife and one child
KLEMMACHER, Etienne		Wife and three children
ANDRE		Wife and one child
PAIS, Jean George		Wife and one child
CAUSEMAN, Matite		Wife and two children
CHIN, Jean		Wife and two children

JULY 20, 1721

LIST OF PASSENGERS EMBARKED ON THE
SAONE BOUND FOR LOUISIANA FROM
LORIENT.

Name	Comments
CHANTRAU DE BEAUMONT, M.	Storekeeper. His wife is with him.
LA COSTE, Dumas de	(Position or occupation unknown)

There are four wives and thirteen children of workers on the Kolly
concession who have boarded this ship to join their husbands and
fathers.

JULY 21, 1721

LIST OF PASSENGERS EMBARKED ON THE
L'ADOUR WHO ARE GOING TO THE LE BLANC
CONCESSION IN LOUISIANA FROM LORIENT.

Name	Comments
DESFONTAINES, Sieur	Director. His wife and daughter are with him.
LA LOERE, Sieur	Clerk
FAGUIER, Sieur	Clerk
One servant & One valet	Attached to the DESFONTAINES party.

SEPTEMBER 30, 1724

LIST OF PERSONS FOR THE CONCESSION OF
PARIS DUVERNAY WHO EMBARKED ON THE
<u>GIRONDE</u> BOUND FOR LOUISIANA FROM
<u>LORIENT</u>.

Name	Comments
DUVERTEUIL, M.	Director of Paris DUVERNAY's Concession. His wife and sister are with him.
DE LA CHAIZE, Sieur	
VILLAINVILLE, Sieur	Lieutenant returning to Louisiana.
DU CHAINE	Constructor
HAMON	Constructor
DE LASSUS (the elder)	Carpenter
DE LASSUS (the younger)	Carpenter
Father MATHIAS	Capucin Missionary
PREVOST, Sieur	Bookeeper

WORKERS FOR THE CONCESSION OF PARIS DUVERNAY

POINCONNIER	Mason
LE TELLIER	Carpenter
GRALLE	Sawyer
MOSSEC	Carpenter
PERRIER, Jacques	Carpenter
DUBOIS, Jean	Metal worker and Edged-tool maker

JANUARY 21, 1721

LIST OF OFFICERS WHO ARE TO COMMAND
THE TWENTY-FIVE COMPANIES OF INFAN-
TRY WHICH THE COMPANY MAINTAINS IN
LOUISIANA.

Name	Date of Commission	Comments
CAPTAINS		
RICHEBOURG	May 30, 1713	Good officer. It is unfortunate for him that rumors of his death aboud in France and have caused a delay in his advancement.
MANDEVILLE	October 2, 1714	Good officer. He has not returned to the colony.
GAUVRIT	(October 2?), 1714	On August 18 (1720?), the Council at New Orleans decided to retain him. Should the Company approve that decision, he will have to demonstrate capability or he will be placed at the tail end (demoted).
DARTAGUIETTE	February 11, 1719	He is in Illinois. He is a good officer, very capable and attentive.
DUTISNE	February 11, 1719	He is also in Illinois. He, too, is a good officer, most capable and attentive.
LE BLANC	February 11, 1719	He is at Biloxi. He is a good officer, without reproach.
CARRIE DE NANCRE	February 11, 1719	He is at Biloxi. He has not been assigned a company because he is not capable. Therefore, he is useless.
JEAN KXER (?)	July 1, 1719	He has not come to the colony
ST BEURRE	July 1, 1719	He is at Biloxi. Good officer. There is nothing more to say about him.

Name	Date of Commission	Comments
JOBERT	July 1, 1719	He has not come to the colony
LONGUEVILLE, Chevalier de la	January 2, 1720	He is in France. Good officer.
BERNAVAL	January 2, 1720	He is at Natchez. There have been some complaints about him, however, he is a good officer.
MONMARQUET	July 1, 1719	He is at Biloxi, having arrived on the MARIE. At the moment he appears to be a good officer.
DUMONTCHELLE DE TILLAINVILLE	July 1, 1719	He is at the Alibamons. The council has proposed that he be given a company in April, being that he is a very good officer and is most wise.
TONTY	March 19, 1720	He has been advised of his promotion in Canada. There is no doubt that he will not go to Illinois where he has been assigned by the Company.
DE CLARE	March 19, 1720	He is at New Orleans. He has little sense and is capable of very little.
RABOUL	March 19, 1720	He is at Biloxi, having arrived on the MARIE. At the moment he appears to be a good officer.
CARPOT DE MONTIGNY	March 19, 1720	He is at Pensacola. He has a drinking problem but promises to correct it.
TAUCHER DE LA TARDIERE	March 19, 1720	He has not been in the colony for some time, having gone to Carolina to get married.
LE SUEUR	March 19, 1720	He is at Mobile. Good officer.
ST. DENIS	March 21, 1720	He is at Biloxi. He is most wise.

Name	Date of Commission	Comments
COUSTILLAC	(March 21, 1720)?	He is at New Orleans. In April, 1720, he was named a lieutenant. Good officer.
ANDRIOT	(March 21, 1720)?	He was named a lieutenant at the same time as Sieur Coustillac. He performs the duties of major at Biloxi, just as he did at Dauphin Island. He is most capable to fill this post, being very diligent.
LUSSER	(March 21, 1720)?	He was named lieutenant at the same time as Sieur Coustillac. He is a good officer, most capable.
MACARTY	April 30, 1720	He died last November.
SUBERCAZEAUX	January, 1720	He is not in the colony.
MARCHAND DE COURCELLES	March 23, 1720	He is at the Alibamons. His work is satisfactory.
RENAULT D'HAUTERIVE	March 23, 1720	He is at Natchitoches. There is nothing more to say about him. He was sent a short time ago to replace M. Blondel who died.
MAGOIRE	?	He died last November 18th.
DU MERBION	?	He died in France. He was a good officer.

LIEUTENANTS

Name	Date of Commission	Comments
MELICQ	February 11, 1719	He is in Illinois. According to the reports of MM. Boisbriant and Diron, this man performs his duties well.
DE COUBLANS DE DIRON	February 11, 1719	He is in New Orleans. He must be satisfied with the rank of lieutenant.
DESVAUX DE BLANCHE-FONTAINE	February 11, 1719	He has not come to the colony.

Name	Date of Commission	Comments
LIEUTENANTS (cont.)		
DOUTAILLON DESPINAL	February 11, 1719	He has not come to the colony.
DETCHEPARRE	February 11, 1719	He is at New Orleans. Good officer, very capable.
CHAILLION	February 11, 1719	He has not come to the colony.
SAINTRAY DE BIRAGUE	February 11, 1719	He is in Natchez. He is a good lieutenant but is incapable of commanding a company.
DE GARON DE QUINCY	July 1, 1719	He has not come to the colony.
LEBOIS, René	July 1, 1719	He has not come to the colony.
VERMENELLE	July 1, 1719	He has not come to the colony.
DUFAURE	July 1, 1719	He is in France. Good officer, most capable.
DE LA ROQUE DE LA FOND	July 1, 1719	He is in France. Good officer, most capable
DE BASSEE	July 1, 1719	He is in New Orleans. Good officer, capable.
RECLOS	July 1, 1719	He is in Natchez, Good officer, capable.
SUB-LIEUTENANTS		
ROUVEYRE	February 11, 1719	He has not come to the colony.
BOUCHARD	February 11, 1719	The Company had named him major for the Illinois post, but because he is not qualified for that command, and has no knowledge of his intended promotion, the Company has decided to let him remain at Natchez.
DEISAUTIER DU PETIT CHEUSE	February 11, 1719	He is at Mobile. Good officer. He is wise and merits promotion.

Name	Date of Commission	Comments
SUB-LIEUTENANTS (cont.)		
DE MOUY	July 1, 1719	M. Bienville has selected him as his aide-de-camp in place of Sieur Moullon, who deserted.
CHASSIN	July 1, 1719	He is still performing the duties of storekeeper at the Illinois post. We will advise him that he can take command of some of the surplus troops. We are satisfied with his work.
CHARREAU	July 1, 1719	He has returned to France according to the wishes of the Company.
THIERRY CHASSIN	July 1, 1719	He is in New Orleans preparing to depart for the Illinois post. He appears to be a good officer.
DE LISLE	July 1, 1719	He is at the Illinois post. He is a good officer and, according to the reports of MM. Boisbriant and Diron, he merits promotion.
BENOIST	July 1, 1719	He is at Mobile. Good officer, most prudent.
PELLERIN	July 1, 1719	He is in Biloxi. He is most exact in all his duties. We a quite pleased with him.
BIZEUL DE VARENNES	March 23, 1720	He is in New Orleans. He is an unsettled and blundering person.
MAILLARD	March 23, 1720	He has gone to Natchitoches. He is a good officer.
CERLANDRE	March 23, 1720	He is not in the colony.
VILLEMERIEN	March 23, 1720	He is at the Alibamons. We are most satisfied with him.

Name	Date of Commission	Comments
SUB-LIEUTENANTS (cont.)		
TERRISSE DE TERNANT	?	He has returned to France
VAUVRE	?	He arrived without a commission from the Company. He was put in Sieur De Mouy's place. He was sent with a good recommendation from M. de Rigby.
SAUVAGE	?	He died at Dauphin Island last November.
FLAMINQUE	?	He has returned to France. Bad subject.
ENSIGNS		
HERSANT (the younger)	January 5, 1719	He is at the Alibamons. He is hated by his brother who has been returned (to France)
SIMARE	January 5, 1719	We believe he is presently at Natchitoches.
ROUVROY	January 5, 1719	He has not come to the colony.
FRANCHOMME	January 5, 1719	He is at the Yazoo post. We are satisfied with him.
SAGOT	July 1, 1719	He has not come to the colony.
ST. ESTEVES. Chevalier de	July 1, 1719	He is in Biloxi. He is a good officer and deserves promotion.
REGIS DU ROULLET	July 1, 1719	He is at Dauphin Island. He diligent but blunders.
DEISAUTIER LACOUIN	July 1, 1719	He is at Mobile. There are no complaints about him. He performs his duties well.
DU QUARTIER	July 1, 1719	He is at the Yazoo post. He is a good officer.

Name	Date of Commission	Comments

ENSIGNS (cont.)

Name	Date of Commission	Comments
MARREST DUPUY (the elder)	July 1, 1719	He is in New Orleans. He is wise and we are satisfied with him.
MARREST (the younger)	July 1, 1719	He is at Natchitoches.
LA DROITIERE	March 23, 1720	He has not come to the colony.
SALMON DE LA FERTIERE	?	He has not come to the colony.
DUTERPUY	?	He is at Biloxi and has been appointed.
GUERIN	?	He is at Mobile and has been appointed
CASENEUVE	?	He is at Natchez and has been appointed
DAMEROAL	?	He is at Pensacola and has been appointed.
GIRARDEAU	?	He is at Illinois and has been appointed.
DUPUY BLANCHARD	?	He is at New Orleans and has been appointed. He performs the duties of aide-major.
DEVIEUGE	?	He is in Biloxi and was named an ensign by the Council in April, 1720
PACQUIER	?	He is in Mobile and has been appointed. He is a good officer. We are satisfied with him and he merits promotion.

OFFICERS OF DETACHED COMPANIES

Name	Date of Commission	Comments
ST. GEORGE, Chevalier de		Captain. He is in Mobile. Very good officer. He has had the misfortune of accidentally shooting off three fingers of his left hand.

Name	Date of Commission	Comments

OFFICERS OF DETACHED COMPANIES (cont.)

Name	Date of Commission	Comments
MALOZA		"Lieutenant en Pied". He is at Mobile. Good soldier
CAUDER		"Lieutenant en Pied". He is at Mobile. Good officer.
ENDRIEUX		"Lieutenant en Pied". He died the previous November 4th.
LALLIERE		Lieutenant on half pay. He is at Mobile
ENDRIEUX, Chevalier		Lieutenant on half pay. He has returned to France.
MAISONNEUVE, M. de		Captain. Died October 4, 1720.
CHAMPEAUX		Captain. He is in Biloxi. Good officer.
POTIER		"Lieutenant en Pied" He is in Biloxi
VILLARD		"Lieutenant en Pied". He is in Biloxi.
LACHAUSSEE		"Lieutenant en Pied". He is in Biloxi
MASSE		Lieuteant on half pay. He is in Biloxi.

OFFICERS OF TWO COMPANIES OF INFANTRY WHO WILL SERVE ON THE CONCESSION OF M. LE BLANC, SECRETARY OF STATE FOR WAR.

CAPTAINS

Name	Date of Commission	Comments
BIZARD	February 6, 1720	
DESLIETTES	February 6, 1720	M. DE LA TOUR has testified to the abilities of these men. They are all good officers.

LIEUTENANT

Name	Date of Commission	Comments
BAURET	January 1, 1720	

SUB-LIEUTENANTS

Name	Date of Commission	Comments
GUILLERNY	January 1, 1720	
PETIT LEVILLIER	February 24, 1720	

Name	Date of Commission	Comments

OFFICERS FOR THE LEBLANC CONCESSION (cont.)

ENSIGNS

LACOMBE	February 24, 1720	
LA SUZE	February 24, 1720	

CAPTAINS ON HALF-PAY

DILLON		
FABRY		
DEQUAILAS		He arrived three days ago. He is in Biloxi suffering from an illness.

Done at Biloxi the 21st day of January, 1721

(signed)

Bienville   C. Legac   Leblond de la Tour

Delorme   Diron

SEPTEMBER 5, 1721

THE SALARY OF MAJOR OFFICERS IN LOUISIANA

Name	Comments	Salary in "livres" for one year
BIENVILLE	Beginning January 1, 1722, a salary of	12,000
LA TOUR	Lieutenant General. He has no appointment other than Engineer in Chief	(See salary of LA TOUR under "Engineers."
BOISBRIANT	First Lieutenant of the King, a salary of	5,000
CHATEAUGUE	Second Lieutenant of the King, a salary of	4,000
BARBAZAN DE PAILHOUX	Major General	2,000
DIRON	Inspector General of Troops and Militia, a salary of	3,000

COMMANDERS OF PARTICULAR POSTS

Name	Comments	Salary
LOUBOEY	Captain. Commander at Biloxi	720
LA MARQUE, de	Captain. Commander at Ship Island	720
RICHEBOURG	Captain. Commander at New Orleans	720
BOURMONT	Captain. Commander at the Missouri River post	1,080

COMMANDERS   (The following posts have not yet been established)

Name	Comments	Salary
LA HARPE	Captain. Commander at St. Bernard Bay	1,080
ST. DENIS	Captain. Commander at the Cane River post	1,080

Name	Comments	Salary in "livres" for one year
MAJORS AT CERTAIN POSTS		
FORTEVAL	Major at Biloxi	900
BEAUCHAMP	Major at Mobile	900
PECHON DE COMTE	Major at the Alibamons	900
DE BANNEZ	Major at New Orleans	900
ENGINEERS		
LA TOUR, M. de		8,000
A draughtsman		1,200
PAUGER, Sieur de		5,000
BOISPINEL, Sieur de		5,000
FRANQUET DE CHAVILLE, Sieur		2,400
DE VINS, Sieur	Draughtsman	600
INSPECTORS		
DALLERY		600
MORAND		500
AUBERT		400

SEPTEMBER 5, 1721

LIST OF OFFICERS FOR THE SIXTEEN COM-
PANIES OF INFANTRY EMPLOYED IN LOUISI-
ANA ALONG WITH A LIST OF HALF-PAY
CAPTAINS AND LIEUTENANTS ALSO EMPLOYED
IN LOUISIANA

CAPTAINS

RICHEBOURG	DU TISNE	JOBERT
MANDEVILLE	LA MARQUE	BERNEVAL
LA TOUR	LE BLANC	MARCHAND DE COURCELLES
DARTAGUIETTE	ST. BEURE DE MONT-MORT	RENAULT D'AUTRIVE
PRADEL	BIZARD	DE GRAVES
NOYAN		

LIEUTENANTS

HERSENT	RECLOS	COUSTILLAS
MELIQUE	VILAINVILLE	ANDRIOT
DES COUBLANS	TONTY	BAUVREL
DETCHEPARRE	RABOUL	PETIT DE LEVILLIERS
BIRAGUE	CARPOT DE MONTIGNY	CAUDER
MONTMARQUE	ST. DENIS	MARQUIS (by order of His
BASSEE	LE SUEUR	Royal Highness, The Regent)

SUB-LIEUTENANTS

DE MOUY	LA BOULAYE	HERSANT
THIERY CHASSIN	BIZEUL DE VARENNES	GUILLERMET
LUSSER	MAILLARD	SIMARE
DE LILLE	TERISSE	BENOIST
VILLEMERIEN		

ENSIGNS

FRANCHOMME	MARETZ (the younger)	DE VIEUGE
ST. ESTEVES	DELALOE DULONDEL	GUERIN
REGIS DU ROULET	CAZENEUVE	DUPUY
DUQUARTIER	GIRARDOT	LA SUZE
MARETZ DUPUY (the elder)	DOMERVAL	LA COMBE

CAPTAINS (Half-Pay)

DILLON	DU QUAILA	FABRY
GAUVRY	CHAMPOUX	ARENTZBOURG

LIEUTENANTS (Half-Pay)

CRESPY	NOLAN	POTTIE
COMBETTE	VILLARS	PIGNON
LA CHAUSSEE	CHALUET	LALLIE
DESTOF CHULTZ	MASSE	NICOLAS BLOM
DUMONT DE MONTIGNY	CLAIR JANSEN	

LIST OF OFFICERS FOR THE SIXTEEN
COMPANIES OF INFANTRY IN LOUISIANA

CAPTAINS

RICHEBOURG	LA MARQUE	MARCHAND
MANDEVILLE	LE BLANC	D'HAUTERIVE
LA TOUR	MONTMORT	PRADEL
DARTAGUIETTE	BARNAVAL	LOUBOEY
DU TISNE	DE GRAVES	DETCHEPARRE

LIEUTENANTS

COUSTILLAS	REBOUL	BASSEE
HERSANT	MONTMARQUET	ST. DENIS
LE SUEUR	PETIT DE LEVILLIERS	DES COUBLANS
TONTY	MARQUIS	CAUDER
MELIQUE	VILANVILLE	
DE MOUY	RECLOS	

SUB-LIEUTENANTS

THIERY	SIMARE DE BELLEISLE	TERRISSE
LUSSER	LALLIER	VILLEMERIEN
BENOIST	PATON DU BROUSSET	MASSE
DE LILLE	GUILLERMET	LANNOY DE GOURNAY
LA BOULAYE	HERSANT	
NOLAN	MAILLARD	

ENSIGNS

DUPUY PLAUCHARD	MARETZ (the younger)	MARETZ DUPUY (the elder)
DAMERVAL	NOYAN	DE MARITE
GUERIN	DUTERPUIS VERCHIERES	LEGENOIS
GIRARDEAU	DEMONT DE MONTIGNY	FRANCHOMME
STE. THERESE DE LAN-GLOISIERE	DUPLESSIS FABERT	CAZENEUVE
	REGIS DU ROULET	

HALF-PAY OFFICERS

GAUVRIT	Captain	50 livres per month
ARENTZBOURG, Charles	Captain	
JAUSSEN, Claude	Lieutenant	40 livres per month
BOURDON	Lieutenant	40 livres per month
ST. ANGE (father)	Lieutenant	40 livres per month
VINCELLES	Lieutenant	40 livres per month
ST. ANGE (son)	Ensign	30 livres per month

OCTOBER 21, 1723

LIST OF OFFICERS OF THE TWELVE COM-
PANIES OF INFANTRY IN LOUISIANA
WITH THE DATES OF THEIR COMMISSION.

CAPTAINS

Name	Date of Commission
MANDEVILLE	October 2, 1714
LA TOUR	October 28, 1717
DARTAGUIETTE	February 11, 1719
DU TISNE	February 11, 1719
LA MARQUE	February 11, 1719
LE BLANC	February 11, 1719
MONTMORT	July 1, 1719
DES LIETTES	February 6, 1720
MARCHAND DE COURCELLES	March 23, 1720
RENAULT D'HAUTERIVE	March 23, 1720
PRADEL	March 23, 1720
LOUBOEY	October 1, 1720

LIEUTENANTS

Name	Date of Commission
MELIQUE	February 11, 1719
MONTMARQUE	July 1, 1719
BASSEE	July 1, 1719
RECLOS	July 1, 1719
VILAINVILLE	January 2, 1720
TONTY	March 19, 1720
RABOUL	March 23, 1720
LE SUEUR	March 23, 1720
ST. DENIS	March 23, 1720
CAUDER	October 30, 1720
COUSTILLAS	October 30, 1720
PETIT DE LIVILLIERS	November 4, 1720

SUB-LIEUTENANTS

Name	Date of Commission
THIERRY CHASSIN	July 1, 1719
LUSSER,	March 23, 1720
DE LILLE	March 23, 1720
BENOIST	March 23, 1720
LA BOULAYE	March 23, 1720
MAILLARD,	March 23, 1720
TERISSE	October 30, 1720
VILLEMERIEN	October 30, 1720
HERSAN	October 30, 1720
SIMARRE DE BELLEISLE	September 5, 1721
LALLIER	December 19, 1722
MASSE	December 19, 1722

Name	Date of Commission

ENSIGNS

Name	Date of Commission
FRANCHOMME	February 11, 1719
ST. ESTEVES	July 1, 1719
REGIS DU ROULET	July 1, 1719
MARETZ DUPUY (the elder)	January 2, 1720
MARETZ (the younger)	January 2, 1720
DU TERPUY VERCHIERS	October 30, 1720
CAZENEUVE	October 30, 1720
GIRARDOT	October 30, 1720
DOMERVAL	October 30, 1720
GUERIN	October 30, 1720
DUPUY PLANCHARD	October 30, 1720
STE. THEREZE DE LANGLOISIERE	May 19, 1722

SUPERNUMERARY OFFICERS FOR THE FOUR HALF-PAY COMPANIES

BERNAVAL	Captain
GRAVES	Captain
NOYAN	Captain
DETCHEPARRE	Captain
MARQUIS	Lieutenant
DE MOUY	Lieutenant
NOLAN	Sub-Lieutenant
PATON DE BROUSSET	Sub-Lieutenant
LAGENOIS	Ensign
Noyan (the younger)	Ensign

OCTOBER 21, 1723

ASSIGNMENT OF THE OFFICERS OF THE TWELVE
INFANTRY COMPANIES IN LOUISIANA AS WELL
AS THE ASSIGNMENTS OF SUPERNUMERARY AND
HALF-PAY OFFICERS

AT NEW ORLEANS

The four companies at New Orleans must furnish two
detachments composed of one lieutenant, one ensign,
one sargeant and nineteen soldiers each to serve
at Balize and at Biloxi.

MANDEVILLE'S COMPANY

MANDEVILLE	Captain
ST. DENIS	Lieutenant
VILLEMERIEN	Sub-Lieutenant
DUTERPUY VERCHUR	Ensign

Supernumerary Officer
DE MOUY   Lieutenant

HALF-PAY OFFICER
GAUVRIT   Captain

LA MARQUE'S COMPANY (formerly Richebourg's company)

LA MARQUE	Captain
COUSTILLAS	Lieutenant
THIERRY	Sub-Lieutenant
DUPUY PLANCHARD	Ensign

Supernumerary Officers
DE NOYAN (the elder)   Captain
DE NOYAN (the younger)   Ensign

LE BLANC'S COMPANY

LE BLANC	Captain
REBOUL	Lieutenant
SIMARRE DE BELLEISLE	Sub-Lieutenant
MARETZ (the younger)	Ensign

HALF-PAY OFFICER

ARENTZBOURG   Captain. Detached. At the
                                German village.

PRADEL'S COMPANY

PRADEL	Captain
BASSEE	Lieutenant
LALLIER	Sub-Lieutenant
ST. ESTEVES	Ensign

HALF-PAY OFFICER

JANTZEN	Lieutenant. Detached. At the German village.

AT MOBILE

The three companies at Mobile must furnish two detachments composed as follows: For Dauphin Island, one sub-lieutenant, one sargeant and fourteen soldiers; For the Alibamons, one lieutenant, one ensign, one sargeant, one corporal, one drummer and twenty-three soldiers.

LOUBOEY'S COMPANY (formerly Mandeville's company)

LOUBOEY	Captain
VILLAINVILLE	Lieutenant
LUSSER	Sub-Lieutenant
DAMERVAL	Ensign

SUPERNUMERARY OFFICERS

BERNAVAL	Captain
LAGENOIS	Ensign

LA TOUR'S COMPANY

LA TOUR	Captain
LE SUEUR	Lieutenant
BENOIST	Sub-Lieutenant
GUERIN	Ensign

SUPERNUMERARY OFFICER

PATON DU BROUSSET	Sub-Lieutenant

MARCHAND DE COURCELLES' COMPANY

MARCHAND DE COURCELLES	Captain
CAUDER	Lieutenant
HERSANT	Sub-Lieutenant
REGIS DU ROULET	Ensign

AT NATCHITOCHES

The company at Natchitoches must furnish a detachment of sixteen men for the Cadodaquious.

RENAULT D'HAUTRIVE'S COMPANY

RENAULT D'HAUTRIVE	Captain
RECLOS	Lieutenant
MAILLARD	Sub-Lieutenant
MARETZ DUPUY (the elder)	Ensign

SUPERNUMERARY OFFICERS

DETCHEPARRE	Captain
MARQUIS	Lieutenant

AT NATCHEZ

The company at Natchez must furnish a detachment composed of two officers, one sargeant and nineteen soldiers for the Yazoo Post.

MONTMORT'S COMPANY

MONTMORT	Captain
PETIT DE LIVILLIERS	Lieutenant
MASSE	Sub-Lieutenant
FRANCHOMME	Ensign

SUPERNUMERARY OFFICERS

DE GRAVES	Captain
NOLAN	Sub-Lieutenant

AT THE WABASH POST

The following company must be divided as follows: For the Wabash Post, the captain, the sub-lieutenant, the half-pay lieutenant, one sargeant, one corporal, one drummer and twenty-two soldiers. The remaining officers and men are to be stationed at the Arkansas Post.

DES LIETTES' COMPANY

DES LIETTES	Captain
MONTMARQUET	Lieutenant
TERISSE	Sub-Lieutenant
CAZENEUVE	Ensign

HALF-PAY OFFICERS

VINCELLES	Lieutenant
ST. ANGE (son)	Ensign

AT THE ILLINOIS POST

This company must detach two officers and fifteen men to serve at the Missouri River Post.

DU TISNE'S COMPANY

DU TISNE	Captain
MELIQUE	Lieutenant
LA BOULAYE	Sub-Lieutenant
STE. THEREZE DE LANGLOISIERE	Ensign

HALF-PAY OFFICER

ST. ANGE (father)	Lieutenant

DARTAGUIETTE'S COMPANY

DARTAGUIETTE	Captain
TONTY	Lieutenant
DE LILLE	Sub-Lieutenant
GIRARDOT	Ensign

HALF-PAY OFFICER

BOURDON	Lieutenant

SEPTEMBER 23, 1724

OFFICER ASSIGNMENTS FOR THE TEN COMPANIES STATIONED IN LOUISIANA

AT NEW ORLEANS

MANDEVILLE'S COMPANY

MANDEVILLE	Captain	Present
DE MOUY	Lieutenant	Present
LALLIER	Sub-Lieutenant	Present
DU TERPUIS VERCHIER	Ensign	Present

LA MARQUE'S COMPANY

LA MARQUE	Captain	Present
COUSTILLAS	Lieutenant	Present
THIERRY CHASSIN	Sub-Lieutenant	Present
DUPUY PLANCHARD	Ensign	Present

LE BLANC'S COMPANY

LE BLANC	Captain	Present
RABOUL	Lieutenant	Assigned to Balize
SIMARE DE BELLEISLE	Sub-Lieutenant	Assigned to Missouri
MARETZ (the younger)	Ensign	Present

DARTAGUIETTE'S COMPANY

DARTAGUIETTE	Captain	At the Illinois Post
DU CAUDER	Lieutenant	At the Missouri Post
STE. THEREZE DE LANGLOI-SIERE	Ensign	At the Missouri Post
DE LILLE	Sub-Lieutenant	At the Missouri Post

RENAULT D'HAUTRIVE'S COMPANY

RENAULT D'HAUTRIVE	Captain	Present
BASSEE	Lieutenant	At Natchitoches
MAILLARD	Sub-Lieutenant	At Natchitoches
DE NOYAN	Ensign	Present

AT NATCHEZ

DU TISNE'S COMPANY

DU TISNE	Captain	At the Illinois Post
PETIT DE LIVILLIERS	Lieutenant	Present
MASSE	Sub-Lieutenant	Present
CAZENEUVE	Ensign	Present

PRADEL'S COMPANY

PRADEL	Captain	At the Missouri Post
VILAINVILLE	Lieutenant	Has left the colony
TERISSE	Sub-Lieutenant	Present
GIRARDEAU	Ensign	At the Illinois Post

AT THE ILLINOIS POST

DES LIETTES' COMPANY

DES LIETTES	Captain	At Natchez
MELIQUE	Lieutenant	Present
LA BOULAYE	Sub-Lieutenant	At Arkansas
FRANCHOMME	Ensign	Present

Note: It will be necessary to give DES LIETTES the lieutenant that he asks for. If that is impossible then MELIQUE must be moved to another company.

AT MOBILE

LA TOUR'S COMPANY

LA TOUR	Captain	Present
MONTMARQUET	Lietuenant	Present
LUSSER	Sub-Lieutenant	Present
REGIS DU ROULET	Ensign	Present

MARCHAND DE COURCELLES' COMPANY

MARCHAND DE COURCELLES	Captain	Present
--------	Lieutenant	-------
BENOIST	Sub-Lieutenant	Present
ST. ESTEVES	Ensign	At New Orleans

Note: HERSANT, Sub-Lieutenant assigned to the Alibamons will become Sub-Lieutenant in MARCHAND DE COURCELLES' Company, and BENOIST will fill the vacancy for Lieutenant.

SUPERNUMERARY OFFICERS

BERNAVAL	Captain	At New Orleans
LOUBOEY	Captain	At New Orleans
NOYAN	Captain	At New Orleans
DETCHEPARRE	Captain	At Natchez
DE LA HARPE	Captain	In France
NOLAN	Sub-Lieutenant	At Mobile

HALF-PAY OFFICERS

GAUVRIT	Captain	At New Orleans
ARENTZBOURG	Captain	At the German village
DUMONT DE MONTIGNY	Lieutenant	At Natehez
JANTZEN	Lieutenant	At Natchitoches
ST. ANGE (father)	Lieutenant	At the Illinois Post
VINCENNES	Lieutenant	At Oyatanons
ST. ANGE (son)	Ensign	At the Missouri Post

DECEMBER 12, 1725

LIST OF OFFICERS WHO ARE TO COMMAND THE
EIGHT INFANTRY COMPANIES STATIONED IN
LOUISIANA.

CAPTAINS

MANDEVILLE	DES LIETTES
LA TOUR	MARCHAND DE COURCELLES
DARTAGUIETTE	RENAULT D'HAUTRIVE
DU TISNE	PRADEL

LIEUTENANTS

MELIQUE	CAUDER
MONTMARQUET	COUSTILHAS
BASSEE	PETIT DE LEVILLIERS
VILLAINVILLE	DE MOUY

SUB-LIEUTENANTS

DE LISLE	HERSANT
LA BOULAYE	SIMARE DE BELLISLE
MAILLARD	LALLIER
TERISSE	MASSE

ENSIGNS

FRANCHOMME	MARETZ DE LA TOUR
ST. ESTEVES	DUPUY PLANCHARD
REGIS DU ROULET	DU TERPUYS VERCHIER
MARETZ DUPUY	CAZENEUVE

SUPERNUMERARY OFFICERS

CAPTAINS

BERNAVAL (Returning to France)
MERVEILLEUX
LOUBOEY
NOYAN
DETCHEPARRE

LIEUTENANTS

LUSSER

SUB-LIEUTENANT

NOLAN

ENSIGNS

GIRARDEAU
STE. THEREZE DE LANGLOISIERE
LE CHEVALIER DE NOYAN

1728-1777

LIST OF OFFICERS WHO SERVED IN LOUISI-
ANA WITH DATE OF VARIOUS PROMOTIONS

Name	Titles (in French)	Date

GOVERNOR

Name	Titles (in French)	Date
KERLEREC, M. de	Garde de la Marine	1720
	Enseigne de Vaisseau	1731
	Lieutenant de Vaisseau	1741
	Chevalier de St. Louis	1746
	Capitaine de Vaisseau	1751
	Gouverneur de La Louisiane	1752
AUBRY, M.	Lieutenant au Regiment de	
(Aubry drowned in the	Lyonnois, Infanterie	1742
wreck of the Pére de	Capitaine a La Louisianne,	
Famille, February 17,	18 Octobre	1750
1770, while returning	Chevalier de St. Louis,	
to France.)	10 Juillet	1761

LIEUTENANTS OF THE KING

Name	Titles (in French)	Date
MACARTY	Mousquetaire	---
(Macarty died in Louisi-	Ayde-major	1732
ana April 20, 1764)	Capitaine	1735
	Chevalier de St. Louis	1750
	Lieutenant of the King at	
	New Orleans	1759
VELLE, Chevalier de	Mousquetaire	---
	Lieutenant à la Louisiane	1732
	Capitaine	1736
	Ayde-major à La Mobile	1744
	Chevalier de St. Louis	1750
	Major à La Mobile	1752
	Lieutenant du Roy à La Mobile	1759

MAJORS

Name	Titles (in French)	Date
BELLISLE, Scimars de	Ancien enseigne en pied	---
(Dead. He was demoted and	Lieutenant	1734
dismissed from the ser-	Ayde-major à La Nouvelle	
vice October 1, 1759.	Orléans	1735
Kerlerec, however, re-	Commission de Capitaine	1740
ceived word from the king	Major de La Nouvelle Orléans	1752
on January 18, 1762 that	Chevalier de St. Louis	1752
the matter against BELL-		
ISLE would not be pursued		
and that he should be kept		
on as long as thought		
appropriate.)		

Name	Titles (in French)	date
MAJORS (cont.)		
LA HOUSSAYE, Chevalier de	A servi dans les Gardes Francoises dans le regiment de Vintinielle et dans les Garde--costes du pays d'Aunis	
	Chevalier de St. Louis	
	Capitaine à La Louisiane	1750
	Major de La Mobile	1759
NEYON DE VILLIERS	Enseigne au Regiment de Choiseul	1735
	Réformé	1738
	Lieutenant au Regiment de Merinville	1742
	Aide-major au Regiment de Lorraine	1744
	Capitaine du Regiment de Lorraine	1747
	Capitaine réformé	1748
	Major, commandant aux Illinois	1759
	Chevalier de St. Louis	1759

AYDE-MAJORS

Name	Titles (in French)	date
AUBERT (He was made Capitaine en Pied, July 1, 1759)	Lieutenant au Regiment de Grassin	
	Lieutenant à La Louisiane	1750
	Ayde-Major de La Mobile	1752
DORVILLE	Capitaine Ayde-major du Regiment de Grassin	
	Capitaine à La Louisiane	1750
	Ayde-major de La Nouvelle Orléans	1754
DU BARRY	Lieutenant en Second au Regiment de La Couronne	1743
	Lieutenant dans le même Regiment	1745
	Réformé	1749
	Lieutenant à La Louisiane	1751
	Ayde-major de La Mobile avec commission de Capitaine	1759
	Chevalier de St. Louis	1770

ENGINEERS

Name	Titles (in French)	date
DU VERGEZ	Ingenieur à La Nouvelle Orléans	
	Chevalier de St. Louis	1752

Name	Titles (in French)	Date

ENGINEERS (cont.)

AMELOT — Lieutenant dans le Regiment de Grassin

Capitaine à La Louisiane — 1750

Ingenieur — 1752

Chevalier de St. Louis — 1759

MONIN DE CHAMPIGNY
(He was made Captain
in the Legion of the
Isle de France,
8 Nivose, Year VIII

Cadet à l'Aiguellette — 1754

Ingénieur — 1762

Commission de Capitaine — 1762

Passé à La Guyanne pour servir en la même qualité — 1763

ANDRY

Lieutenant réformé — 1762

Sous Ingénieur — 1762

ARTILLERY COMPANIES

DESSALLES
(He was given 400 livres
as an half-pay officer
in 1763. In 1771 he
received a pension of
600 livres per year.)

Garde de la Marine — 1749

Garde du Pavillon — 1750

Lieutenant réformé chargé du détail de l'artillerie — 1752

Capitaine Commandant de la compagnie des Canoniers — 1759

Rang et ancienneté de Capitaine d'Infanterie à comptes du 1 Janvier — 1759

Chevalier de St. Louis — 1762

RENARD DE COUDREAU

Enseigne en Second — 1752

Enseigne en Pied — 1754

Lieutenant des Canonier — 1759

LA BOUCHERIE FROMENTEAU
(He went to Louisiana
to serve in the capacity
of Lieutenant in 1762)

Enseigne en Second à l'Isle Royale — 1750

Sous-lieutenant de la Compagne de Canoniers Bombardiers à l'Isle Royale — 1755

Lieutenant de la Compagnie — 1758

LOPINOT DE BEAUPORT
(He went to Louisiana
in 1762 as a lieutenant.
He was made captain in
1769 and Major in the
Colonial Army in 1770.

Enseigne en Second à l'Isle Royale — 1754

Enseigne in Pied de la Deuxième Compagnie de Canoniers Bombardiers à l'Isle Royale — 1758

Name	Titles (in French)	Date

ARTILLERY COMPANIES (cont.)

| LAVAU TRUDEAU | Enseigne de la Compagnie d'artillerie à La Louisiane | 1762 |

CAPTAINS

DE BLANC	Capitaine au service de la Compagnie	
	Cassé par la dite Compagnie, rétabli capitaine 18 Juillet	1734
	Commandant aux Natchitoches	1745
	Chevalier de St. Louis	1750
D'ERNEVILLE, Chevalier	Enseigne en Second	1732
	Enseigne en Pied	1733
	Lieutenant	1734
	Capitaine	1740
	Chevalier de St. Louis	1754
MAREST DE LA TOUR	Ancien enseigne	
	Lieutenant	1736
	Capitaine	1741
	Chevalier de St. Louis	1759
DE GRANDPRE (He died in Louisiana, July 1, 1763.)	Enseigne	1732
	Lieutenant	1736
	Capitaine	1741
	Chevalier de St. Louis	1754
NOYAN, Chevalier de	Officier au service de la Compagnie	
	Enseigne à l'Isle Royale	1730
	Lieutenant à La Louisiane	1735
	Ayde-major de La Mobile	1736
	Commission de Capitaine	1740
	Capitaine en Pied	1744
	Chevalier de St. Louis	1752
HAZEUR (He died in December, 1758.)	Enseigne	1732
	Lieutenant	1736
	Capitaine	1746
DE MONCHERVAUX	Enseigne	1732
	Lieutenant	1736
	Capitaine	1747

Name	Titles (in French)	Date

CAPTAINS (cont.)

Name	Titles (in French)	Date
DE BONNILLE	Enseigne	1728
	Lieutenant	1735
	Capitaine	1750
	Chevalier de St. Louis	1759
FAVROT	Enseigne	1732
	Lieutenant	1736
	Capitaine	1750
	Chevalier de St. Louis	1759
DELFAU DE PONTALBA (He retired in 1759)	Enseigne en Second	1732
	Enseigne en Pied	1735
	Lieutenant	1740
	Capitaine	1750
	Chevalier de St. Louis	1759
DE BELLENOS	A servi 14 ans dans le Regiment des Gardes Suisses	
	Lieutenant de Grenadiers dans le Regiment de Louvendal	1744
	Capitaine dans le Bataillon de Milias de Dinan	1748
	Capitaine à San Domingue	1750
	Capitaine à La Louisiane	1758
	Chevalier de St. Louis	1762
MONTBERAULT (His full name was Henry Elizabeth Aimé de Montberault.)	Lieutenant réformé	1738
	Lieutenant en Pied	1744
	Capitaine réformé	1749
	Capitaine en Pied	1750
	Chevalier de St. Louis	1751
VAUGELADE DE GRANDCHAMP	Garde du Corps du Roy	
	Capitaine en Second de Hussards dans les Volontaires de Gantis	1746
	Capitaine à La Louisiane	1750
	Chevalier de St. Louis	1770
DE VILEMONT (He went to Canada in 1760 but returned to Louisiana to serve in the Spanish army (1763).	Capitaine réformé au Regiment de Ferrary	1745
	Capitaine en Pied audit Regiment	1747
	Capitaine à La Louisiane	1750
	Chevalier de St. Louis	1760
	Lieutenant Colonel de Cavalerie	

Name	Titles (in French)	Date

CAPTAINS (cont.)

DES MAZELLIERES

Capitaine en Second au Corps
de Chasseurs de Colonne — 1747
Capitaine à La Louisiane — 1750

GAMON DE LA ROCHETTE

Capitaine des Milices du Dau-
phiné — 1747
Capitaine à La Louisiane — 1750
Chevalier de St. Louis — 1759

DE REGGIO

Lieutenant avec commission de
Capitaine dans les Grenediers
Royaux Genois en — 1748
Capitaine à La Louisiane — 1750

AUBRY

Lieutenant au Regiment de
Lyonnois Infanterie — 1742
Capitaine à La Louisiane — 1750
Chevalier de St. Louis — 1761

DE MURAT
(Retired.)

Lieutenant a été 8 ans au
Régiment de La Tour d'Auvergne
Capitaine à La Louisiane — 1750

DE TRANT

Enseigne dans le Regiment de
Louvendal — 1744
Lieutenant en Second audit
Regiment — 1746
Capitaine à La Louisiane — 1750

DU TILLET

Enseigne dans le Regiment de
Foix — 1747
Capitaine à La Louisiane — 1750

GOURDON

Lieutenant réformé en France — 1747
Capitaine à La Louisiane — 1750

CHABERT

Lieutenant au Régiment Royal
Infanterie — 1747
Capitaine à La Louisiane — 1751
Chevalier de St. Louis — 1776

ARTAUD

Avoit servi 5 years en qualité
de volontaire dans le Regiment
du metre de Camp general suivant
le certificat de M. Le Duc de
_____ — 1746
Lieutenant au Regiment de La
Morliere — 1747
Capitaine à La Louisiane — 1751
Chevalier de St. Louis — 1762

Name	Titles (in French)	Date

CAPTAINS (cont.)

Name	Titles (in French)	Date
PAUPULUS	Enseigne en Second	1733
	Enseigne en Pied	1736
	Lieutenant	1746
	Capitaine	1752
	Chevalier de St. Louis	1777
HARPAIN DE LA GAUTRAYE (He died at the hospital of Angers on May 15, 1776)	Cadet a Rochefort	
	Enseigne à La Louisiane	
	Lieutenant	1740
	Capitaine	1754
	Chevalier de St. Louis	1775
MACARTY, Chevalier de	Sous lieutenant en France	
	Enseigne en Second à La Louisiane	1736
	Lieutenant	1741
	Capitaine	1754
DE SOMME DE MONTY	Lieutenant dans Raugrade	1743
	Lieutenant à La Louisiane	1750
	Capitaine	1759
VILLIERS, Chevalier de	Enseigne	1736
	Lieutenant	1746
	Capitaine	1754
	Chevalier de St. Louis	1759
DE GRANDMAISON	Cornette de cavalier dans Grassin	1745
	Lieutenant à La Louisiane	1750
	Capitaine	1754
	Chevalier de St. Louis	1762
	Major de La Nouvelle Orléans	1763
D'AUTERIVE (Bernard)	Lieutenant en Second des Volontaires Royaux	1748
	Lieutenant réformé	1749
	Lieutenant à La Louisiane	1750
	Capitaine	1755
DUPLESSIS	Enseigne	1738
	Enseigne en Pied	1741
	Lieutenant	1750
	Capitaine	1758
	Chevalier de St. Louis	1762
AUBERT	Lieutenant dans Grassin	1747
	Lieutenant à La Louisiane	1750
	Ayde-major de La Mobile	1752
	Capitaine	1759
	Chevalier de St. Louis	1774

Name	Titles (in French)	Date
DU FOSSAT, Chevalier	Lieutenant au Régiment de Monaco	1747
	Lieutenant à La Louisiane	1750
	Capitaine	1759
TRUDEAU	Enseigne en Second	1735
	Enseigne en Pied	1740
	Lieutenant	1747
	Capitaine	1759
LE BOSSU	Avoint servi 15 ans dans le Regiment de Poitou et a été blessé à l'attaque de Rétranchement du Chateau Dauphin en	1744
	Lieutenant au Regiment de La Dauphine Allemand	1747
	Lieutenant à La Louisiane	1750
	Capitaine	1759
	Chevalier de St. Louis	1773
DE L'HOMMER	Lieutenant au Régiment de Saxe Allemand Infanterie	1747
	Lieutenant à La Louisiane	1750
	Capitaine	1759
DE LUSSER	Enseigne en Second	1736
	Enseigne en Pied	1740
	Lieutenant	1747
	Capitaine	1759
FLEURIAU	Expectative de Lieutenant	1748
	Lieutenant en Pied	1750
	Capitaine	1759
DE PORTNEUF	Enseign en Second	
	Enseigne en Pied	1740
	Lieutenant	1750
	Capitaine	1759
VOISIN	Enseigne en Second	1736
	Enseigne en Pied	1746
	Lieutenant	1752
	Capitaine	1759
DE GRUY (He died in 1759.)	Enseigne en Second	1740
	Enseigne en Pied	1746
	Lieutenant	1752
	Capitaine	1759

Name	Titles (in French)	Date

CAPTAINS (cont.)

DE BRESSAY	Cornette dans le Regiment de Brancas	1746
	Lieutenant dans la même Regiment	1748
	Lieutenant à l'Isle de Ré	1751
	Capitaine à l"Islede Ré	1757
	Capitaine d'infanterie à San Domingue	1761
	(Arrived in Louisiana)	1761
	Chevalier de St. Louis	1773

LOMBARD	Lieutenant au Regiment de Bearn	
	Lieutenant à l'Isle de Ré	1752
	Capitaine à l'Isle de Ré	1757
	Capitaine à San Domingue	1761
	(Arrived in Louisiana)	1761

DE CHABRILLARD	Lieutenant réformé en France	
	Lieutenant à La Louisiane	1751
	Capitaine	1762

LE DOUX	Lieutenant au Regiment de Custine	
	Lieutenant à La Louisiane	1750
	Capitaine	1762

DE SANTILLY	Enseigne en Second	1738
	Enseigne en Pied	1744
	Lieutenant	1752
	Chevalier de St. Louis	1775

COPPIN	Lieutenant en Second en France	1745
	Enseigne à La Louisiane	1750
	Lieutenant	1754
	Capitaine	1762
	Chevalier de St. Louis	1774

CABARET D'ETREPIS	Lieutenant	1754
	Capitaine	1762
	Chevalier de St. Louis	1770

HUREAU DE LIVOIS	Lieutenant au Bataillon de Milices de Montargis	1747
	Une interruption	
	Lieutenant à La Louisiane	1751
	Capitaine	1762

Name	Titles (in French)	Date

CAPTAINS (cont.)

Name	Titles (in French)	Date
LA PIERRE	Lieutenant dans le Régiment de Montboissier	
	Garde du Roy en	1749
	Lieutenant à La Louisiane	1751
	Capitaine à St. Domingue	1762
	Capitaine à La Louisiane	1763
	Chevalier de St. Louis	1763
VAUGINE DE NUISMAN	Cadet dans Royal Artillerie	1744
	Lieutenant au Régiment Royal Baviere Allemand	1746
	Lieutenant à La Louisiane	1750
	Capitaine	1763

LIEUTENANTS

Name	Titles (in French)	Date
DU CODER	Enseigne en Second	1733
	Enseigne en Pied	1740
	Lieutenant	1746
DE MANTOIULLET	Lieutenant	1750
FOURCROY (He resigned and returned to France in 1751 (1756?).	Lieutenant au Régiment d'Orléans Infanterie	
	Lieutenant à La Louisiane	1751
LA PERLIERE	Enseigne en Second	1740
	Enseigne en Pied	1746
	Lieutenant	1750
DE MANDEVILLE	Enseigne en Second	1740
	Enseigne en Pied	1746
	Lieutenant	1752
ROCHEBLAVE	Lieutenant en France	1748
	Lieutenant à La Louisiane	1752
MONTREUIL	Enseigne en Second	1740
	Enseigne en Pied	1746
	Lieutenant	1754
DE LORRY	Lieutenant	1754
DE CLOUET, Chevalier	A servi 14 ans dans le Régiment d'Egmont dragons	
	Lieutenant à La Louisiane	1758

Name	Titles (in French)	Date

LIEUTENANTS (cont.)

LA NOUE BOGARD	Enseigne d'infanterie au Régiment de Bresse	1743
	Lieutenant au même Régiment	1744
	Réformé à la fin de	1748
	Enseigne en Second à l'Isle Royale	1750
	Enseigne en Pied	1754
	Lieutenant à La Louisiane	1758
	Chevalier de St. Louis	1771
DOUIN DE LA MOTTE	Lieutenant	1758
	Capitaine à St. Domingue	1762
LE BRUN	Lieutenant en Second au Régiment d'Alsace	
	Enseigne en Pied à l'Isle Royale	1750
	Enseigne en Pied à La Louisiane	1755
	Lieutenant	1759
ROULLIN	Lieutenant dans le Bataillon de Milice de Neufchâtel	1742
	Volontaire au Régiment d'Orléans dragons	1743
	Lieutenant en Second au Régiment d'Orléans Infanterie	1744
	Lieutenant dans le même Régiment	1745
	Enseigne à La Louisiane	1750
	Lieutenant	1759
	(Captain)	1770
	Chevalier de St. Louis	1770
DORIOCOURT	Lieutenant en Second des Milices au Bataillon de St. Dizier	1743
	Lieutenant dans le même Bataillon	1745
	Porte Drapeau au Régiment de Grenadier Daulon	1748
	Lieutenant de Grenadiers au Bataillon de St. Dizier	1750
	Enseigne à La Louisiane	1750
	Lieutenant	1759
	Chevalier de St. Louis	1771
LA FOREST DE LAUMONT (Drowned as a result of the wreck of the Père de Famille, February 17, 1770.)	Lieutenant des Grenadiers du Bataillon de St. Maixant	1746
	Enseigne à La Louisiane	1750
	Lieutenant	1759

Name	Titles (in French)	Date
LIEUTENANTS (cont.)		
PESCHON	Enseigne en Second	1746
	Enseigne en Pied	1750
	Lieutenant	1759
ROUVILLE, Chevalier de	Enseigne en Second	1746
	Enseigne en Pied	1750
	Lieutenant	1759
LA RONDE, Chevalier de	Enseigne en Second	1746
	Enseigne en Pied	1750
	Lieutenant	1759
LE BLANC	Lieutenant au Bataillon de Rhodez	
	Enseigne a La Louisiane	1750
	Lieutenant	1759
ADAM	Lieutenant au Bataillon de St. Lo	
	Enseigne à La Louisiane	1750
	Lieutenant	1759
DUSSEAU	Enseigne en Pied	1750
	Lieutenant	1759
DE LUSSER, Chevalier	Enseigne en Second	1746
	Enseigne en Pied	1752
	Lieutenant	1759
HEUGON DESDEMAINE (Retired October 26, 1762 with a pension.)	Enseigne en Second	1746
	Enseigne en Pied	1752
	Lieutenant	1759
	Chevalier de St. Louis	1770
ST. DENIS (the elder)	Enseigne en Second	1746
	Enseigne en Pied	1752
	Lie utenant	1759
DE NOYAN (Retired July, 1760.)	Enseigne en Pied	1752
	Lieutenant	1759
DE BELLISLE	Enseigne en Second	1747
	Enseigne en Pied	1754
	Lieutenant	1759
BOISSEAU	Enseigne en Second	1747
	Enseigne en Pied	1754
	Lieutenant	1759

Name	Titles (in French)	Date
LIEUTENANTS (cont.)		
DE LIVAUDAIS (the elder)	Enseigne en Second	1752
	Enseigne en Pied	1754
	Lieutenant	1759
DE VILLIERS, Chevalier (Ricard)	Enseigne en Second	1725 (?)
	Enseigne en Pied	1754
	Lieutenant	1759
DESSALLES, Chevalier	Lieutenant	1759
	Cadet à l'Eguillette	1759
DE NESLE	Lieutenant de cavallerie au Régiment de Frennes	
	Lieutenant à la suite des Recrues à l'Isle de Ré	1757
	Lieutenant à St. Domingue	1761
	Lieutenant à La Louisiane	1761
RAIMBAULT LA MOELE	Enseigne en Second en Canada	1750
	Enseigne en Pied en Canada	1755
	Lieutenant en Canada	1759
	Lieutenant en La Louisiane	1762
BAILLEUL CANUS (He was taken prisoner en route to Louisiana from Canada and ulti- mately returned to Rochefort.)	Enseigne en Second en Canada	1750
	Enseigne en Pied en Canada	1755
	Lieutenant en Canada	1759
	Chevalier de St. Louis	1761
	Lieutenant à La Louisiane	1762
FONTENELLE	Lieutenant de Grenadiers au Bataillon de Poitiers	1747
	Enseigne à La Louisiane	1750
	Lieutenant	1762
BOULANGER	Lieutenant de Grenadiers au Bataillon de Péronne	
	Enseigne à La Louisiane	1750
	Lieutenant	1762
DE VOLSEY	Officier réformé de Lancize	
	Enseigne à La Louisiane	1750
	Lieutenant	1762
	(Captain)	1775
	Chevalier de St. Louis	1775

Name	Titles (in French)	Date
ROBERT DE LA MORANDIERE	Expectative d'Enseigne en Second	1748
	Enseigne en Second	1750
	Enseigne en Pied	1754
	Lieutenant	1762
GIRARDEAU (the elder)	Enseigne en Second	1750
	Enseigne en Pied	1754
	Lieutenant	1762
DU TISNE (the elder)	Enseigne en Second	1752
	Enseigne en Pied	1754
	Lieutenant	1762

ENSIGNS "EN PIED"

Name	Titles (in French)	Date
DE ROCHE DE BEAUMONT	Officier réformé de Lancize	
	Enseigne à La Louisiane	1750
DU CLOS	Enseigne en Second	1740
	Enseigne en Pied	1754
DE COURT DE PRESLES	Enseigne en Second	1750
	Enseigne en Pied	1754
FERRAND	Enseigne en Second	1752
	Enseigne en Pied	1754
DES COUDREAUX (Renard) (Promoted to Lieutenant in September, 1759.)	Enseigne en Second	1752
	Enseigne en Pied	1754
DE BONREPOS	Page du Roy	
	Enseigne en Second	1752
	Enseigne en Pied	1754
DE BELLEISLE	Enseigne en Pied	1754
LE GROS DE LA GRANDCOUR	Enseigne en Pied	1758
DE CHATEAUBODAU	Enseigne en Pied	1758
FOUBERT (He did not come to Louisiana because he was arrested and imprisoned at Brest.)	Enseigne en Pied	1758
DE VAUCORET	Enseigne en Pied	1759

Name	Titles (in French)	Date
ENSIGNS (cont.)		
DE LANTAGNAC	Enseigne en Pied	1759
GIRARDEAU (the younger)	Enseigne en Second Enseigne en Pied	1752 1759
DE BACHEMIN	Enseigne en Second Enseigne en Pied	1752 1759
LA LANDE DALCOURT	Enseigne en Second Enseigne en Pied	1752 1759
BAUDIN	Enseigne en Second Enseigne en Pied	1752 1759
VEDRINE	Enseigne en Second Enseigne en Pied	1752 1759
DE VIN	Enseigne en Second Enseigne en Pied	1752 1759
PELLERIN	Enseigne en Second Enseigne en Pied	1752 1759
DARENSBOURG (the elder)	Enseigne en Second Enseigne en Pied	1752 1759
DU VERGEZ (the elder)	Enseigne en Second Enseigne en Pied	1752 1759
DE LAVAU	Enseigne en Second Enseigne en Pied (Captain) Chevalier de St. Louis	1752 1759 1774 1776
ROCHEBLAVE, Chevalier de (Imprisoned by order of the governor and will be released only if he returns to France.)	Enseigne en Second Enseigne en Pied	1752 1759
DE LA TOUCHE	Enseigne en Second Enseigne en Pied	1754 1759
DU VERGEZ SOUBADON	Enseigne en Second Enseigne en Pied	1754 1759
GLAPION, Chevalier de	Enseigne en Second Enseigne en Pied	1754 1759

Name	Titles (in French)	Date
ENSIGNS (cont.)		
MONGIN	Enseigne en Second Enseigne en Pied	1754 1759
DARENSBOURG (the younger)	Enseigne en Second Enseigne en Pied	1754 1759
PHILIPPE	Enseigne en Second Enseigne en Pied	1754 1759
DE VELLE	Enseigne en Second Enseigne en Pied	1754 1759
ENOULD DE LIVAUDAIS	Enseigne en Second Enseigne en Pied	1754 1759
KERNION	Enseigne en Second Enseigne en Pied	1754 1759
DU TISNE (the younger)	Enseigne en Second Enseigne en Pied	1754 1759
DE SOIZY	Enseigne en Pied	1759
BEAURANS	Enseigne en Second à l'Isle Royal Enseigne en Pied à La Louisiane	1750 1756
DE KERLEREC	Enseigne en Pied	1762
CHAUVET DUBREUIL	Enseigne en Pied	1762
DE LIGNERIS	Enseigne en Second en Canada Enseigne en Pied en Canada Enseigne en Pied à La Louisiane	1757 1760 1762
DE JUZAN	Enseigne en Second Enseigne en Pied	1752 1762
DE MOUY	Enseigne en Second Enseigne en Pied	1758 1762
DE TREMILLEC	Enseigne en Pied	1762
TIXERANT	Enseigne en Second Enseigne en Pied	1772 (sic.) 1762
ST. DENIS (the younger)	Enseigne en Second Enseigne en Pied	1752 1752

Name	Titles (in French)	Date

ENSIGNS (cont.)

| FAZENDE | Enseigne en Second | 1754 |
| | Enseigne en Pied | 1762 |

ENSIGNS "EN SECOND"

BROUTIN	Enseigne en Second	1752
VALENTIN DES ILLETS	Enseigne en Second	1762
DES ILLETS DU MANOIR	Enseigne en Second	1762
DAUTHERIVE DES VALLIERES	Cadet à l'Aiguillette	1755
	Enseign en Second	1762
DAUTHERIVE DUBUCLET	Cadet à l'Aiguillette	1755
	Enseigne en Second	1762
BROSSARD	Cadet à l'Aiguillette	1756
	Enseigne en Second	1762
DE BRÉMOND	Cadet à l'Aiguillette	1758
	Enseigne en Second	1762
DENOIS	Enseigne en Second	1762
LIGNERIS, Chevalier de	Cadet à l'Aiguillette en Canada	
	Enseigne en Second à La Louisiane	1762
DE LONGUEVAL	Enseigne en Second	1762
DE GENTILLY	Enseigne en Second	1762
MAREST DE LA TOUR	Enseigne en Second	1762
POPULUS (the elder)	Enseigne en Second	1762
TRUDEAU (the elder)	Enseigne en Second	1762
DE CHEVENNES	Enseigne en Second	1762
DUBREUIL ST. CYR	Enseigne en Second	1762
DUVERGER St. LUC	Enseigne en Second	1762
MACARTY (the elder)	Enseigne en Second	1762

Name	Titles (in French)	Date
ENSIGNS "EN SECOND" (cont.)		
DE LA GAUTRAIS	Enseigne en Second	1762
DE CIRCE (Drowned when he fell from the _Thétis_ while returning to France in June, 1770.)	Enseigne en Second	1762
VILLEBOEUVE	Enseigne en Second	1762
ACHART	Enseigne en Second	1762
DE MONTBERAULT (the elder) (Louis Augustin de Montberault. Aged 23 years in 1770.)	Cadet à l'Aguillette Enseigne en Second	1753 1762
DE MONTCHERVAUX (son)	Enseigne en Second	1762
FAGOT	Enseigne en Second	1762
DE LAURE	Enseigne en Second	1762
DUCLOS	Enseigne en Second	1762
SAUSSIER	Enseigne en Second	1762
TOULON	Cadet à l'Aguillette Enseigne en Second	1754 1762
DE BERQUEVILLE	Enseigne en Second	1762
DE VILLIERS (the elder)	Enseigne en Second	1762
POILLEVE	Enseigne en Second	1762
DESPALIERES	Enseigne en Second	1762
COULON DE VILLIERS	Enseigne en Second	1762
FAVROT	Enseigne en Second	1762
DUVERGER ST. SAUVEUR	Enseigne en Second	1762
LA LOIRE	Enseigne en Second	1762
VILLARS DUBREUIL	Enseigne en Second	1762
DUBREUIL	Cadet à l'Aguillette Enseigne en Second	1753 1762

Name	Titles (in French)	Date

ENSIGNS "EN SECOND")cont.)

| BERNAUDY | Enseigne en Second | 1762 |
| CHAUVIN | Enseigne en Second | 1762 |

CAPTAINS "REFORME"

DARENSBOURG	Capitaine réformé	1732
	Chevalier de St. Louis	1759
DE LA VERGNE	Lieutenant réformé	1738
	Capitaine réformé	1747
	Chevalier de St. Louis	1759
ST. ANGE	Capitaine réformé	1748
DE MEZIERES	Cadet à l'Aguillette	
	Expectative d'Enseigne en Second	1748
	Lieutenant réformé	1749
	Capitaine réformé	1754
	Chevalier de St. Louis	1772
MONIN DE VAUCORET	Lieutenant en Pied	1753
	Capitaine réformé	1759
	Chevalier de St. Louis	1760

LIEUTENANTS "REFORME"

DESSALLES	Lieutenant réformé chargp du détail d l'artillerie	1752
LANTAGNAC	Lieutenant réformé	1762
SARRAZIN	Lieutenant réformé	1762

OTHER OFFICERS

DE LIVAUDAIS	Capitaine de port à La Nouvelle Orléans avec brevet de Capitaine de flute du 18 Juillet	1734
	Chevalier de St. Louis	1759
FONTENELLE (Dismissed by the order of October 1, 1759. Died the same year at Havana while en route to France.)	Medecin du Roy	1748
	Coner au Conseil Superieur	1757

Name	Titles (in French)	Date

OTHER OFFICERS (cont.)

| GARDRAT | Chirurgien Major | 1754 |

| OLIVIER DE VEZIN | Grand Voyer et Arpenteur Général | 1747 |

| VALLETTE | Arpenteur | 1759 |

| LE BEAU | Medecin du Roy par Brevet du 9 Janvier
Pour la Botanic (sic.) et les recherches sur l'histoire naturelle | 1761 |

CIVIL ADMINISTRATORS
(not necessarily civilians)

| DE ROCHEMORE
(Recalled to France by order of August 1, 1759) | Commissaire général de la Marine Ordonnateur | 1757 |

| D'ABBADIE
(Died in Louisiana) | Comissaire de la Marine Commissaire général Ordonnateur à La Louisiane | 1761 |

| BOBE DESCLOZEAUX
(Retired in January, 1762, with a pension) | Commissaire de la Marine Ordonnateur | 1759 |

| FOUCAULT
(Note: Foucault carries an order of the King, dated January 1, 1762, to perform the functions of ordonnateur in Louisiana in the event that the Sieur D'Abbadie does not arrive there, or in the case that D'Abbadie should die there.) | Ecrivain de la Marine Passé à La Louisiane Controlleur | 1762 |

| DE LA GROUE
(Dead) | Ecrivain principal de la Marine faisant fonction de Controleur par order du 22 Octobre | 1758 |

| MIGNOT
(He eventually went to Guadeloupe.) | Ecrivain de la Marine Controlleur à La Louisiane order du 1 Janvier | 1762 |

Name	Titles (in French)	Date

OTHER OFFICERS (cont.)

Name	Titles (in French)	Date
BUCHET (Dead)	Ecrivain principal	
LOBINOIS (Dead)	Ecrivain principal	
CARLIER	Ecrivain ordinaire faisant fonctions de Controlleur par ordre du 20 May	1759
VILLERE	Ecrivain ordinaire	
BOBE DESCLOZEAUX (son)	Ecrivain ordinaire faisant fonctions de Controlleur à La Louisiane par order du 15 May	1765
FAZENDE	Ecrivain ordinaire	
NERMAN (Recalled by order of January 1, 1762 to serve at Rochefort.)	Ecrivain	1758

SUPERIOR COUNCIL

Name	Titles (in French)	Date
RAGUET (Dead)	Oldest member of the Council	
DE LA LANDE	Councilor, January 10,	1762
KERNION	Councilor, January 10,	1762
LA FRESNIERE	Councilor, January 1,	1762
FONTENETTE	Medecin du Roy, Councilor	
CHANTALOU	Greffier du Conseil	
PIOT DE LAUNAY	Councilor, January 10,	1762
GARIC	Greffier du Conseil Supérieur January 10,	1762
LE SASSIER	Conseiller au Port-au-Prince, assesseur	

MARCH 6, 1730

LIST OF OFFICERS TO SERVE IN LOUISI-
ANA ALONG WITH THE DATE OF THEIR
COMMISSION.

CAPTAINS

GAUVRIT	Mar. 12, 1716	MARCHAND DE COURCELLES	March 23, 1720
DU TISNE	Feb. 11, 1719	PRADEL	March 23, 1720
DARTAGUIETTE	Feb. 11, 1719	RENAULT D'HAUTRIVE	March 23, 1720
MERVEILLEUX	Jan. 4, 1720	LUSSER	Dec. 1, 1728

LIEUTENANTS

MONTMARQUET	July 1, 1719	PETIT DE LEVILLIERS	Nov. 4, 1720
BASSEE	July 1, 1719	DE MOUY	Dec. 12, 1722
VILLAINVILLE	Jan. 2, 1720	LA BOULAYE	March 6, 1730
COUSTILHAS	Aug. 30, 1720	BENOIST	March 6, 1730

SUB-LIEUTENANTS

MAILLARD	Mar. 20, 1720	MARETZ DUPUY	Mar. 6, 1730
TERISSE	Oct. 30, 1720	MARETZ DE LA TOUR	Mar. 6, 1730
SIMAR DE BELLISLE	Sept. 5, 1721	DUPUY PLANCHARD	Mar. 6, 1730
REGIS DE ROULLET	Mar. 6, 1730	GIRARDEAU	Mar. 6, 1730

ENSIGNS

DU TERPUY VER-CHIER	Oct. 30, 1720	DESROCHES	Commission
STE THERESE DE LANGLOISIERE	May 19, 1722	DAQUIN	dates are
ST. ANGE (son)	Dec. 19, 1722	CHAMBELLAN GRATON	not given.
DU TISNE	Sept. 24, 1723	BESSAN	

HALF-PAY OFFICERS

CAPTAINS

BROUTIN	Mar. 21, 1720	(He receives no salary.)

LIEUTENANTS

JANTZEN	Jan. 9, 1721	ST. JULIEN	Mar. 21, 1720
ST. ANGE (père)	Dec. 19, 1722	MONDRELOIS	Oct. 17, 1727
DE VINCENNES	Dec. 19, 1722	JUZAN	Mar. 6, 1730
DU VERGER	May 27, 1724	LIRON	Mar. 6, 1730
DEVIN	May 27, 1724	LA BUISSONNIERE	Mar. 6, 1730

ENSIGN

BONNILLE	Dec. 1, 1728

APRIL 1, 1730

LIST OF OFFICERS IN LOUISIANA AND
THEIR ASSIGNMENTS

Name	Assigned to
PERIER, Governor	New Orleans
DIRON, Lieutenant of the King	Mobile
LOUBOEY, Major	New Orleans
ST. DENIS, Commander	Natchitoches
BEAUCHAMP, Major	Mobile
CAPTAINS	
GAUVRIT	New Orleans
DU TISNE	Illinois
DARTAGUIETTE	New Orleans
MERVEILLEUX	Mobile
DES LIETTES (Died April 8, 1729)	Illinois
PRADEL	New Orleans
MARCHAND DE COURCELLES	Alibamons
RENAULT D'HAUTERIVE	New Orleans
LIEUTENANTS	
MONTMARQUE	Alibamons
BASSEE	Mobile
VILLAINVILLE	New Orleans
DE CAUDER (killed by the Indians at Natchez, November 28, 1729)	Yazoo
COUSTILHAS	New Orleans
PETIT DE LIVILLIERS	New Orleans
DE MOUY	New Orleans
SUB-LIEUTENANTS	
BENOIST	Mobile
LA BOULAYE	New Orleans
MAILLARD	Natchitoches
TERISSE	Illinois
SIMARE DE BELLISLE	New Orleans
MACE (killed by the Indians at Natchez, November 28, 1729)	Natchez
FRANCHOMME (killed by the Indians, July, 1728)	Illinois
ENSIGNS	
REGIS DU ROULET	Mobile
MARETZ DUPUY	New Orleans
MARETZ DE LA TOUR	New Orleans
DUTERPUY VERCHIER	Mobile
GIRARDEAU	Illinois
STE. THERESE DE LANGLOISIERE	New Orleans
ST. ANGE (son)	Illinois
DU TISNE (son)	Balize

Name	Assigned to

SUPERNUMERARY OFFICERS

CAPTAINS
DECHEPARRE (killed at Natchez, Nov. 28,
        1729)   Natchez
LUSSER   Mobile

HALF-PAY OFFICERS

CAPTAINS
BROUTIN   New Orleans
ST. JULIEN, Chevalier de   - - - - -

LIEUTENANTS
DUMONT DE MONTIGNY   (resigned)
JANTZEN   Natchitoches
ST. ANGE (father)   Illinois
DE VINCENNES   Wabash
DUVERGES   Balize
DEVINS   Mobile
DE MONDRELOIS   New Orleans

ENSIGNS
DES ROCHES (killed in the Natchez massacre) Yazoo
DAQUIN   Mobile
DUBOIS   killed by Indians in the spring
        of 1728)   Illinois
CHAMBELLAN GRATON   New Orleans
DES NOYERS (killed during the Natchez
        massacre)   Natchez
BESSAN   New Orleans
BONNILLES   Mobile

1731

LIST OF OFFICERS STATIONED IN LOUISIANA

Name	Comments
LOUBOEY, Chevalier de	Lieutenant of the King at New Orleans
CRENAY, Baron de	Lieutenant of the King at Mobile
DARTAGUETTE	Major at New Orleans
BEAUCHAMP	Major at Mobile
BESSAN	Aide-major at New Orleans
ST. DENIS	Commander at Natchitoches
ST. ANGE (father)	Half-pay Lieutenant and Commander at the Illinois post.
VINCENNES	Half-pay Lieutenant and Commander at the Wabash post.

CAPTAINS

GAUVRIT	At Balize
PRADEL	At Natchez
MARCHAND DE COURCELLES	At Mobile
RENAULT D'HAUTERIVES	- - - - -
NOYAN, Chevalier de	At New Orleans
LUSSER	At Mobile
ST. JULLIEN, Chevalier de	At New Orleans

LIEUTENANTS

MONTMARQUES	At the Alibamons
BASSE	At Mobile
COUSTILLAS	At New Orleans
PETIT DE LIVILLIERS	At New Orleans
BENOIS	At Mobile
MAILLARD	At the Illinois post
JANTZEN	At Natchitoches

SUB-LIEUTENANTS

TERISSE DE VUSSAN	At the Illinois post
SIMARE DE BELLEISLE	AT New Orleans
REGIS DU ROULET	At the Choctaw post
MARIN DE LA TOUR	At New Orleans
MARIN DUPUY	At New Orleans
DUPUY PLANCHARD	At Balize
DUTERPUY VERCHIER	At Mobile

ENSIGNS

STE. THEREZE DE LANGLOISERE	At New Orleans
ST. ANGE (son)	At the Illinois post
DU TISNE	At the Illinois post
CHAMBELLON GRATON	At the Choctaw post
BONNILLE	At Mobile
GRANDPRE	At New Orleans
D'HERNEVILLE, Chevalier	At Natchez

Name	Comments

HALF-PAY OFFICERS

DARENSBOURG	Captain at the German villages.
MOUDRELOIS	Lieutenant at New Orleans
JUZAN	At the Tunica post
LA BUISSONNIERE	At Natchez

OFFICERS WITHOUT COMMISSION

| COULANGE | At the Arkansas post |
| ISET | At Natchez |

JANUARY 19, 1724

LIST OF SOLDIERS FROM PLANTIN'S COM-
PANY FORMING A DETACHMENT TO GO TO
LOUISIANA ON THE SHIP PROFOND

Name	Age	Comments
BELHOTE, Charles	25	Called LA LUNE. Son of Thomas and Charlotte TERRIER. Native of St. Brieux in Brittany. Metal worker.
ROGUIE, Charles	30	Called DEVERTU. Native of Dévertu in Champagne, Electorate of Challon. Carpenter.
GODARD, Martin	21	Called FORGERON. Native of Sarcelle, near Paris. Edged-tool maker.
CORNU, Pierre Aubert	21	Called ARTOIS. Son of Claude CORNU and Marie Agnesse. Carpenter.
PENOT, Pierre	20	Called TAILLANDIER. Native of Fontainebleau. Edged-tool maker.
PELTIER, Antoine	16	Called BATAILLE. Native of Paris, parish of St. Nicolas des Champs. Carpenter.
LEGER, Jacques Denis	23	Called ST. LEGER. Native of Paris, parish of St. Sulpice. Carpenter.
LARQUET, Joseph	17	Called LA JAUGE. Native of Reims in Champagne. Carpenter.
PLEYARD, Antoine	21	Called LA PATIENCE. Native of Sens in Burgundy. Carpenter.
FAURE, François	18	Called PONTARLIER. Native of Baligne in Franche-Comté, Electorate of Pontarlier. Carpenter

MARCH 27, 1724

LIST OF FIFTEEN SOLDIERS OF PLANTIN'S
COMPANY WHO EMBARKED ON THE BALINE AT
LORIENT FOR SERVICE IN LOUISIANA.

Name	Age	Comments
HORAUX, Maturin	21	Called LA BONTE. Native of Ingrande in Anjou. Metal worker.
DUHAMEL, Marcelin	25	Called LA POMPE. Native of Paris, parish of St. Louis. Block-maker
DESGRANGES, Jean Bapte	25	Called ST. SULPICE. Native of Paris, parish of St. Sulpice. Carpenter.
LA CHAMPAGNE, François	27	Called VANDOEUVRE. Native of Vandoeuvre in Champagne. Metal worker and gunsmith
DRIGNY, Antoine	18	Called COMMERCY. Native of Commercy in Lorraine. Cutler.
D'ARGENT, Pierre	17	Called DARGENT. Native of Commercy in Lorraine. Cutler.
DESVILLES, Estienne	18	Called VERSAILLES. Native of Versailles. Wagon-maker.
GARDE, Jean	20	Called LYONNAIS. Boat builder.
GIRARD, Joseph	18	Called GIRARD. Native of Paris, parish of St. Sulpice. Metal worker.
HULCE, Vilhem	31	Called L'ALLEMAND. Native of Quemis-lande in Franconia. House builder.
PIPIN, Thomas	25	Called BONNEFOY. Native of St. Quintin in Picardy. Metal worker.
LAMBERT, Claude	15	Called ST. LAMBERT. Native of Paris, parish of St. Eustache. Carpenter.
CHEVERY, Laurent	20	Called VITRY. Native of Vitry le François. Metal worker.
LA CROIX, Claude	17	Called LA CROIX. Native of Paris. Wheelwright.
AUBRY, Jean	19	Called ST. SEVERIN. Native of Paris, parish of St. Severin. Carpenter.

AUGUST 25, 1725

LIST OF TWENTY SOLDIER-WORKERS FROM
PLANTIN'S COMPANY WHO EMBARKED ON THE
BALEINE, AUGUST 14, 1725, BOUND FOR
LOUISIANA FROM LORIENT.

Name	Age	Comments
LOISEL, Gilles	17	Called LOISEL. Native of St. Pierre de Pleguen, Bishopric of Dol. Rope-maker. Engagé, January 11, 1722.
CHASSIGNON, Pierre Louis	18	Called ST. FELIX. Native of Paris, parish of St. Remy. Founder. Engagé, February 14, 1722.
POULIGUEN, Yves	26	Called BOISDANGER. Native of the parish of Mordel, Bishopic of Remis in Brittany. Farmer. Engagé, July 16, 1724.
BOURGEOIS, Pierre	20	Called LA RIVIERE. Native of Paris, parish of St. Nicolas des Champs. Harness-maker. Engagé, December 9, 1724.
LAMBERT, Claude	17	Called DAUPHINE. Native of Grenoble in Dauphiné. Shoemaker. Engagé, November 9, 1724
GOUFFIER, Jacques	28	Called GOUFFIER. Native of St. Germain in Laye. Mason and carpenter. Engagé, November 18, 1724.
MENUET, Jullien	23	Called MENUET. Native of Guemené Ponefau, Bishopric of Nantes. Cooper. Engagé, December 5, 1724.
LE CLERC, Nicolas	25	Called TROUJOLY. Native of St. Germain in Laye. Cooper. Engagé, December 20, 1724.
RYAU, François	25	Called LA BRULURE. Native of the parish of St. Salomon de Vannes in Brittany. Rope-maker. Engagé, January 16, 1725.

Name	Age	Comments
BAUGE, Augustin	18	Called LA LIME. Native of Joigny in Burgundy. Metal worker. Engagé, January 27, 1725.
MAGRET, Michel	21	Called L'AMOUREUX. Native of Nantes in Brittany. House builder. Engagé, January 27, 1725.
ETIENNE, Jean	25	Called ROCANCOURT. Native of the parish of Carnot, Bishopric of Quimper in Brittany. Carpenter. Engagé, January 27, 1725.
THEBAUT, Jean	26	Called VA DE BON COEUR. Native of the parish of St. Gilles, Bishopric of Remes in Brittany. Ship-builder. Engagé, March 12, 1725.
DURAND, François	25	Called FRAPE DABORD. Native of Poitier, parish of St. Savin. Tailor. Engagé, January 27, 1725.
BASSET, Nicolas	31	Called BONTEMPS. Native of Conty Le Chateau in Picardy. Tailor. Engagé, December 9, 1724.
BORDERY, Marc	17	Called ST. SULPICE. Native of Paris, parish of St. Sulpice. Ribbon-maker. Engagé, December 3, 1724.
BRANCOURT, Joseph	27	Called STRASBOURG. Native of Strasbourg. Mason. Engagé, January 27, 1725.
DURANT, Denis	26	Called ST. ROMAIN. Native of Sevrès, near Paris. Cooper. Engagé, January 27, 1725.
LE GOFFE, Yvon	20	Called QUIMPER THE YOUNGER. Native of the parish of St. Mathew, Bishopric of Quimper in Brittany. Mason. Engagé, March 20, 1725.
ASSELINE, Pierre	18	Called ROCHEFORT THE YOUNGER. Native of Rochefort. Stonecutter. Engagé, January 27, 1725.

MAY 22, 1727

LIST OF SOLDIERS FROM PLANTIN'S COM-
PANY WHO EMBARKED ON THE <u>DROMADAIRE</u>
FOR SERVICE IN LOUISIANA.

Name	Age	Comments
DAVID, Daniel	37	Called LA DOUCEUR. Native of Cork in Ireland. Tailor. <u>Engagé</u>, June 6, 1726. His wife is with him.
TRAVERS, Jean	36	Called BRUNEAU. Native of the parish of Beton, diocese of Mans, province of Perche. <u>Engagé</u>, April 25, 1726.
LE GALLIOU, Marc	18	Called L'ENCLUME. Son of Jean LE GALLIOU. Native of the parish of Languidic, diocese of Vannes in Brittan <u>Engagé</u>, August 6, 1726. Nail-maker.
BREHELIN, Jean	20	Called LA VIOLETTE. Son of Pierre BREHELIN. Native of Lorient, parish of St. Louis in Brittany. <u>Engagé</u>, October 14, 1726. Ship-builder.
LOR, Henry	30	Called QUENUAN. Native of the parish of Cleguerec, diocese of Vannes in Brittany. <u>Engagé</u>, October 14, 1726. Carpenter.
LE GUENE, Jean Baptiste	19 1/2	Called ST. JEAN. Son of Jean LE GUENE. Native of the parish of St. Gilles à Humebond, diocese of Vannes in Brittany, <u>Engagé</u>, December 2, 1726. House-builder.
BOUGILLAUD, Claude Joseph	33	Called BRISETOUT, Son of Jean BOUGILLAUD. Native of Ran in Franche Comté. <u>Engagé</u>, January 12, 1727. Nail-maker. His wife is with him.
DUBAUX, Pierre	20	Called MENDON. Son of Grégoire DUBAUX. Native of the Parish of Paul, diocese of Vannes in Brittany. <u>Engagé</u>, January 22, 1727.
CHANDELLIER, Sebastien	18	Called CHATEAULIN. Son of Pierre CHANDELLIER. Native of Chateaulin, diocese of Quimper in Brittany. <u>Engagé</u>, February 1, 1727. Nail-maker and metal worker.
LE BRETON, Claude	22	Called SANS SOUSSY. Son of Joseph LE BRETON. Native of Ville de Fahouet, diocese of Quimper in Brittany. <u>Engagé</u>, March 4, 1727. Nail-maker.

AUGUST 17, 1727

LIST OF SOLDIERS FROM PLANTIN'S COMPANY
WHO ARE BEING SENT TO LOUISIANA ON THE
SHIP DEUX FRERES WHICH DEPARTED FROM
LORIENT.

Name	Age	Comments
GUILLOTEL, Gilles	31	Called LA CHENAYE. Native of the parish of Guere, diocese of St. Malo in Brittany. Engagé, August 21, 1726.
MOISAN, Vincent	21	Called ST. VINCENT. Native of Josselin, diocese of St. Malo in Brittany. Engagé, March 31, 1727.
DAUPHIN, Estienne	19	Called ST. SAUVEUR. Native of Paris, parish of St. Gervais. Engagé, May 3, 1727.
HUET, Pierre	18	Called LA PALME. Native of Josselin, diocese of St. Malo in Brittany. Engagé, May 12, 1727.
LE GUEGUN, Jean	23	Called LA TIMBALE. Native of the parish of Lamezelec, diocese of Leon in Brittany. Engagé, June 18, 1727.
LE LARGE, Joseph	17	Called L'ENCLUME. Native of Nantes, parish of St. Saubin, in Brittany. Engagé, June 22, 1727.
BREJON, Pierre Jean François	23	Called LA POUSSIERE. Native of Dal in Flanders. Engagé, June 27, 1727.
DURAND, Pierre François	24	Called DURAND. Native of Rouen in Normandy. Engagé, July 11, 1727.

AUGUST 27, 1728

LIST OF CADETS AND SOLDIERS FROM PLANTIN'S
COMPANY WHO ARE EMBARKED ON THE BALEINE
BOUND FOR LOUISIANA FROM LORIENT.

Name	Age	Comments
CADETS		
FAVROT, Sieur	--	--
POPULUS DE ST. PROTAIS, Sieur	--	--
SOLDIERS		
CAUE, François	27	No particular profession. Engagé February 4, 1728. Native of Calais.
MIGUET, Jullien	27	Called ST. JULLIEN. Native of the parish of Plevigner, diocese of Vannes in Brittany. Sawyer. Engagé, December 16, 1727.
IYGROME (?), Guillaume	24	Called IYGROME (?). Native of the parish of Lotady, diocese of Quimper in Brittany. Aged 24 years. Sawyer. Engagé, December 22, 1727.
IYGROME (?), Jean	18	Called PONT LABE. Native of the parish of Lotady, diocese of Quimper in Brittany. Farmer. Engagé, December 22, 1727.

JUNE 9, 1728

LIST OF SOLDIERS FROM PLANTIN'S COM-
PANY WHO EMBARKED ON THE <u>AURORE</u>
BOUND FOR LOUISIANA FROM LORIENT.

Name	Age	Comments
PAJOT, Jean	30	Called PAJOT. Native of the parish of Dattée in the Province of Anjou. Without profession. <u>Engagé</u>, May 19, 1728.
GOSSE, Antoine Mathias	16	Called GOSSE. Native of Paris, parish of St. Mery. Without profession. <u>Engagé</u>, June 1, 1728.

JULY 12, 1728

LIST OF SOLDIERS FROM PLANTIN'S COM-
PANY WHO EMBARKED ON THE PRINCE DE
CONTY BOUND FOR LOUISIANA FROM LORIENT.

Name	Age	Comments
GATBOIS, Jean	27	Called FRANCOEUR. Native of Vitrě, parish of Notre Dame, diocese of Rennes en Brittany. Carpenter and Sawyer. Engagé, February 11, 1727.
TANGUY, Yves	25	Called LA DOUCEUR. Native of Pimpon, diocese of St. Malo en Brittany. Nail-maker. Engagé, July 16, 1727.
LE MEUR, Yves	18	Called D'ALBERT. Native of the parish of Fahouet, diocese of Quimper in Brittany. Cooper. Engagé, December 2, 1727.
PANICQ, Pierre	18	Called LA RUINE. Native of the parish of Langrudic, diocese of Vannes in Brittany. Farmer. Engagé, November, 17, 1727.
BELEGUEUX, Pierre	23	Called LA PITTIEE. Native of the parish of Carnat, diocese of Vannes in Brittany. Farmer Engagé, February 27, 1728.
PRIOU, Denis	18	Called ST. PRIX. Native of Reddon, diocese of Vannes in Brittany. Nail-maker. Engagé, April 14, 1728.

AUGUST 23, 1728

LIST OF SOLDIERS FROM PLANTIN'S COM-
PANY WHO EMBARKED ON THE DROMADAIRE
BOUND FOR LOUISIANA FROM LORIENT.

Name	Age	Comments
RYAU, Jean	50	Called SANS CRAINTE. Native of the parish of Plaudrin, diocese of Vannes in Brittany. Nail-maker. Engagé, August 29, 1726.
RODE, Jacques	20	Called ST. CREPIN. Native of the town of Heimebond, parish of St. Gilles, diocese of Vannes in Brittany. Shoemaker. Engagé, March 18, 1728.
TANGUY, Alain	25	Called LA FORME. Native of the parish of Riecq, diocese of Quimper in Brittany. Shoemaker. Engagé, June 23, 1728.
LOZET, Jean	18	Called CARHAYS. Native of the parish of Paul, diocese of Quimper in Brittany. Farmer. Engagé, June 23, 1728.
LOBJOY, Jean	28	Called BELLAIR. Native of Luçon in Poitou. Edged-tool maker. His wife is with him. Engagé, July 10, 1728.
CUISY, Remy Rolland	28	Called ENTRENGOUST. Native of Paris, parish of St. Jacques de la Boucherie. Engagé, July 11, 1728
JOLY, Pierre	19	Called BOURGUIGNON. Native of La Ville de Sure in Burgundy. Mason. Engagé, July 21, 1728
VIMONT, Pierre	18	Called LA GIROFLEE. Native of Lambale, diocese of St. Brieuc in Brittany. Tailor. Engagé, July 23, 1728.
AUDIONNE, François	24	Called LA NOE. Native of the parish of St. Lauveux, diocese of Dol in Brittany. Mason. Engagé, July 26, 1728.
TOURRE, Pierre	23	Called BELLEGARDE. Native of Maussa in Languedoc. Weaver. Engagé, August 7, 1728.

NOVEMBER 26, 1728

LIST OF SOLDIERS FROM PLANTIN'S COM-
PANY EMBARKED ON THE <u>DUC DE NOAILLES</u>
BOUND FOR LOUISIANA FROM LORIENT.

Name	Age	Comments
BAUDET, Yves		Called SANS CRAINTE. Carpenter
ACRAL, Thomas		Called LANDIVISIAU. Carpenter
PAULET, Jean		Called LA PALME. Gunsmith.
LE BRUN, François		Called NANTOIS. Carpenter
POULIQUAIN, Jacques		Called LA GIROFFLE. Nail-maker
DE BRAY, Jean		Called L'ARDOISE. Tiler
SABATTIER, Philipes		Called ST. MEDARD. Tiler
STEPHANT, François		Called MAILLET. Caulker.
LAUNAY, Charles de		Called ST. SULPICE. Glazer.
ROCHETON, Pierre		Called LANGEVIN. Turner
CHEVERT, Guillaume		Called FRESNE. Carpenter
LE DUC, Joseph		Called LA PARADE. Farmer.
DAGE, Pierre Joseph		Called ST. ELLOY. Cooper
PENIN, Theodor		Called LA VIOLETTE. Tailor

MARCH 17, 1729

LIST OF SOLDIERS FROM PLANTIN'S COM-
PANY WHO ARE EMBARKED ON THE <u>DURANCE</u>
BOUND FOR LOUISIANA FROM LORIENT.

Name	Comments
OFFRET, Pierre	Called LA PLACE. Nail-maker.
LA HAYE, René	Called LA LIME. Metal worker.
JUQUIOLE, Charles	Called LA GRANGE. No profession.
DOUCET, Sebastien	Called ST. MARTIN. Edged-tool maker.
BRAY, Jacques	Called LA FORGE. Marshal
STEPHANICQ, Henry	Called LA HARDRESSE. House builder.
BRISSARD, Germain	Called LA VIGNE. Silk worker.
VILLEMERRY, Alexandre de	Called VILLEMERRY. Carpenter.
AIGNES, Pierre Antoine	Called LA PALUT. Sawyer.
LE FEVRE, Jean	Called DU TERTRE. Tiler.
BONIN, Alexandre	Called NAMURE. No profession.
THIEVION, Jean	Called CHALON. No Profession.
ST. GILLES, Jacques Chas.	Called BONTEMS. Messanger
BERNARD, Jean	Called LA VIRDURE. Tiler
LE GLOAHECQ	Called LOCOALE. Tailor
RYAU, Julien	Called L'ENCLUME. Founder
BENARD, Joseph	Called DESMARETS. Tapestry maker.
LAURENT, Nicolas	Called LAURIN. Miller
ANNICQ, François	Called BELHUMEUR. Ribbon-maker.
LAINE, Vincent	Called MILLY. Tanner.

AUGUST 10, 1729

LIST OF SOLDIERS FROM PLANTIN'S COM-
PANY WHO ARE EMBARKED ON THE ALEXANDRE
BOUND FOR LOUISIANA FROM LORIENT

Name	Comments

CORPORAL

DIREY, Jean	Called PROMPT

SOLDIERS

Name	Comments
DU CODERC, Sieur Laurens	A cadet.
LE MOILE, Prigent	Called DUBOIS
JEAN, Jean Baptiste	Called MONACAU
TRISTANT, Jean	Called ST. LOUIS
BOURNAY, François	Called DUVAL
DUPONT, Jullien	Called DUPONT
MORAU, Nicolas	Called LANGEVIN
L'ORPHEVRE, René	Called DESLAURIERS
BAUGUYON, ?	Called VA DE BON COEUR
GALARD, Jullien	Called LA MUZE
ROBE, Guillaume	Called LA CROIX
LE FERE, Jean	Called ST. JEAN
BIXAUX, Jullien François	Called BIDAUX
BLONDEL, Jean	Called LA FORME
TROHOT, Maurice	Called BEAUSEJOUR
MAZE, François	Called JOLYCOEUR
LE GALAU, Jullien	Called LA HOUSSAYE
LE LICURECHE, Yves	Called BEAULIEUX

Name	Comments
TRAVERS, Thomas	Called TRAVERS
FERRON, Jean	Called L'EPINE
BOULAY, Mathurin	Called LA BOULAYE
LE FEVRE, Paderne	Called LA CHENAYE
GUYCHARD, Joseph	Called GUYCHARD
BLOUIN, Pierre	Called CHEVALLIER

OCTOBER 17, 1729

LIST OF SOLDIERS FROM PLANTIN'S COM-
PANY WHO ARE EMBARKED ON THE BALEINE
BOUND FOR LOUISIANA FROM LORIENT.

Name	Comments
SARGEANT	
LA BOUCHARDIERE, Jean Baptiste	Called LA BOUCHARDIERE
BODEREL, René Laurens	Called BODEREL
GOUVELLO, Jean	Called Baron
BODEREL, Jacques Laurens	Called DU ROCHER
BOULANGER, Louis Roch	Called SANLIS
BONBLED, François	Called TOURANGEAU
GORDRIN, Honnoré	Called LA GRENADE
JARNO, François	Called JARNO
LA ROCHE, Pierre	Called LA ROCHE
PAPY, André	Called LANGUDOC
KHALLIC, Toussaint de	Called KHALLIC
KHALLIC, Yves de	Called DU KGOUET
TANGUY, Jean	Called LA TOURMENTE
PIRE, Antoine	Called LA BATTERIE
BAHUOT, Pierre	Called L'ESPERENÇE
CRUCHERON, Paul	Called ST. ANTOINE
LA VALLE, Jean Etienne	Called LA VALLE

JULY 3, 1730

LIST OF SOLDIERS FROM PLANTIN'S COM-
PANY WHO ARE EMBARKED ON THE VENUS
BOUND FOR LOUISIANA FROM LORIENT

Name	Comments
SARGEANTS	
BORDEMONT, Louis	Called DES LORIERS
CLERMONT, Antoine	Called ST. ANTOINE
CORPORALS	
REGUISTON, Antoine	Called LA RAMEE
BEZIAC, Antoine	Called LAURAGUE
DRUMMER	
VILARS, Michel	Called VILARS
TROOPS	
MELON (MELOU?), Michel	Called LA SONDE. Surgeon
ROUGET, Etienne	Called BELHUMEUR. Printer
VERNAY, Jacques	Called SANS SOUCY
PEPIN, François	Called LA LIBERTE
GUILLOT, Jean	Called LA ROZE. Mason
ELLAY, François	Called ST. FRANCOIS. Mason
BABIN, René	Called LA FLAME. Marshal
BUFET, François	Called CHAMPAGNE. Marshal
BESSE, Jean	Called ORIGNAC. Sawyer.
GRUYER, Jean	Called LA ROZE. Sawyer
PERAUD, François	Called ST. MICHEL
AUSNY, Jean Baptiste	Called VAT DE BON COEUR
DU ROZAT, Pierre	Called BLONDIN. Gardener
TISSIER, Charles	Called JOLLY COEUR. Gardener
FLAMAND, Jean	Called MAURICE. Gardener
CROQUY (CROGUY?), Louis	Called LA BEAUSSE. Gardener
MEUNIER, François	Called LA PIERRE. Linen worker.
VACQUERY, Jean	Called CARIGNAN. Linen worker.
MARCHAND, François	Called ST. FRANCOIS. Linen worker.
BEAUGARD, Charles Joseph	Called ST. CHARLES. Linen worker
FOURNIER, François	Called BELLEROZE. Linen worker.
PERONNY, Jacques	Called BLONDIN. Saddler
LE MALE, Jean	Called LA JEUNESSE. Saddler
MOTET, Etienne	Called LA PENSEE. Saddler
ROBERT, François	Called LA DOUCEUR. Saddler
HOLL, Nicolas Pierre	Called LA SONDE. Surgeon
PUGET, Jean	Called ST. JEAN. Shoemaker
MONTEVARY, Jean	Called TOUSSAINT. Shoemaker

Name	Comments
ALARIS, Jean	Called SANS FACON. Gardener
CABRIE, Pierre	Called MONTLEMARD. Silk worker
BOET, Nicolas	Called BELLEGARDE. Silk worker
ROMAIN, Antoine	Called ROMAIN
GRAU, Jean Baptiste	Called LA TENDRESSE
LE ROUX, Antoine	Called SANS SOUCY
PARIER, Paul	Called LA PRAIRIE
PLEAU, René	Called BELLEROZE. Farmer
GALE, Etienne	Called COMDE. Cook
LOTH, Jean	Called POITEVIN. Cook
MASSEROLLES, Jean	Called ETIENNE. Cook
CHANTAL, François	Called FRANCOIS. Tailor
SIET, Jean	Called LA JEUNESSE. Weaver
FRANCIS, Gilles	Called JOLLYBOIS, Weaver
DREANEAU, Yves	Called VILLAGAUTIER. Weaver
LARDIN, Pierre	Called MONTREUIL. Carpenter
CANTET, Pierre	Called LA ROCHELLE. Tailor
MAUBU, André	Called MAUBU. Tailor
SIMON, Louis Alexis	Called DOUVILLE. Tailor

Nine wives and eleven children are with the above-listed soldiers.

SEPTEMBER 5, 1730

LIST OF SOLDIERS FROM PLANTIN'S COM-
PANY EMBARKED ON THE AURORE BOUND
FOR LOUISIANA FROM LORIENT

Name	Comments
SARGEANTS	
CHELAYE, Jacques	Called JACOB
BARACHE, Pierre	Called BELHUMEUR
COLAS, Jean	Called GRANDVILLE
CORPORALS	
ROMBLAY, Claude	Called CHATEAUGONTIER
VAUTIER, Louis	Called LA MONTAGNE
LE COMTE, Jean	Called LE COMTE
TROOPS	
DU NAU, Etienne	Called DESCOUDRAY
AYGMORTE, François	Called ST. FRANCOIS
FOURNIER, Jean	Called FOURNIER
RAMONT, Claude	Called SANS QUARTIER
GOBEROILLE, Jean Baptiste	Called SANS SOUSSY
URGENOUX, Alain	Called LA JEUNESSE
PICARD, Pierre	Called JEAN DE PARIS
CANDELON, Rémont	Called BELLEROZE
DUC, Joseph	Called VILLEFRANCHE
L'ALEMAND, Augustin	Called VAT DE BON COEUR
DUVAL, Joseph	Called LE BRETON
GIBERT, Antoine	Called LA MONTAGNE
RICOUS, Jean	Called LANGUEDOC
LAMOUREUX, René	Called LA FORTUNE
BERLAN, Jean	Called ST. JEAN
GIRAUTON, Joseph	Called STE. CICILE
DE FASSY, Claude	Called CORNEILLE
GUILLAUME, Jean	Called LANGUEDOC
HERY, Claude	Called LA TOURMONTE
DU MUY, Jean	Called FRANCOEUR
CHAUVIN, Pierre	Called FLEUR D'EPINE
LE DEUIL, Estienne	Called LA FLEUR
BERE, Pierre	Called BELLEFIN
TASSE, Pierre	Called MARCHE A TERRE
QUATRESOLS, Antoine	Called BRISETOUT
GRIGNON, François	Called BELLE ETOILLE
GUIBERT, Pierre	Called SANS RANCUNE
VERCE, Prudent	Called JEAN BAPTISTE

Name	Comments
GOUPILLE, Pierre	Called ST. ANGE
DE LA NOE, Jullien	Called ST. JULLIEN
HEMON, Jean	Called BRINDAMOUR
MANNIERE, Antoine	Called LA BASTILLE
GRATIA, Joseph	Called CASTILLE
CHEVALIER, Jacques	Called STE. MARIE
MARYON, Jean Baptiste	Called RICHEVILLE
CHAUVIN, Antoine	Called ANTOINE
DROUIN, Nicolas	Called PORTEMAY
HERVE, François	Called HERVE

DECEMBER 2, 1731

LIST OF THOSE PERSONS COMPRISING THE
FOUR COMPANIES STATIONED AT NEW ORLEANS

Name	Comments
GAUVRIT'S COMPANY	
D'ARENSBOURG	Half-pay Captain. Present
MONDRELOIS	Half-pay Lieutenant. Present
JUZAN	Half-pay Lieutenant. Present
STE. THEREZE DE LANGLOISIERE	Ensign. Present
Sargeants	
ROBERT, Jacques	
LE VASSEUR, Etienne	Called BARCELONNE
GILLET, Jacques	
Corporals	
BEAT	Called LAVERGNE
LEBERCHER, François	
LE COMTE, Jean	
Drummer	
FREDERIC	Called LA FONTAINE
Soldiers	
DESTHUILLETTES, Vauparis	Cadet
DUCODERE, Laurent	Cadet
GUERIN	Cadet
PROMPT A BOIRE	
LEMAIRE, Jacques	
pinet, Jean	
BAUDET, Yves	Called SANS CRAINTE
GUYOT	Called LA PENSEE
BRAY	Called LA FORGE
GOUVELLE	Called BARON
BAUDEREL, Laurent	
DAMIENS	Called LA GUERRE
BOISSIERE	Called DUFRESNE
ROBLOT	Called ST. AUBIN
BABIN	Called LA FLAME
MEUNIER	Called LA PIERRE
VACQUERIE	Called CARIGNAN
VIGNERON	Called LA VIOLETTE
TASSE	Called MARCHEATERRE
DEYMAR, Thomas	
DEMAU	Called DESCOUDRAIS
LE CAMU, Antoine	
LERY	Called LA TOURMENTE
JACOB	

Name	Comments

DARTAGUIETTE's COMPANY

DE NOYAN	Captain. Present
MAREST DE LA TOUR	Sub-Lieutenant. Present
DU TISNE	Ensign. Present

Sargeants
BARBIER	Called FRANCOEUR
BORDEMON	Called DESLAURIERS

Drummer
COUSSOT, Simon

Soldiers
FAVROT	Cadet
RICHEVILLE	Cadet
LE PRINCE	Cadet
POMEL	Called ST. OMER
GIRARD	Called FAIOL
GIGON	Called DUBOURG
MERAND	Called ST. PIERRE
LEVEL	Called BELLEROSE
BORRE	Called BRISE BATAILLE
RODE	Called ST. CRESPIN
ST. PELLE	
BERNARD	Called LAVERDURE
LA FONTAINE	Called BELLEFLEUR
KHALLIC	
BOTH	CALLED MONTAUBON
PIERRE	Called LARASNE
VICDEBEC	Called SARLOUIS
MECHINET	Called DUBREUIL
BOURMAUX	Called PARISIEN
STEIBRE, François	Called - - - -
FLAMAND	Called MAURICE
CHAMPAGNE	Called MELIQUE
CUCU	Called LA FRANCE
LOISEAU	
VILLEGAUTIER	
HERVE	

PRADEL'S COMPANY
PRADEL	Captain. Present
PETIT DE LIVELLIERS	Lieutenant. Present
SIMART DE BELLEISLE	Sub-Lieutenant. Present

Sargeants
DARNAULT	
LANCIEN	Called DE ROUEN

Name	Comments

PRADEL'S COMPANY (cont.)

Corporals
METTAY — Called LARIVIERE
CIVADE — Called LA JEUNESSE
REGUISTON — Called LARAME

Drummer
RICOU — Called LANGUEDOC

Soldiers
SERARD — Cadet
MACE — Cadet
FRETEL — Called PICQUARD
BRANCOURT — Called STRASBOURG
BENOIST, Claude
GOSSE, Mathias
RIAU — Called SANS CRAINTE
THIERION — Called CHALONS
LORFEVRE — Called DESLAURIERS
TROHOT — Called BEAUSEJOUR
BONBLED — Called TOURENJEAU
LA ROSE, Alix
LE ROUX — Called ST. MARTIN
AUBREUILLE — Called LA RENCONTRE
CHAUVIN — Called FLEUR D'EPINE
CARDON — Called LA JEUNESSE
MILAN, Denis
DUVERGER — Called STE. CROIX
DESJARDINS, Thomas
DAMIENS — Called LA GUERRE

RENAUT'S COMPANY

RENAUT D'HAUTERIVE — Captain. Absent, in France.
COUSTILLAS — Lieutenant. Present
MAREST DUPUY — Sub-Lieutenant. Present
D'HERNEVILLE, Chevalier — Ensign. Present

Sargeant
SANS SOUCY

Corporals
ROBERT, Pierre
LE GUCHARD — Called VAUCHEL

Drummer
MINARD — Called DESLAURIERS

Name	Comments

RENAUT'S COMPANY (cont.)

Soldiers

DE MOUY	Cadet
LA HOUSSAY	Cadet
LAGRANDECOURT	
LAMBERT	Called DAUPHINE
LAMBERT	Called LENTURLU
GONICH	Called COUTOIS
COADIT	Called JOLICOEUR
OUATIE	Called DUCHENE
DUBIT, Barthelemy	
LEMOILLE	Called DUBOIS
FERON	Called LEPINE
BIGNARD	Called LA JOIE
MEUNIER	Called LA LIME
DROINEAU	Called TRANCHEMONTAGNE
DUMANCHE	Called DUTEMPLE
FAUCHON	Called ST. JEAN
BERNARD	Called BELLEROSE
CHEREL, Robert	
D'ORLEANS	Called ST. DENIS
GOURMEVELLE	Called STE. ANNE
FOUQUET	Called LA FRAMBOISE
VERNAY	Called SANSOUCY
MANIERE	Called LA BASTILLE
MAILLARD	Called CHAMPAGNE
RIEN	Called LA BRULURE
BEAUFORT	Called STE. REINE
HUMBERT	Called ST. LAURENT

DECEMBER 9, 1721

LIST OF COMPANY WORKERS WHO ARE
ACTUALLY IN LOUISIANA.

Name	Comments

CARPENTERS

SERINGUE, Michel	Master carpenter
COUTURE, Jean Baptiste	Journeyman
GUILLAIN, Robert	Journeyman
POURE, Hans	Good
LAURE, Leonard	Good
CARPENTERAS, Pierre	Passable

METAL WORKERS

CHALINNE, Jean	Master
MENNEROLLE, Mathieu	Good
ROMAGOU (ROMAGON?), Jean	Passable
LE CAILLE, Simon	Passable
JEANBON, Nicolas	Passable
D'AIGREMONT, Antoine	Passable
PAMEL, François	Passable

EDGE-TOOL MAKERS

POTTIER, François	Journeyman
VALETTE, François	Passable
TAIBRE, François	Master

TILERS

RAFFLAUP, Denis	Master
HAYS, Jean	Journeyman
DUPRE, Jacques	Journeyman
AMIOT, Jacques	Journeyman
NOEL, Claude	Journeyman
LIGNER, François	Journeyman
MENESCEAUX, François	Journeyman
TABOURET, Pierre	Journeyman
BOURET, Jean	Journeyman
BRYE, Cristophe	Journeyman

FOUNDERS

JEANNOT, David	Good
COUVENT, Estienne	Good
DE LA HOUSSAY, Jacque	Good

Name	Comments

MASONS

AUGRAN, Nicolas	Master
ALBRET, Magnus	Master
ANGRAN, Michel	Journeyman
LESTIMIER, Charles	Journeyman
DEJARDIN, Thomas	Journeyman
CAPEL, Antoine	Journeyman
ESPEGLE, Alexandre	Journeyman
KATDINBERGUE, Jean	Good

BRICK MAKERS

CHERASSE, François	Master
MARCUIT, Charles	Master
KELLE, Laurens	Master
LAMPRE, Simon	Good
MESLER, Joseph	Good

COOPER

BENET, Yves	Good

SHOEMAKERS

DAVID, Joseph	Good
MADRON, François	Good

WHEELWRIGHTS

BUNEL, Antoine	Master
PIGNY, Maurice	Master
MOUZEL, Pierre	Master

SAWYER

MEUNIER, Martin	Passable

GUNSMITH

BODART, Jacques	Good

MARSHALS

BOURLON, Louis	Passable
BON, Jean	Passable

TURNERS

FOUREAU, Pierre	Passable

Name	Comments
"GAZONNEURS"	
DUBOS, René	Passable
JULIEN, Pierre	Passable
NAIL-MAKERS	
PINCHON, Jacques	Master
LE BON, Joseph	Passable
GILDER	
GENIER, Jean	Passable
CUTLER	
FOURTOUT, Pierre	Good for nothing
MINER	
PORTHUYS, Pierre	Passable
TILE-MAKER	
FONTAINE, Maximilien	Passable
BUTCHER	
FANACEL, Jean	Good
CANLE-MAKER	
BLANQUET, Robert	Passable
BREWERS	
PARE, Joseph	Good
MENECAIN, André	Good
TAILORS	
FONTAINNE, Pierre François	Passable
GOBEAU, Alexandre	Passable
STORME, Romaine	Good
BOOKSELLER	
DUBUC, Jacques	

Name	Comments

GARDENERS

CAMUS, Pierre	Pasable
AVIGNON, Mathieu	Good
DUROCQ, Jacques	Good
LEONARD, Jean Baptiste	Good
LEONARD, Jean	Passable

BAKER

BENARD, René	Good

LABORERS

ANDRONIC, Honoré	Good
VATTIER, Jean	Good
LE CAILLOU, Joseph	Good
CARPENTIER, Pierre	Passable
ROBA, Jacques	Good
LEJEUNE, Antoine	Good
CARPENTIER, Thomas	Passable
FONTAINNE, François	Good
BOTSON, Jean	Good
GONNET, Claude	Good
RICHY, Henry	Passable
GOBERT, Gilles	Next to nothing

SEAMEN

SANTORUM, Pitre	Passable
VERNAY, Pierre	Good
DUVAL, Jean	Good
RAIZEL, Jean	Good
BOURGEOIS, Henry	Good
BLOQUET, Jean	Passable
MADRE, Barthelemy	Good
CASTEL, Joseph	Good
CORDIER, Jacques	Good
JOUANNE, Charles	Passable
COCHART, François	Passable
BLANGRENON, Vincent	Good
CAUBE, Martin	Good
VILLENEUVE, Robert	Good
BERTIN, Louis	Good

WORKERS OUTSIDE OF NEW ORLEANS

ROBIN, Jean	Master Locksmith
MOREL, Jean Pierre	Journeyman carpenter
ROBERT, Pierre	Passable carpenter
MAZELIERS, Jean Baptiste	Good seaman

LIST OF COMPANY WORKERS WHO ARE EM-
PLOYED AT NEW ORLEANS ALONG WITH
THEIR WAGES FOR ONE YEAR

Name		Salary for one year in "livres"

CARPENTERS

SERINGUE, Michel	Master	400
COUTURE, Jean Baptiste		300
GUILLAIN, Robert		250
POURE, Hans		250
LAURE, Leonard		250
CARPENTERAS, Pierre		200
HAYS, Nicolas	Master	500
DUPRE, Jacques		350
AMIOT, Jacques		300
HAYS, Jean		300
NOEL, Claude		250
LIGRE, François		150
MENEMEAU, François		130
TABOURE, Pierre		150
BOURE, Jean		150
BRIE, Christophe		150
MOREL, Jean Pierre		275
ROBERT, Pierre		250

METAL WORKERS & LOCKSMITHS

ROBIN, Jean	Master	500
CHALY, Jean	Master	450
MENEROL, Mathieu	Master	450
LA CAILLE, Simon	Journeyman	100
JAMBON (JEANBON?), Nicolas		150
D'AIGREMONT, Antoine		150
PAMEL, François		150

EDGED-TOOL MAKERS

TEBRE (TAIBRE?), François	Master	400
VALET, François		300
POTTIER, François		250

MARSHALS

BOURBON, Louis		150
BON, Jean		100

NAIL-MAKERS

PINCHON, Jacques	Master	150
LE BON, Joseph		100

Name		Salary

BRICK MAKERS

CHERASSE, François	Master	250
MARCUIT, Charles	Master	250
KELLE, Laurent	Master	250
LAMPRE, Simon		120
MESLER, Joseph		100

MASONS

ANGRAN (AUGRAN?), Nicolas	Master	400
ALBRE, Magnus	Master	400
ANGRAN, Michel		150
LESTEINIER, Charles		100
DESJARDINS, Thomas		80
CAPEL, Antoine		100
ESPEGLE, Alexandre		120
BERGUE, Jean Kadin		100
FONTAINE, Maximilien		100

COOPER

| BENET, Yves | 275 |

WHEELWRIGHT

| BUNEL, Antoine | Master | 250 |

SAWYER

| MEUSNIER, Martin | 150 |

BREWERS

| PARE, Joseph | 150 |
| MENECAIN, André | 100 |

GARDENERS

| DUCROQ, Jacques | 150 |
| AVIGNON, Mathieu | 120 |

BAKER

| BENARD, René | 120 |

LABORERS

| ANDRONIQUE, Honoré | 200 |
| VATTIER, Jean | 200 |

Name	Salary

WORKERS FOR THE ILLINOIS POST

One carpenter	400
One journeyman carpenter	200
One gunsmith	400
One edged-tool maker	400
One mason	300
Another mason	150
PIGUY, Maurice (Wheelwright)	250
MORISSE, Pierre (Wheelwright)	200

JANUARY 15, 1723

LIST OF WORKERS RETAINED IN LOUISIANA

CARPENTERS	Salary in "livres"	BRICK MAKERS	Salary in "livres"
PINAULT, Pierre	600	KELLE, Laurens	300
SERINGUE, Michel	400	CHERASSE, François	250
COUTURE, Jean Baptiste	300	CAUBE, Martin	150
CARPENTRAS, Pierre	200	LAMPRE, Simon	150
PERAULT, Toussaint	400	MILLER, Joseph	150
BUREAU, Jean	250	FURET, Guillaume	90
PAURE, Hans	250		
MOUZET, Pierre	200	TILER	
SCHEMIT, Nicolas	200		
KATSEBERGUE, Jean	150	RAFLAUP, Daniel	150
LAORDE, Leonard	150		
HAYS, Nicolas	500	MASONS	
DUPRE, Jacques	350		
HAYS, Jean	300	ANGRAND, Nicolas	400
NOEL, Claude	250	ALBERT, Magnus	200
MOREL, Pierre	250	LETIMIER, Charles	100
ROBERT, Pierre	250	SPEGLE, Alexandre	120
CRISTIAN, Charles	200	ANGRAN, Michel	---
METAL WORKERS		COOPER	
ROBIN, Jean	500	BENET, Ives	275
CHALINE, Jean	450		
MENNEROLLE, Mathieu	450	TURNER	
ROMAGON, Jean	400		
LAILLIE, Simon	100	FOUREAU, Pierre	200
JANBON, Nicolas	150		
		EXCAVATORS	
EDGED-TOOL MAKERS			
		DUBOS, René	200
TAIBRE, François	250		
VALETTE, François	250	CHARCOAL MAKERS	
BON, Jean	100		
		CRELY, Jean Baptiste	150
WHEELWRIGHTS			

The following are men who were hired to saw lumber because the work of their trade was no longer required.

WHEELWRIGHTS			
PIGNY, Maurice	---	MEUNIER, Martin	150
BUNEL, Antoine	250	PAUMIER, Louis	150
		DECROCQ, Jacques	150
NAIL-MAKERS			
PINCHON, Jacques	150		

Name	Salary in "livres"

WORKERS (cont.)

Name	Salary
GONNET, Claude	200
CASTEL, Joseph	150
MADRE, Barthelemy	150
VATTIER, Jean	200
AVIGNON, Mathieu	120
VILLENEUVE, Norbert	75
PORTIUS, Pierre	80
LIGNE, François	150
PAMEL, François	100
ANDRONICQ, Honoré	200
BERNARD, René	150
MANSIEAU, François	130
JULIEN, Pierre	200
FONTAINE, Pierre François	50
BLOQUET, Jean	150
DAVID, Joseph	150
CHANLOT, Louis	100
CORDIER, Jacques	100
BLANGRENON, Vincent	100
CHARPANTIER, Pierre	60
RICHY, Henry	150
FANASSELLE, Jean	100
GOBEAU, Alexandre	180
FUMA, Jean	150

SEPTEMBER 23, 1723

LIST OF WORKERS WHO HAVE FULFILLED
THEIR CONTRACT WITH THE COMPANY OF
THE INDIES AND WHO ASK TO RETURN
TO FRANCE

Name	Comments
AUGRAND (ANGRAND?), Nicolas	
AUGRAND (ANGRAND?), Michel	
COUTURE, Jean Baptiste	
ROBIN, Jean	
BE(?), Ives	(More than likely Ives BENET)
LIGNER, Jacques François	
PIGNE, Maurice	
MOREL, Pierre	His wife is with him
CHALINES, Jean	Called BAZONNOIS
MEROLLE, Mathieu	His wife and one child are with him.
VALETTE, François	His wife is with him.
JEANNOT, David	His wife and one child are with him.
DUPRE, Jacques	
PIGEON, Jacques	
NOEL, Claude	
ROBERT, Pierre	
HAYS, Jean	
BUREL, Nicolas	His wife is with him.
DUBOS, René	His two daughters are with him.
BLOQUE, Jean	
MADRE, Barthelemy	His wife is with him.
CASTEL, Joseph	
JULIEN, Pierre	His wife is with him.
CORDIER, Jacques	
BLANGRENON, Vincent	
ROMAGON, Jean	His wife and son are with him.

All of these workers arrived at Old Biloxi November 24, 1720 aboard the ship CHAMEAU

The three following workers ask to return to France because of hardship.

PINAULT, Pierre	Master Carpenter. Native of La Rochelle where he has a wife and two children.
PERRAULT, Toussaint	Master Carpenter. Native of St. Denis Jouaye in Brie. He has a wife and five children in France who have been reduced to a miserable state because of his absence.
BUREAU, Jean	Master Carpenter. Native of Benest in Anjou.

MARCH 8, 1724

LIST OF COUNCILORS AND CLERICAL EM-
PLOYEES OF THE COMPANY OF THE INDIES
IN LOUISIANA.

Name	Position	Salary per year in "livres"
	COUNCIL	
BRUSLE	First Councilor	4000
FAZENDE	Second Councilor	4000
PERRY	Third Councilor	4000
FLEURIAU	Attorney General and Fourth Councilor	4000
ROSSART	Clerk of Court	600
DE CHAVANNES	Secretary	1500
GIRAUT	Clerk	1000
PICHOT	Clerk	1000
MICHEL	Clerk	800
MONTORGES	Clerk	800
	OFFICE OF RECORDS AND ACCOUNTS	
DUVAL	Bookkeeper	3000
BYON	Bookkeeper	1200
	CASHIER'S OFFICE	
BRU	Cashier	2000
ST. QUENTIN OR MORISSET	Accoutant	1200
-------	Clerk	400
	GENERAL STORES	
BONNAULT	General Storekeeper	2000
BION	Bookkeeper	1200
LA COUR	Clerk	400
CRESPIN	Clerk	400
	DISTRIBUTION OF SUPPLIES	
DRILLANT		600
	At Mobile	
LALOIRE (the younger)	Head Clerk	1500
HURAULT		400

Name	Position	Salary in "livres"

AT THE ALIBAMONS

The Company has decided that this position is no longer necessary.

At Natchez

	one clerk	600

At Balize

	one clerk	800

At Illinois

LALOIRE (the elder)	Head Clerk	2000
CHASSIN		800
	A secretary-recorder	600

All of the above-named employees, except the Clerk of Court will continue to receive gratis two barrels of flour, one barrel of lard, a small cask of wine, and a small cask of brandy per year.

EMPLOYEES UNDER ORDERS FROM THE COUNCIL

LA RENAUDIERE		600
CADOT	At the Cashier's Office	600
MORISSET	At the General Stores	800
LANGLOIS	At the General Stores	800
JACOTEAU	At the General Stores	800
LALANDE	At the Alibamons	600
D'HERBANNE	At Natchitoches	1200
DE FLANDRES	At Natchitoches	1200
GOUIN	At the Missouri River Post	500
DUFRESNE	At the Arkansas Post	500
LA SALLE	At Biloxi	600
MICHEL	At Balize	800
MALO	At Natchez	600

EMPLOYEES WHO HAVE BEEN DISMISSED

DALCOURT	Former cashier.
ESTIENNES	Former secretary.
DURANT	Formerly principal clerk at Mobile

SEPTEMBER 28, 1726

LIST OF EXPENSES FOR THE YEAR 1727

Name	Position	Salary (in "livres")
PERIER, M.	General Commander	12,000
BOISBRIANT, M. de	First Lieut. of the King	5000
DIRON, M.	2nd Lieut. of the King	4000
(omitted)	Major at New Orleans	1200
DES LIETTES	Commander at Illinois	720
ST. DENIS	Commander at Natchitoches	1080
BROUTIN	Commander at Natchez	1080
PECHON	Major at the Alibamons	900
BEAUCHAMP	Major at Mobile	900
DUPUY PLANCHARD	Performing the functions of Aide-Major at New Orleans. A token salary of	150
MANDEVILLE	First Captain. A token salary of	300

CAPTAINS

MANDEVILLE		1080
LA TOUR		1080
DARTAGUIETTE		1080
DU TISNE		1080
DES LIETTES		1080
MARCHAND DE COURCELLES		1080
RENAULT D'HAUTRIVE		1080
PRADEL		1080

SUPERNUMERARY CAPTAINS

GAUVRIT		600
MERVEILLEUX		600
LOUBOEY		1080
DETCHEPARRE		1080

LIEUTENANTS

MELIQUE		720
MONTINARQUE		720
BASSEE		720
VILLAINVILLE		720
CAUDER		720
COUSTILHAS		720
PETIT DE LIVILLIERS		720
DE MOUY		720

Name	Position	(Salary (in "livres")
SUPERNUMERARY LIEUTENANTS		
LUSSER		720
SUB-LIEUTENANTS		
DE LISLE (absent)		600
BENOIST		600
LA BOULAYE		600
MAILLARD		600
TERISSE		600
HERSANT		600
SIMARE DE BELISLE		600
LALLIER		600
SUPERNUMERARY SUB-LIEUTENANTS		
MASSE		600
NOLAN		600
ENSIGNS		
FRANCHOMME		480
ST. ESTEVES		480
REGIS DU BOULET		480
MARETZ DUPUY		480
MARETZ DE LA TOUR		480
VERCHIER DU TERPUY		480
CAZENEUVE		480
DUPUY PLANCHARD		480
SUPERNUMERARY ENSIGNS		
GIRARDEAU		480
STE. THEREZE DE LANGLOISIERE		480
HALF-PAY LIEUTENANTS		
DUMONT DE MONTIGNY		480
JANTZEN		480
ST. ANGE (father)		480
VINCENNES		480
VERGIER		480
VINS		480
HALF-PAY ENSIGN		
ST. ANGE (son)		360

Name	Position	Salary (in "livres")

ENSIGNS "EXPECTATIVES"

DU TISNE (son)
DES ROCHES
DUPUY PLANCHARD (son)
DAGUIN
DUBOIS

NUMBER OF NON-COMMISSIONED OFFICERS AND TROOPS AT VARIOUS POSTS

Place	Sargeants	Corporals	Drummers	Fusilliers	Total
Mobile	4	4	2	75	85
Biloxi				7	7
Balize	1	1	1	17	20
New Orleans	5	5	2	118	130
Alibamons				15	15
Natchitoches	1	1		23	25
Natchez	1	2	1	31	35
Yazoo	1			14	15
Wabash	1	1	1	27	30
Illinois & Missouri	2	2	1	33	38

CAPUCHINS	Salary (in "livres")

At New Orleans
Father Raphaël — 600
Father Hyacinthe — 600

At the German Village
Brother St. Julien, Schoolmaster — 600

At Balize
Father Gaspard — 600

At Mobile
Father Mathias — 600

AT Appalachee
Father Victorin (Recollect) — 600

At Natchitoches
(vacant)

At Natchez
Father Philibert — 600

Note: Father François de Neau and Theodore de Besançon will fill the vacancies at New Orleans and Natchitoches.

Name	Position	Salary (in "livres")

JESUITS

Jesuit missionaries at the following posts.

Kaskaskia		600
Fort de Chartres		800
Wabash		800
Arkansas		800
Yazoo		800
Alibamons		800
Caokias and Tamarois		600
Missouri		600

URSULINES

Six Ursulines at a salary per year of 600 livres each.
300 livres for the maintenance of their buildings.

PRAT, Dr.	Payed by the King	1070
ALEXANDRE	Surgeon major	1200
LA TOUR	Assistant surgeon for the city	800
DAMARON	Apothicary	1000
Hospital expenses		15,000

SURGEONS

At New Orleans
DAUVILLE, Dame	Mid-wife	1200

At Balize
BALDIE	600

At Mobile
NAVARRE	600
VAUTIER	300

At the Alibamons
MELISAN	300

At Natchitoches
TOTIN	200

At Illinois
GIRARD	600

Name	Position	Salary (in "livres")
FORTIFICATIONS		
PAUGER, M. de	Engineer-in-Chief	5000
DUVERGIER, Sieur		1200
VINS, Sieur de		800
MORAND	Inspector of Works	700
ARTILLERY		
CHESNEAU	Master Gunner at New Orleans	600
PARISIS	Master Gunner at Mobile	360
PIERRE, Michel	Master Gunner at Balize	300
Three assistant gunners		900
GUNSMITHS		
BRANTAIN		400
PINET	(Came from Senegal)	300
MARINE		
SENET, Sieur	Captain of the Port	1200
SENET (son)	Clerk	400
CAPTAINS OF BRIGANTINES		
LAZOU		1200
(vacant)		1200
PILOTS		
FION, François	At Balize	900
TIREL	At Balize	480
COOPERS		
OZANNE, Jacques	At New Orleans	600
PANNETIER	At New Orleans	600
LURAT, Phelix	At Mobile	500
EMPLOYEES "DE PLUME"		
LA CHAISE	First Councilor	10,000
BRULE		4000
AMYAULT D'AUSSEVILLE		400
BRU	Assistant at Mobile	3000
LA LOERE DES URSINS	Assistant at Natchez	2000
CHAVANNES	Secretary	1500
PICHOT	Head Clerk	1200
MICHEL		1200
DUBUISSON		1000
MONTORGE		1000
BELLEVEUE	Concierge	300

Name	Position	Salary (in "livres")
BOOKKEEPING DEPARTMENT		
PREVOST	Head Bookkeeper	2400
BAILLY	Assistant Bookkeeper	1800
BERNAUDAT		600
CASHIER		
DUVAL	Head Cashier	2000
MAISONNEUVE		400
STORES		
ROUSAULT	Storekeeper	2400
PELLERIN		1200
DE COUR	Distributor of merchandise	600
FERVE	Distributor of Powder	400
SUPPLIES DISTRIBUTION		
NOLIN DE TOUR		600
MERLE, Jean		240
At Balize		
LA LOERE FLAUCOURT		1500
At Mobile		
BRU	Councilor	- - -
HURAND	Distributor of Supplies	400
INTERPRETERS		
DUCHE	Chief Interpreter	400
At the Alibamons		
LA LANDE		800
(vacant)		250
At Natchez		
LA LOERE (the elder)	Councilor	- - -
RICARD		300
PAPIN	Interpreter	200
At Illinois		
(vacant)	Interpreter	250
PERILLAND	Clerk	600

Name	Position	Salary (in "livres")

PERSONS EMPLOYED FOR THE SERVICE OF THE COLONY

For the Superior Council
FLEURIAU	Attorney General	2000
ROSSARD	Recorder	600

Surveyors
LASSUS (the elder)		2000
LASSUS (the younger)		600

ESTIMATED COST OF INDIAN PRESENTS		12,000